# THE W

## AND

# THE WOMAN-HATER

# THE WITLINGS

# AND

# THE WOMAN-HATER

Frances Burney

*edited by Peter Sabor and Geoffrey Sill*

broadview literary texts

**National Library of Canada Cataloguing in Publication Data**
Burney, Fanny, 1752-1840
    The witlings; and, The woman-hater / Frances Burney; edited by Peter Sabor and
Geoffrey Sill.

(Broadview literary texts)
Includes bibliographical references.
ISBN 1-55111-378-3

I. Sabor, Peter II. Sill, Geoffrey M., 1944-   . III. Title. IV. Series.
V. Title: Woman-hater.

PR3316.A4W57 2002      822'.6      C2002-902986-4

Broadview Press Ltd. is an independent, international publishing house, incorporated in
1985. Broadview believes in shared ownership, both with its employees and with the general public; since the year 2000 Broadview shares have traded publicly on the Toronto
Venture Exchange under the symbol BDP.

We welcome comments and suggestions regarding any aspect of our publications–please
feel free to contact us at the addresses below or at broadview@broadviewpress.com.

North America
PO Box 1243, Peterborough, Ontario, Canada K9J 7H5
3576 California Road, Orchard Park, NY, USA 14127
Tel: (705) 743-8990; Fax: (705) 743-8353
email: customerservice@broadviewpress.com

UK, Ireland, and continental Europe
Thomas Lyster Ltd., Units 3 & 4a, Old Boundary Way
Burscough Road, Ormskirk
Lancashire, L39 2YW
Tel: (01695) 575112; Fax: (01695) 570120
email: books@tlyster.co.uk

Australia and New Zealand
UNIREPS, University of New South Wales
Sydney, NSW, 2052
Tel: 61 2 9664 0999; Fax: 61 2 9664 5420
email: info.press@unsw.edu.au

www.broadviewpress.com

Broadview Press Ltd. gratefully acknowledges the financial support of the Government of
Canada through the Book Publishing Industry Development Program for our publishing
activities.

Series editor: Professor L.W. Conolly
Advisory editor for this volume: Rebecca Conolly
Text design and composition by George Kirkpatrick

PRINTED IN CANADA

# Contents

FRANCES BURNEY,
a steel engraving of a portrait painted in 1782 by Edward Francesco
Burney. The original painting hangs in Parham Park, Sussex.

## Acknowledgements

The manuscripts of the plays on which this edition is based are held at the Berg Collection in the New York Public Library, Astor, Lenox and Tilden Foundations, which has kindly given permission to print Burney's holographs in its possession. For permission to reprint passages from journals and letters in the appendices and introduction, we thank the Clarendon Press for *The Early Journals and Letters of Fanny Burney*, edited by Lars E. Troide *et al.*; *The Letters of Dr. Charles Burney*, edited by Alvaro Ribeiro; and for *Thraliana: The Diary of Mrs. Hester Lynch Thrale (later Mrs. Piozzi), 1776-1809*, Second Edition, edited by Katharine C. Balderston. We also thank Penguin Books for permission to reprint from Frances Burney, *Journals and Letters*, edited by Peter Sabor and Lars E. Troide.

We are indebted to Lars Troide, director of the Burney Papers at McGill University, and to other Burney scholars, especially Stewart Cooke, Barbara Darby, Margaret Anne Doody, Victoria Kortes-Papp, Alvaro Ribeiro, Betty Rizzo, and Janice Thaddeus. At Broadview Press we have enjoyed the support of Don LePan, as well as the editorial advice of Barbara Conolly and Julia Gaunce.

For financial support for his research, Peter Sabor is grateful to the Social Sciences and Humanities Research Council of Canada; for Marie he is always grateful. Geoffrey Sill extends his thanks to Paul D. Taylor, who made the first transcription of the text of *The Woman-Hater*, and to Susan Chromiak, for assistance in every other way.

# Short Titles

| | |
|---|---|
| Burney, *Complete Plays* | *The Complete Plays of Frances Burney.* Ed. Peter Sabor; associate editor (*Tragedies*) Stewart J. Cooke; contributing editor (*Comedies*) Geoffrey M. Sill. 2 vols. (London: Pickering & Chatto, 1995). |
| Burney, *Camilla* | Frances Burney, *Camilla; or, A Picture of Youth.* Ed. Edward A. Bloom and Lillian D. Bloom (Oxford: Oxford University Press, 1972). |
| Burney, *Cecilia* | Frances Burney, *Cecilia; or Memoirs of an Heiress.* Ed. Peter Sabor and Margaret Anne Doody, with an introduction by Margaret Anne Doody (Oxford: Oxford University Press, 1988). |
| Burney, *Evelina* | Frances Burney, *Evelina; or, The History of a Young Lady's Entrance into the World.* Ed. Edward A. Bloom, with the assistance of Lillian D. Bloom (Oxford: Oxford University Press, 1968). |
| Burney, *The Wanderer* | Frances Burney, *The Wanderer; or, Female Difficulties.* Ed. Margaret Anne Doody, Robert L. Mack, and Peter Sabor, with an introduction by Margaret Anne Doody (Oxford: Oxford University Press, 1991). |
| Burney, *Early Journals* | *The Early Journals and Letters of Fanny Burney.* Ed. Lars E. Troide *et al.* 6 vols. (Oxford: Clarendon Press, 1988-). |
| Burney, *Journals and Letters* | *The Journals and Letters of Fanny Burney (Madame d'Arblay).* Ed. Joyce Hemlow *et al.* 12 vols. (Oxford: Clarendon Press, 1972-84). |
| Doody, *Frances Burney* | Margaret Anne Doody, *Frances Burney: The Life in the Works* (New Brunswick, NJ: Rutgers University Press, 1988). |
| *OED* | *A New English Dictionary on Historical Principles.* 2nd ed. (Oxford: Clarendon Press, 1989). |

# Introduction

Frances Burney is familiar to readers of English literature as the author of a series of brilliant novels—*Evelina* (1778), *Cecilia* (1782), *Camilla* (1796), and *The Wanderer* (1814)—works in which, as Jane Austen declares, "the greatest powers of the mind are displayed, in which the most thorough knowledge of human nature, the happiest delineation of its varieties, the liveliest effusions of wit and humour, are conveyed to the world in the best chosen language."[1] Burney is also celebrated for the voluminous journals and letters she wrote for over seventy years, from 1768 to 1840, which are at once a major primary source for the history of late eighteenth- and early nineteenth-century England and the psychological drama of a woman writer struggling to gain recognition in a highly patriarchal society. But there was another dimension to Burney as a writer, another personal aspiration that she strove to fulfil, which was that of a dramatist. Even as her first novel, *Evelina*, enjoyed the acclaim of literary London in the winter of 1778-79, Burney was lifting her sights to what was then regarded as a higher form of art. She had always loved the theatre, and now her friends, including Samuel Johnson, Hester Thrale, Sir Joshua Reynolds, Arthur Murphy, and Richard Brinsley Sheridan, who had just purchased the Theatre Royal on Drury Lane, were advising her to try her hand at drama. Even her "two Daddys," by whom she meant her father, Dr. Charles Burney, and her elderly friend and literary censor, Samuel Crisp, encouraged her to capitalize on her popularity by writing a comedy. "This is your time," Crisp wrote to her—though it seems he had something very different in mind from the play that she produced.[2]

It was both a blessing and a curse for Burney, as an aspiring young dramatist, that she had so many influential counsellors advising her on how best to write a successful comedy. In September 1778, Burney recorded "*such* a Conversation," in which Hester Thrale told her that a play "is the Road both to Honour &

---

[1]  Jane Austen, *Northanger Abbey*, ed. Claire Grogan (Peterborough, ON: Broadview, 1996) 60.

[2]  Crisp to Burney, 11 November 1778; *Early Journals*, III, 179.

Profit." Burney, continued Thrale, had "the right & true talents for writing a Comedy,—— you would give us all the fun & humour we could wish, & you would give us a scene or 2 of the pathetic kind that would set all the rest off."[1] For Samuel Crisp, however, the task was not so simple. In a typically pedantic letter of December 1778, he warned Burney against the "very fine-Spun, all-delicate, Sentimental Comedies ... brought forth, on the English, & more particularly on the French Stage," which "are such sick things so Void Of blood & Spirits! that they may well be call'd *Comedies Larmoyantes!*" Nevertheless, Crisp wanted Burney, for the sake of decorum, to avoid "lively Freedoms": "it appears to me extremely difficult, throughout a whole spirited Comedy, to steer clear of those agreeable, frolicksome *jeux d'Esprit*, on the one hand; and languor & heaviness on the other."[2]

Burney's other famous advisers on *The Witlings* had different ideas. Dr. Johnson envisaged the comedy as a satire, and even supplied a working title, "*Stretham, a Farce,*"[3] thus encouraging Burney to mock the group of writers and would-be writers who assembled at the Thrales' country residence, Streatham Park. Johnson also laughingly offered his services as collaborator on the play, eliciting Murphy's remark: "I wish you would Beaumont & Fletcher us!"[4] Sheridan, meanwhile, egged on by Sir Joshua Reynolds, was promising to produce the still incomplete play "*Unsight unseen.*"[5] And Murphy himself, almost as great a name as Sheridan in the theatre world of the 1770s, read at least the first two acts of *The Witlings* in May 1779 and pronounced himself "extremely pleased with it indeed."[6] In a letter to Crisp of 30 July 1779, Burney describes the play as "of an enormous length, though half as short again as the *original*";[7]

---

1 Letter to Susanna Burney, 3 September 1778; *Early Journals*, III, 133. See Appendix B.2.
2 Crisp to Burney, 8 December 1778; *Early Journals*, III, 187-89.
3 Letter to Susanna Burney, 28 August 1778; *Early Journals*, III, 111.
4 Letter to Susanna Burney, February 1779; *Early Journals*, III, 245. See Appendix B.6. For Burney's apparent interest, over twenty years later, in one of Beaumont and Fletcher's collaborations, *The Woman Hater* (1607), see pp. 29-31.
5 Letter to Susanna Burney, 11 January 1779; *Early Journals*, III, 235. See Appendix B.4. The phrase "unsight unseen" appears in Addison's *The Spectator* 511 (October 16, 1712).
6 Letter to Susanna Burney, 30 May 1779; *Early Journals*, III, 282. See Appendix B.8.
7 *Early Journals*, III, 342; see Appendix B.9.

evidently she had revised the play considerably between May and July.

*The Witlings* is a sharp satire in the comedy of manners tradition, written very much in the spirit of Molière's *Les Femmes Savantes*. The play depicts the manners of a circle called the Esprit Party, led by Lady Smatter, who affects the right as a patron of literature to form judgements about it. The party also includes Mrs. Sapient, who is unable to form judgements of her own but peddles secondhand opinions on every subject; Mrs. Voluble, who talks without any intention of judging what she is saying; and Mr. Dabler, a witless poet. A final member of the party, Codger, is a plodding pedant whose deliberate style clashes with that of his son Jack, who is always in haste to be somewhere else. To leaven her satire of the group, Burney introduces a romantic subplot in which Lady Smatter's nephew and adopted son, Beaufort, is interested in the orphaned heiress, Cecilia. Lady Smatter will not hear of such a match after the news arrives that Cecilia's fortune has been lost. Beaufort's friend Censor, who is outraged by the pretensions of the Esprit party, forces Lady Smatter, under the threat of a public lampoon, to relinquish her prohibition of the marriage, and restores Cecilia to her financial independence, thus enabling her freely to accept Beaufort's humble addresses.

Burney's satire of pretentious witlings, male and female, still seems fresh today: the would-be poet Dabler, the pedantic Codger, the self-proclaimed arbiter of taste Lady Smatter, and the sententious Mrs. Sapient are among her best comic creations. The play probably takes its title from a line in Pope's *The Rape of the Lock* (1717): "A *Beau* and *Witling* perished in the throng" (V, 59). Burney alludes to *The Rape of the Lock* on three occasions in journals and letters written while she was at work on *The Witlings*,[1] and at its best her play has something of the satirical force and comic sparkle of Pope's poem. But the laboured romance between Cecilia and Beaufort holds less appeal: the sentiments designed to move Burney's audience to tears are more likely to make us queasy. It is to Burney's credit that she anticipates such a reaction within the play itself, making fun of her young lovers' declamations as fast as they are declaimed. Thus in the final act

---

1 See *Early Journals*, III, 34, 129, 345.

the impoverished Cecilia declares portentously, "sooner will I famish with want, or perish with Cold,—faint with the fatigue of labour, or consume with unassisted Sickness, than appropriate to my own use the smallest part of my shattered Fortune, till your— and every other claim upon it is answered" (p. 145). Her debtor, Mrs. Wheedle, replies, "Well, ma'am, that's as much as one can expect," turning the heroine's flight of fancy into a precise financial settlement. Similarly, in response to Cecilia's rhetorical question, "is, then, reason another word for baseness, falsehood and Inconstancy?", Mrs. Wheedle returns to the matter at hand: "I only wish my money was once safe in my Pocket" (p. 146).

The play was read privately in August 1779 to an audience that included Samuel Crisp, Frances's sisters Susanna and Charlotte, and others, by Dr. Burney, who had not read it through before. Despite his lack of preparation and strength to carry it off, his reading of the play highly amused the audience: Susanna wrote to Frances that "the first act diverted us *extremely* all round ... Charlotte laugh'd till she was almost black in the face," and that the sentimental subplot "made me for to cry in 2 or 3 places—I wish there was more of this Sort—so does my Father—so, I believe, does Mr. Crisp."[1] Indeed, Dr. Burney and Crisp were alarmed that Burney's devastating satire of female wit came uncomfortably close to a recognizable portrait of some influential literary women of the time, particularly the leader of the Bluestocking group, Elizabeth Montagu. In a letter to Crisp written just before the fatal reading took place, Burney had asked her "dear Daddy" for his comments on *The Witlings*, reminding him that it was still "a play in manuscript, & *capable* of alterations." She hoped that friendly criticism would enable her to give Sheridan a much improved play for production: at least "the *manager* will have nothing to reproach me with: is not that some comfort?"[2] Instead, Burney received what she memorably described as a "Hissing, groaning, catcalling Epistle" jointly written by her two "daddies."[3] The metaphors are apt: instead of analyzing her play with a view

---

1 Susanna Burney to Frances Burney, 3 August 1779; see Appendix B.10.
2 Letter of 29-30 July 1779; *Early Journals*, III, 343. See Appendix B.9.
3 Letter to Samuel Crisp, c. 13 August 1779; *Early Journals*, III, 350. See Appendix B.12.

to making it fitter for the stage, treating it as a work in progress, Crisp and Dr. Burney had acted like a hostile first-night audience, determined that the play should be taken off the boards.

The correspondence between Burney and the "daddies" that follows their rejection of *The Witlings* is painful to read. Burney, warned by her father to expect the collaborative epistle, assured him that though she had "little hope of ever writing what you will both approve," she would be "a Beast & a monster not to do the best I can when I have two such Daddys for my Judges, & two such Friends for my Critics."[1] Two long letters to her father and Crisp follow, in which Burney strives to express gratitude for the wisdom of their verdict while showing herself well aware that her play could be staged and could succeed. Sheridan, for his part, continued to take an interest in the play, telling Dr. Burney that "he had much rather see pieces before their Authors were contented with them than afterwards, on account of sundry small changes always necessary to be made by the managers, for Theatrical purposes, & to which they were loath to submit when their writings were finished to their own approbations." And Murphy, likewise, urged Burney to put *The Witlings* on stage, assuring her that "if it wants a few Stage Tricks, trust it with me, & I will put them in … I will promise not to let it go out of my Hands without *engaging* for its success."[2]

Since Crisp and Dr. Burney were determined that the play should not be staged, however, all such talk of revision and potential production was in vain. Crisp's final verdict was that "the Play has *Wit* enough, & enough—but the Story & the incidents dont appear to me interesting enough to seize & keep hold of the Attention."[3] The extent of Dr. Burney's fears can be seen in his remark that "not only the Whole Piece, but the *plot* had best be kept secret, from every body"[4]—as though even a report that his daughter was satirizing witlings could damage her reputation.

---

1   Letter to Dr. Burney, 4 August 1779; *Early Journals*, III, 343-44.
2   Burney to Samuel Crisp, 22 January 1780; *Early Journals*, IV, 13. See Appendix B.15.
3   Letter to Burney, 23 February 1780; *Early Journals*, IV, 17. See Appendix B.16.
4   Letter to Burney, 29 August 1779; *The Letters of Dr. Charles Burney*, ed. Alvaro Ribeiro (Oxford: Clarendon Press, 1991), I, 280. See Appendix B.14.

In a perceptive discussion of *The Witlings*, Margaret Anne Doody contends that the two "daddies" suppressed Burney's play as a sacrifice to preserve Dr. Burney's career as a historian of music, a profession that depended upon the patronage of persons of Mrs. Montagu's class, while they pretended to act out of concern for Frances's own interests.[1] Doody contends that the withdrawal of *The Witlings* was a mistake that cost Burney and the English stage what would almost certainly have been a dramatic success to rival her earlier triumph in the novel. Here she contradicts some earlier critics, who have concurred with the "two daddies" that *The Witlings* is apprentice work, and that Burney might have been hurt by a theatrical production. In the first article written on Burney as a playwright, Joyce Hemlow found in *The Witlings* "fewer comic transcriptions of life than readers of *Evelina* might have expected," while Michael Adelstein feared that "the formidable Mrs. Montagu would have retaliated" in ways that "would have been highly injurious to the sensitive young woman."[2]

Surprisingly, at least two feminist critics have taken a similar position. Ellen Moers writes that "had Dr. Burney allowed *The Witlings* to go on the boards, his daughter would have been convicted of a tasteless gaffe equivalent to, say, the submission by an aspiring young authoress of a nasty satire on Gloria Steinem to *Ms.* magazine." And Katharine Rogers finds Burney's "choice of subject ... singularly perverse, since the main object of satire is intellectual women."[3] These critics, however, ignore the fact that Burney's witlings are not a bluestocking group. The founding members of the Esprit Club are Lady Smatter, Dabler, Mrs. Sapient, and Codger, and Burney's satire of the two men is no gentler than that of the two women.

Such satire of would-be intellectuals, moreover, was a com-

---

1  Doody, *Frances Burney*, 91–98.

2  Hemlow, "Fanny Burney, Playwright," *University of Toronto Quarterly*, 19 (1949–50): 171; Adelstein, *Fanny Burney* (New York: Twayne, 1968) 60.

3  Moers, *Literary Women: The Great Writers* (New York: Oxford University Press, 1985) 117; Rogers, *Frances Burney: The World of Female Difficulties* (London: Harvester, 1990) 19. Rogers maintains this position in her anthology of women dramatists, writing of Burney's "strange perversity" in focusing her ridicule on the Bluestockings (*The Meridian Anthology of Restoration and Eighteenth-Century Plays by Women* [New York: Meridian, 1994] 290).

monplace of the eighteenth-century stage: then as now, playwrights had to take certain risks if they were to succeed. Hester Thrale was relieved when the play was suppressed, since she felt implicated in the satire, yet she had the honesty to acknowledge that the play was "likely to succeed."[1] Oliver Goldsmith was urged by both George Colman and David Garrick, managers of Covent Garden and Drury Lane in 1771, to suppress *She Stoops to Conquer*, with its supposedly dangerous attacks on current theatrical fashions. And when *The Rivals* opened at Covent Garden in 1775, reviewers were highly critical of Sheridan's first play, which was at once withdrawn for revisions. Only eleven days later, however, the production reopened, and *The Rivals* became not only a resounding success during the 1775 theatre season but, together with *The School for Scandal* (1777), among the most popular of all English comedies.[2]

Had Burney displayed the tenacity of Goldsmith and Sheridan, defying Crisp and Dr. Burney and risking Mrs. Montagu's wrath, she might have made her name as a playwright in the same decade as Goldsmith and Sheridan, and had her premiere produced by Sheridan at Drury Lane. This, of course, is mere speculation, but when, over two hundred years later, *The Witlings* was finally given a public performance on November 9, 1994, the American audience's reaction proved the aptness of Susanna Burney's remark that the play "diverted us *extremely* all round," and no one seemed to take offence at the satire.[3] A year earlier, in summer 1993, the opening scene of Act V of *The Witlings* was staged at a theatre history workshop, again by an American cast. Ellen Donkin, the organizer, found the work a "joy to perform: it timed out beautifully, it created deliciously controlled comic moments, and it also made a very pointed and thought-provoking contrast

1   *Thraliana: The Diary of Mrs. Hester Lynch Thrale (later Mrs. Piozzi), 1776-1809*, ed. Katharine C. Balderston, 2nd ed., (Oxford: Oxford University Press, 1951) I, 401. See Appendix B.13.
2   See Tom Davis, ed., *She Stoops to Conquer* (London: New Mermaids, 1979) xv; and John Loftis, *Sheridan and the Drama of Georgian England* (Cambridge, MA: Harvard University Press, 1977) 59-61.
3   The production, sponsored by Jo Gillikin, was directed by Robert Hulton-Baker at the Willowbrook Campus of the College of Staten Island, City University of New York, 9-13 November 1994.

between women who have some control over their livelihood (the milliners) and women who don't (Cecilia)."[1]

What effect the withdrawal of *The Witlings* had on Burney's development as a writer cannot be determined. Adelstein contends that the traumatic experience of having her play suppressed made her too wary of the reactions of her readers, so that "her work became taut and self-conscious for many years to come."[2] But the young woman who burned all of her literary works in a bonfire at the age of fifteen for fear they would be discovered hardly needed additional lessons in the virtue of discretion.[3] And traumatic as the suppression was, she did not destroy the manuscript of *The Witlings*, only put it away. In a letter to Crisp of August 1779, she wrote "so good Night Mr. Dabler!—good Night Lady Smatter, … & you, *you great Oaf*, Bobby! good Night! good Night!"[4] But goodnight was not goodbye. A few months later, in January 1780, she wrote to Crisp of having "actually new written the 4th Act from beginning to End except for one scene,"[5] in view of Sheridan's continuing desire to see the play. (It is possible that Act IV of the fair copy printed here is this revised version.) In the same letter, Burney writes of her intention to make further radical changes to the text:

> To entirely omit all mention of the *Club*;—
> To curtail the parts of Smatter & Dabler as much as possible;
> To restore to Censor his £5000—& not trouble him even to *offer* it;—
> To give a *new* friend to Cecilia, by whom her affairs shall be retrieved, & through whose means the Catastrophe shall be brought to [a] happy;—
> And to change the Nature of Beaufort's connections with

---

1   Donkin, *Getting into the Act: Women Playwrights in London 1776-1829* (London: Routledge, 1995) 212-13, n. 13.

2   Adelstein, *Fanny Burney*, 61. See Appendix B.12.

3   For the destruction of Burney's early works, see Doody, *Frances Burney*, 35-36.

4   c. 13 August 1779; *Early Journals*, III, 349.

5   The text of Burney's letter quoted here is that prepared by Betty Rizzo for the fourth volume of *Early Journals and Letters*; see Appendix B.15. In the hitherto standard edition, the phrase "new written" is mistranscribed as "now written," giving the false impression that Act IV had only just been completed (*Diary and Letters of Madame d'Arblay*, ed. Austin Dobson [London: Macmillan, 1904-05], I, 316).

Lady Smatter, in order to obviate the unlucky resemblance the *adopted Nephew* bears to our *Female Pride of Literature*.

Few of these proposed revisions seem to have been made, although by deleting a passage in Act I, Burney did soften her satire of the club and removed one of the references to Beaufort's being Lady Smatter's nephew.[1]

In his reply to Burney, Crisp objected, not surprisingly, that the sweeping revisions she contemplated would leave little of the play intact:

> The omissions You propose are right, I think; but how the business of the Piece is to go on, with such omissions & Alterations as You mention, it is impossible for me to know — what you mean to leave out—*the Club, & the larger Share of Smatter & Dabler*—seems to have been the main Subject of the play — Cecilia's loss, & unexpected restoration of her fortune, is not a new Incident by any means — however any thing is preferable to Censor's interfering in the business, by his unaccountable generosity.[2]

After this rebuke, Burney wrote no more about her plans to revise *The Witlings*. Instead, for the next two decades, she put her ambitions as a comic dramatist on hold while she completed a second novel, *Cecilia* (1782), giving Cecilia's name and some of her character traits to the novel's heroine, who also loses (and partly regains) a fortune. Burney subsequently endured five unhappy years as keeper of the Queen's robes, married a French aristocrat, Alexandre d'Arblay, and published a third novel, *Camilla* (1796). She also completed three tragedies, one of which—*Edwy and Elgiva*—was produced at Drury Lane in 1795, closing after the first night.[3]

In her husband she found a companion whose delight in the

---

1  The deleted passage, which followed Act I, line 195, contained a satirical account by Beaufort of the "'Sprit Party," a "fantastic absurdity" directed by "my good aunt." Like Lady Smatter, Mrs. Montagu had a nephew, Matthew Robinson, who was her adoptive son and her heir.

2  Letter of 23 February 1780; *Early Journals*, IV, 17. See Appendix B.16.

3  For an account of Burney's career as tragedian, see Sabor *et al.*, *Complete Plays*, I, xii-xvii, xxx-xxxvii, and the headnote to each play in Volume II, *Tragedies*.

theatre matched her own. "We are both very fond of Plays & Operas," she remarked in a letter to her sister Charlotte in 1798, adding that she was "very indifferent" to any other form of public entertainment. She named six plays that she had attended between November 1797 and March 1798, noting that "after my long abstinence from the Theatre, this was pretty full fare."[1] This reawakening of her passion for theatre-going seems to have coincided with a renewal of her hopes to become a comic dramatist; at about this time she began work on the play that was to be called *Love and Fashion*, which she completed in 1799.[2] Though her hopes to see that play produced were also frustrated, in part through the continuing disapproval of Dr. Burney, she insisted upon attaining her "golden dream" if she could. She protested in a letter to her father in 1800 that she could not combat his "unaccountable but most afflicting displeasure" if she thought she had been "guilty of a crime in doing what I have all my life been urged to, & all my life intended, writing a Comedy."[3] Though she could not prevent her imagination from taking shape in a comedy, she assured her father that she would not bring disgrace upon herself or her family through either the "principles, the moral, or the language" that she intended to employ. Even as she wrote these words, she was probably already at work on her final two comedies, *A Busy Day* and *The Woman-Hater*, both completed by 1802.[4]

Unlike *The Witlings*, which Sheridan was eager to produce at Drury Lane, and *Love and Fashion*, scheduled for production by

---

1   Letter to Charlotte Broome, 3 April 1798; *Journals and Letters*, IV, 129.
2   For the approximate dates of composition of *Love and Fashion* and *A Busy Day*, together with the evidence that supports those dates, see the headnotes to each play in Sabor et al., *Complete Plays*.
3   Letter of 10 February 1800; *Journals and Letters*, IV, 394-95.
4   While the composition of *The Woman-Hater* cannot be dated precisely, some of Burney's notes for the play are written on the backs of letters sent to her in August 1801. Similar scraps used for the first holograph have dates as late as November 1801. The first draft was therefore probably written in autumn 1801, and the fair copy made before Burney left for France in April 1802. Burney's interest in the character of Lady Smatter may have revived after the death of Elizabeth Montagu on 25 August 1800 removed her father's objection that the play might offend the leader of the Bluestockings.

Thomas Harris at Covent Garden in March 1800, before its sudden withdrawal at the behest of Dr. Burney, Burney's last two plays remained entirely private affairs. She did draw up tentative cast-lists, assigning members of the Covent Garden company to parts in *A Busy Day* and Drury Lane actors to *The Woman-Hater*,[1] but neither Harris nor Sheridan, still manager at Drury Lane, was made aware of Burney's intentions. Her departure from England in April 1802 to join her husband in France put an end to any possible productions of her plays, and after her return in 1812 she had no further dealings with theatre managers. Dr. Burney had no need to suppress her final comedies, since he seems never to have been shown them or even told of their existence.

*A Busy Day*, with its trenchant satire of racial prejudice and its breaking down of class distinctions, has something in common with Burney's final novel, *The Wanderer* (1814), which she began writing at about the same time as she wrote her last three plays. *The Woman-Hater* is closer in spirit and character to her first, unpublished play, which she had not forgotten. Like *The Witlings*, *The Woman-Hater* depends for its humour on misquotations from famous authors by Lady Smatter, who affects a capacity for wit and a knowledge of literature that she does not possess. In *The Woman-Hater*, however, Lady Smatter is a single figure, not the leader of a literary club as she is in *The Witlings*, so there is less chance that she could be taken for a portrait of Elizabeth Montagu or any other particular person. *The Woman-Hater* also features several other survivors from that earlier, unknown play, such as Old Waverley, formerly known as Codger, and his son Jack; Bob Sapling, a "looby" in the spirit of Bob Voluble; and Sir Roderick, a woman-hater by virtue of his disappointment in love, who is distantly reminiscent of the crusty but essentially good-hearted Censor from *The Witlings*. But the most important change entails a greater emphasis on the sentimental aspect of the play. Eleonora here is restored to her reputation and to her husband's love, while her daughter, Sophia, is reunited with her father, Wilmot, who has wronged both of them through his hasty suspicions and jealousies. By intensifying the sentimentality, Burney evidently hoped to extract the sympathetic responses, even

1  See Sabor *et al.*, *Complete Plays*, I, 192-93, 289-90.

tears, from her audience that would soften her satiric barbs, and perhaps also supply the moral sentiments that had been found wanting in *The Witlings.*

The development of the sentimental plot in *The Woman-Hater* also allowed Burney to explore the personal relationships and histories of persons who existed only as objects of satire in *The Witlings.* A sheaf of notes bound up with the manuscripts of the first draft and the fair copy of *The Woman-Hater* contains some clues to the creative process by which *The Witlings* became *The Woman-Hater.* The germ of the new play seems to have been the following fragmentary note:

> Adonia and Sir Peppery are engaged to a Brother & Sister, when the Sister, a learned lady, lampoons the Baronet to have done with him. They part, & she marries Ld. Smatter—he vows vengeance on Adonia if she discard not the Brother—but tho' defrauded by her constancy of her fortune, which was all at his disposal, she faithfully wed Kembolton. Distressed in circumstances, they seek their fates in the E. Indies—where he grows jealous & fiery, they are wretched—sundry errors persuade him he is culpable—he tears her from her Infant Daughter [four lines crossed out].[1]

This note, with only minor changes, summarizes the action that precedes the beginning of *The Woman-Hater.* Some sixteen or seventeen years earlier, Eleonora (named Adonia in the above note) and her brother, Sir Roderick (Sir Peppery in the note), are engaged to marry another brother and sister, both named Wilmot (at first, Kembolton).[2] Miss Wilmot breaks off the engagement so

---

1   *The Woman-Hater,* preliminary holograph notes, 99 pp. Cased with *The Woman-Hater,* later holograph draft; Berg Collection, New York Public Library.
2   "Kembolton" is the name used for Wilmot in the preliminary notes. Burney changed the name to "Bolton" in the first draft, then crossed it out and replaced it with "Wilmot." The names "Kembolton" and "Wilmot" both appear to allude to a branch of the Montagu family, whose seat was "Kimbolton" in Huntingdon. Edward Montagu, 3rd Earl of Sandwich, married Elizabeth Wilmot, "the brilliant and largely uncontrollable daughter of that famous rake, the 2nd Earl of Rochester" (Bernard Falk, *The Way of the Montagues: A Gallery of Family Portraits* [London: Hutchinson, 1947] 288).

she can marry Lord Smatter (not, as the note says, by writing a lampoon of Sir Roderick, but because she has received some flattering verses from Lord Smatter). Sir Roderick, deeply angered, swears to disinherit Eleonora if she marries Wilmot, which she does anyway. The Wilmots, now with a child, flee to the West Indies, where Wilmot becomes suspicious of a certain sea-captain and, in a jealous rage, drives Eleonora from her home. As the action of the play begins, Wilmot has returned to England with his grown child to restore her to her rich uncle's favour, and also to clear the name of Eleonora, who he now believes is innocent. Unknown to him, Eleonora has also returned, accompanied by a young woman of the same age as Miss Wilmot. In the course of the play, we learn that the child now recognized as "Miss Wilmot" is not Wilmot's daughter, but a child put in her place by the Nurse when Eleonora secretly took her daughter away with her. Meanwhile, Eleonora and her daughter have been noticed by young Jack Waverley, who drops his cynical courtship of Lady Smatter and her money in order to pursue this new interest. The action of the play terminates in a general unmasking and reconciliation, in which "Miss Wilmot" is revealed as Joyce, the Nurse's daughter, who thereupon becomes a suitable match for Bob Sapling; Eleonora's daughter, Sophia, obtains her rightful place as the real "Miss Wilmot," making her a legitimate partner for Jack Waverley; Eleonora and Wilmot are reconciled, after Wilmot expresses contrition for his excessive passions; and even Lady Smatter and Sir Roderick show signs of renewing the courtship that was broken off many years ago. Along the way, Burney has transformed her earlier satire of literary affectation into a denunciation of misogyny, in the form of Sir Roderick's rage at women, and a warning about the dangers of uncontrolled passions through the example of Wilmot's irrational jealousy.

As Judy Simons suggests, one of Burney's chief satiric targets as a writer is the mis-education of women.[1] The character of Lady Smatter is that of a ridiculous woman whose head is stuffed with snippets of quotations that she attributes to the most unlikely authors and whose fortune has been wasted in a futile effort to

---

1 Simons, *Fanny Burney* (London: Macmillan, 1987) 127-28.

become a patron of the arts. She seems at first to constitute an argument *against* the education of women, on the grounds expressed by Sir Roderick, her frustrated suitor:

> Nay, what's the use of such pedantry, to a woman? Must she study mathematics—to count a Hen's nest?—must she understand Latin,—to stitch her sampler?—must she pore over a library, to find a Greek receipt for a Pudding? (p. 288)

But the reader soon learns to mistrust Sir Roderick's intemperate outbursts, which are as likely to be directed at the sycophantic codger, Old Waverley, or at Sir Roderick's conniving Steward, as they are at women. Sir Roderick's insistence that women should be confined to the domestic sphere of influence is consistent with his contempt for the abilities of everyone besides himself, and says more about his own deficiencies of character than it does about the educability of women. And from Lady Smatter's own mouth, the reader is offered evidence that her attempts at self-education by memorizing bits of poetry have not been successful:

> The learned, Mr. Waverley, are all of one opinion. And yet, study, study, as my friend Waller says, is but a fatiguing thing. It requires such thought! I assure you, sometimes, I think till I am quite stupid. (p. 208)

Lady Smatter is, in fact, not ineducable, but a victim of the practice of depriving women of the systematic education afforded to men. As a victim, Lady Smatter would deserve our sympathy, were it not for her persistent vanity and her willingness to sacrifice the happiness of others to build her reputation as a wit. The return of her brother, Wilmot, and his daughter from the West Indies, for example, gives Lady Smatter an opportunity to be redeemed for some of her selfishness. Wilmot asks her to assume the guardianship of her niece, Miss Wilmot, while he attempts to find his wife, Eleonora, who has fled his jealous accusations. But Lady Smatter, encumbered with the expenses of patronage, plans to palm Miss Wilmot off on the woman-hater Sir Roderick, who is the girl's uncle. So Lady Smatter's vanity is not mere foolishness; it leads to a denial of kinship and of a chance to nurture a young woman who very much needs the sort of literary patronage that Lady Smatter claims to represent.

Sir Roderick's misogyny presents an equally complicated problem. As the incident with the backgammon board shows early in the play, Sir Roderick's irascibility extends to everyone, though it is particularly directed at women. The most obvious reason for his resentment, which he carries so far as not even to allow women in his home, is Lady Smatter's rejection of his suit in favour of the lord who courted her in verse. But the Steward, who has known Sir Roderick since he was a boy, lets slip a more fundamental clue:

> I know it all, Sir: but Sir Roderick means no harm. He is only a spoilt Child, grown into an old Man. His Father died early, and his Mother never gainsay'd him; so that, till Lady Smatter played him false, he never knew what it was to be crossed in his days; though since then, to be sure, he can't so much as see the shadow of a Woman, but it puts him in a passion. (p. 180)

Misogyny therefore originates, at least in Sir Roderick's case, not as the consequence of an offensive action by a woman, nor as an inevitable gender prejudice in a man, but as the result of a lack of discipline in youth. Young Roderick was always permitted to indulge his passions, never required to check them; he has acquired an inflated sense of himself that does not require him to respect the sensibilities of others. His pride in himself is as unfounded as Lady Smatter's vanity, and like hers, his fault is not harmless: it has led him to precipitate his sister Eleonora's tragic predicament by renouncing her and her child, ostensibly on the basis of the rumours of her misconduct that had come back from the Indies. As Young Waverley tells us, however, Sir Roderick's renunciation of Eleonora had no moral basis, but was an act of retribution against the Wilmot family for Lady Smatter's having "crossed" him. The consequences of Sir Roderick's pride, as of Lady Smatter's vanity, are visited on the innocent Sophia, who is the niece of both of them. Misogyny is therefore not just a harmless war between the sexes; it is the consequence of mis-education on the one hand and lack of discipline on the other, abetted by the pride and vanity of the principal elder characters, faults of character that injure both them and their dependents. It would be wrong, however, to blame Sir Roderick and Lady Smatter exclusively for Eleonora's predicament, or to think that their lack of self-control is the play's most significant target. Eleonora's husband, Wilmot, displays as little self-restraint as his sister, Lady Smatter, or his brother-in-law, Sir Roderick. He condemns his wife for infidelities with Captain Ludlow before ascertaining the truth of his suspicions, and insists that she give him the custody of their child. Now, in the present moment of the play, he is equally convinced, on as little evidence, that she is innocent, and has returned to clear her name. As the action advances and he sees her accompanied by a child, while knowing that the girl he recognizes as their daughter is in his custody, he becomes convinced again of her guilt. Each of these convictions is accompanied by a storm of sentimental language expressing the passion with which he holds his present opinion. Wilmot's conduct finally becomes an object lesson in the evils of impetuous behaviour, and his sentimental expressions begin to appear not as the ornaments of a delicate sensibility, but as the symptoms of the inflamed passions that afflict him. Most telling, perhaps, is the degree to which his passionate convictions have blinded him to the true nature of the girl whom he takes to be his daughter, Miss Wilmot. Though she is dutiful to her father, Miss Wilmot's gifts are natural and intuitive, not cultivated. Despite this easily observed fact, Wilmot has given her a rather difficult book of poetry, Thomson's *The Seasons*, with which to amuse herself. Himself unable to read because of his state of mind, Wilmot exclaims:

> I cannot read—the words swim before my Eyes, but paint no images, communicate no ideas. We must share, in some degree, an author's powers, to be capable of enjoying them: and My powers, My faculties, are they not annihilated? Gone, gone—with Thee, Eleonora, gone! (p. 197)

The irony here is that his words apply better to Miss Wilmot than to himself, but he cannot see that because of his self-absorption. His neglect of Miss Wilmot, and his unstable wavering between condemnation and exaltation of his wife, constitute a subtle form of misogyny that is as hurtful, in its way, as the more violent rage of the woman-hater Sir Roderick.

Miss Wilmot, who is metamorphosed into Joyce midway through the play, is perhaps the most intriguing person in the whole cast of characters. A severely repressed personality in her first scene, in which she appears with her father, she soon reveals a playful—even "tricksey," as Old Waverley puts it—side of herself, as she teases her nurse, flirts with simple Bob Sapling, and dances about the room, proclaiming her liberty:

> And I don't chuse to put up with it any longer, Bob. I'm all for Liberty!—Liberty, Liberty, Bob! (p. 244)

At the end of the play, it is her natural and intuitive sense of truth and joy that causes her to expose the masquerade that she now recognizes her life has been, making possible an outcome that resolves everyone's dilemma satisfactorily. Although her character may easily be overread, it is perhaps not straining a point too much to identify Joyce with that revolutionary and romantic spirit that had overturned the social order in France a decade earlier and was bringing rapid social change to England. Both Burney and her aristocratic husband, Alexandre d'Arblay, welcomed the establishment of a constitutional republic in France, despite the personal sacrifices it cost them.[1] Alternatively, the dual personality of Miss Wilmot/Joyce may, as Margaret Doody suggests, express the conflicts that Burney felt over her relationship with her father that divided her psychologically into two daughters, the "quiet, docile, and stiff" Miss Wilmot, and the "perfect hoyden," Joyce. As Doody further observes, the dramatic problem of the play is complicated by the fact that not only are two personalities shared by one daughter, but the role of the Daughter is split between two characters.[2] In this respect, Sophia's predicament in the play is less

---

1  See Doody, *Frances Burney*, 200.
2  Doody *Frances Burney*, 305-308. Doody incorporates Sophia into her autobiographical reading of the daughter's role by identifying her as the "shadowy, if lovely and ideally good" counterpart of the "awkward, physical, un-ideal Joyce," and suggests that the detection of the "cheat" at the close of the play liberates not only the daughter but also the father from the "sexual and emotional misery" under which their relationship has

similar to Cecilia's in *The Witlings* than it is to Evelina's in Burney's first novel, in which the protagonist was deprived of her father by a scheming nurse who substituted her own child for the dispossessed girl. That novel is resolved when the two young women are, in effect, switched back to their rightful identities; but a playgoer might well wonder how Burney will resolve both a psychological drama and a comedy of mistaken identity at the same time.

A clue to Burney's strategy for resolving the comedy is planted in the play's first act. In one of his angry outbursts, Sir Roderick exclaims:

> Ay, that's the way with you! not I, and not I! that's always the case! Every thing's done by Nobody! You are a pretty set of fellows, indeed! a very pretty set of fellows! so not one among you could be found to bring the Letter to my Chamber? And I might have out-slept the Seven Sleepers, if I would, and never have known it was come? (p. 185)

The figure of "Nobody," who is blamed here for having received a letter written by a woman, was one of Burney's favorite devices for disguising the author of an act, literary or otherwise. As several critics have remarked, it was Nobody whom she had addressed in her earliest diaries:

> To Nobody, then, will I write my Journal! since To Nobody can I be wholly unreserved—to Nobody can I reveal every thought, every wish of my Heart, with the most unlimited confidence, the most unremitting sincerity to the end of my Life! For what chance, what accident can end my connections with Nobody?[1]

---

laboured. Doody also recognizes a similarity between Burney's *The Woman-Hater* and *A Winter's Tale*, as well as to Burney's own novel, *Evelina*.

1   Journal entry for 27 March 1768; *Early Journals*, I, 2. Burney's use of "Nobody" as a female character is discussed by Doody, 41, by Joanne Cutting-Gray in *Woman as "Nobody" and the Novels of Fanny Burney* (Gainesville: University Press of Florida, 1992), and by Catherine Gallagher, *Nobody's Story: The Vanishing Acts of Women in the Marketplace, 1670-1820* (Berkeley: University of California Press, 1994), but the figure's appearance in *The Woman-Hater* suggests that Burney did not conceive of Nobody as exclusively female.

The figure of Nobody, which has an ancient pedigree, was often paired in the eighteenth century with Somebody, an over-bearing person who took credit for things he did not do. Nobody was represented by a figure who was all arms and legs, and had no body, while Somebody was a corpulent figure whose body made his arms and legs disappear.[1] In *The Woman-Hater*, Nobody makes an appearance in Act IV in the person of young Jack Waverley, who has put on the Steward's suit as a disguise. Because the Steward's suit is too small for him, it "squeezes me ... horribly," as he admits, and his arms and legs stick out most peculiarly. In a scene of sustained comedy, young Jack fends off Old Waverley's insistence that he is his son, finally admitting that there is a resemblance:

> It's surprising what strong resemblances there sometimes are! I am frequently told nobody would know us asunder— except by our dress! And they say he has quite another taste in dress to what I have! But it's so familiar to me to be taken for him, that I am as much accustommed to be called Jack Waverley, as to be called by my own name. (pp. 258-59)

By employing the guise of Nobody as his double, Jack Waverley hopes to obtain an interview with Sophia, which his father's interest in her prevents. It is no doubt appropriate that Jack's courtship is not successful until it is paid in his proper person, rather than as Nobody. But just as Jack is Somebody masquerading as Nobody, so "Miss Wilmot" is Nobody masquerading as Somebody: from her first appearance in Act II, seated with a book in her hand (though she cannot read it), her physical and emotional being repressed, she is not the person she appears to be. But in the course of throwing off the deceit, she announces her true derivation:

> Why, Papa, I don't tell it very well; but Nurse says that you a'n't my Papa; and that my Mama, there, that should be, i'n't

---

1    An amusing history of Nobody and Somebody, with illustrations by William Hogarth, may be found in *Hogarth's Peregrination*, ed. Charles Mitchell (Oxford: Oxford University Press, 1952) xxiv-xxxi.

my Mama; and that that young lady there is your right earnest Daughter; and as for poor I—now who's daughter do you think I am? Why nobody's but old Nurse's, and a shoe-maker's. — And what do you think is my real Christian name? Why Joyce! (p. 283)

By revealing her identity as a "nobody," as someone whose proper person had been invisible throughout the play, Joyce can shed the expectations and prejudices that had hobbled her as "Miss Wilmot," and can marry simple Bob Sapling, and can eat, as she declares to her mother, as much as she likes.

Perhaps Burney meant nothing more by her puns on the word "nobody" than to enhance the comedy with a private joke. But even if this is granted, the acts committed by "Nobody" in the play alert us to one of the distinguishing features of comedy and to Burney's adept uses of the conventions of that genre. In a tragedy, the fault that precipitates the catastrophe can be laid precisely on a mistake or flaw of character in the protagonist, though it might be shared to a degree by another person in the drama. In *The Woman-Hater*, however, the fault can be laid equally on everybody, and on nobody. Sir Roderick is a misogynist, but he has been provoked by Lady Smatter. Lady Smatter is a vain fool, but she has been deprived of a proper education by her sex. Eleonora ran away from her husband, but only under the provocation of his jealous anger. Wilmot is a man of intemperate passions, but these lead as strongly toward affection and loyalty as they do toward jealousy and cruelty. Joyce has led a life of masquerade, but she was deceived by her mother, the nurse. Only the nurse has no excuse for her behaviour, and she, after all, can claim that it was nobody but a shoemaker who fathered the child whom, at the prompting of "Old Nick," she switched for the Wilmots' daughter. In the end, nobody is entirely to blame, which makes it possible for everyone to be satisfied with the result.

There are several signs that *The Woman-Hater* is the product of a well-tutored knowledge of the tradition of comedy. First there is the accusation made by Samuel Crisp that *The Witlings*, *The Woman-Hater*'s parent play, was drawn in part from Molière's *Les*

*Femmes Savantes.*[1] It is true that the "Esprit Party" that is led by Lady Smatter and Lady Sapient very much resembles Molière's circle of ladies who pretend to a knowledge of poetry, and who dote on the wretched verses of the wit Trissotin, just as Lady Smatter applauds those of Dabler. In both plays, the wit is revealed as a coward who will not acknowledge his own verses when they are criticized by a man of taste. In both plays, the marriageable young woman is prevented from realizing her ambitions by a rumor that her fortune has been lost in a bank failure, and then, when her lover's constancy has been tested and proven, is restored to prosperity in time to present her groom with a handsome dowry. In both plays, the older woman, who claims to be guided by her learning, acts directly against the interest and prospects of the young woman who is dependent on her. These structural similarities argue strongly that Burney, despite her assertion to the contrary, had at least some knowledge of Molière's play, and was paying tribute to it in her own first effort. The absence of any similarities in the phrasing, however, suggests that *The Witlings* is entirely of Burney's own composition, and that, in imitating Molière's model, she was merely following a practice that many other English dramatists had employed.[2]

Whatever model Burney may have used for *The Witlings*, her sources for *The Woman-Hater* place her in the mainstream of English comic drama. The title of the play appears to allude to Francis Beaumont and John Fletcher's *The Woman Hater* (1607), a seminal work in the anti-misogynist tradition.[3] This play is ostensibly the

---

1   In a note of uncertain date attached to her letter to Dr. Burney of c. 13 August 1779, Burney states: "The objections of Mr. Crisp to the MS. Play of the Witlings was its resemblance to Moliere's *Femmes Scavantes*—& consequent immense inferiority." The note is the only source for this objection, which appears in none of Burney's or Crisp's extant correspondences. Burney goes on to declare that "she had literally never read the *Femmes Scavantes* when she composed The Witlings." See *Early Journals*, III, 345.

2   For other uses of Molière in eighteenth-century English comedy, see Richard W. Bevis, *The Laughing Tradition: Stage Comedy in Garrick's Day* (Athens: University of Georgia Press, 1980) 88, and Doody, *Frances Burney*, 80-81. See also Appendix C.

3   *The Woman Hater*, ed. George Walton Williams, in *The Dramatic Works in the Beaumont and Fletcher Canon*, ed. Fredson Bowers (Cambridge: Cambridge University Press, 1966), I, 145-259. Beaumont and Fletcher's *The Woman Hater* reflects the era of Queen Elizabeth, a period in which women enjoyed, in somewhat greater measure than before or since, the privileges of learning and intellectual freedom. Within a dozen

story of the courtship of the virtuous Oriana by the Duke of Milan. Oriana, however, is drawn toward the challenge of reforming the notorious misogynist Count Gondarino, whose first lines establish a character that resembles Burney's Sir Roderick:

> *Servant.* My Lord—
> *Gondarino.* Ha.
> *Servant.* Here's one hath brought you a present.
> *Gondarino.* From whom, from a woman? if it be from a woman, bid him carrie it backe, and tell her shee's a whore: ... Was ther ever any man that hated his wife after death but I? and for her sake all women, women that were created onely for the preservation of little dogges.... O impudence of women, I can keepe dogs out of my house, or I can defend my house against theeves, but I cannot keep out women. (II, i, 1-33)

Gondarino, whose late wife had injured him in some unspecified way, has developed a consuming hatred of women, though he was formerly "the greatest servant to that sexe,/That ever was" (II, i, 119-20). When Oriana persists in her efforts to cure him of his malevolent passion, he destroys her reputation by spreading the rumour that she has spent the night in his bed, much in the way that Sir Roderick, motivated by spite over his rejection by Lady Smatter, ruins his sister Eleonora's reputation by disinheriting her and seeming to credit the rumours of her romance with Captain Ludlow. In both plays, the wronged woman's reputation must be cleared and the misogynist's hatred confronted in order to bring about a resolution. In both plays, the woman is subjected to a severe trial of her virtue, and her success in that trial results in the

---

years after the death of Elizabeth in 1603, however, the "learned lady" became once again the object of virulent satire. One such satire in prose was a pamphlet by Joseph Swetnam entitled *The Araignment of Lewd, Idle, Froward, and Unconstant Women* (1616), in which the author, in "a great choller," denounces the follies of women and their refusal to submit to the authority of their husbands. This pamphlet, which was reprinted frequently in the seventeenth and eighteenth centuries, inspired many responses, including an anonymous feminist play called *Swetnam, the Woman Hater* (1620), in which the misogynist Swetnam is besieged by women until he recants his errors. For the background of the "learned ladies" in English drama, see Jean Gagen, *The New Woman: Her Emergence in English Drama, 1600-1730* (New York: Twayne, 1954).

misogynist's being besieged by "troops" of women who torture him with their presence and break his will to resist. In Beaumont and Fletcher's play, Gondarino is obliged to support the petition of an old gentlewoman who has been seeking a favour from him, and to swear that he will never "meddle" with women again. In Burney's, Sir Roderick is successively attacked by two young women who both claim to be his niece, and then by Lady Smatter herself, who extracts one last tirade from him before he finally succumbs. In both plays, the wronged woman is restored to her good reputation and to her lover/husband's good graces.

Although Burney rooted her play in the tradition of English comedy, she took pains to distance it from its Elizabethan and Restoration predecessors. As we have seen, Eleonora's character was originally called Adonia, a name that would have fitted in well with the list of *dramatis personae* for Beaumont and Fletcher's play, but would hardly do for one set in Georgian England. Sir Roderick had been variously referred to in the notes as Sir Peppery and Sir Marmaduke, names more likely to amuse a Restoration audience than a modern one. By the time that Burney completed the first draft of *The Woman-Hater*, she had evidently come to realize that eponymous names like "Codger" gave too much away and prevented her from using the skill in character development she had acquired as a novelist. Moreover, many of the snatches of dialogue in the discarded notes seem to be backward-looking, as if she were still trying to sound the themes of Restoration comedy:

> *Sir Marmaduke.* Why where may a Man speak his Mind if not in his own House? Hay?
> *Codger.* It is not consonant to the Customs of the World.
> *Sir Marmaduke.* Why then the Customs of the World are consumed stupid, and I shall break thro' them all as fast as I can.
> *Codger.* It is what no Gentleman does.
> *Sir Marmaduke.* So much the Worse! So much the Worse! What, I suppose then if I was a Ragamuffin, if I had not a Coat to my Back, nor a House to my Head, I might live as I please, might I?
> *Codger.* It is an extremely unusual way of receiving visitors.

Besides being too close to the title of Congreve's play, the phrase "Customs of the World" strikes a note that was decidedly flat by 1801. The world's customs had already been rather thoroughly broken through, on the stage and off, and Sir Roderick's ill-humoured insistence on having his own way was no longer particularly comic.

Much more effective as comedy in the finished work is the scene in which the Steward, having heard Sir Roderick say that he wishes to leave his fortune to someone who can neither read nor write, presents his nephew Bob Sapling to Sir Roderick, with the recommendation that he is "a very ignorant young man." In answer to Sir Roderick's incredulous questions, Bob assures him that he has already made plans to "go shares" with a "She" who is "as bad off as I" when he has got Sir Roderick's fortune (pp. 262-63). The audience, knowing of Sir Roderick's prejudices, is moved to laughter as simple Bob Sapling plunges deeper and deeper into dangerous waters. The laughter is directed not at Bob's simplicity so much as it is at the pain felt by Sir Roderick as his two passions, his fear of the loss of his property and his hatred of women, are both aroused at once. In this way, the comedy of the scene is turned toward the ends for which Goldsmith and Sheridan had directed their own "laughing comedies." Burney employs laughter to mock instances of human folly and frailty, particularly the indulgence of unbridled passion, in a way that is at the same time instructive and amusing.[1]

In one other respect, too, Burney shows that she understood recent tendencies in the theory of comedy. Certain scenes, particularly those between Eleonora and Wilmot, resemble the sentimental comedy identified with Richard Steele.[2] Steele's best-known play, *The Conscious Lovers*, resembles Burney's in its story of a young woman's return from the West Indies and her reunion with her father, who believed her lost. Where Burney's play

---

1 For a discussion of the laughing comedies of Goldsmith and Sheridan, see Bevis, *The Laughing Tradition*.

2 A discussion of the difficulties of defining such genres as "sentimental comedy" may be found in Bevis, 47-52. He argues that the term is still useful, provided that one distinguishes among the types of sentiment that were represented and the ends for which it was used.

exceeds Steele's, perhaps, is in the emotional recognition of error that the reunion precipitates. Wilmot cannot accept Sophia as his daughter until Eleonora has brought him to believe in her innocence and until Wilmot has admitted that all of their troubles have resulted from his "fiery" temperament, which predisposed him to believe the worst of his wife. When father, mother, and daughter have at last been reunited, it falls to Wilmot to deliver the moral:

> Now, then, my Eleonora, let me hope the tempest of our days is past. What waywardly I have lost, I will study soberly to regain, convinced, by penitent experience, that not all the ills of pain, pestilence, or War, can be compared with the convulsive tortures of acute and ungoverned passions. (p. 289)

The drama has, in its final moments, come dangerously close to catastrophe, from which it has been saved by Joyce's honest and unforced exposure of her mother's substitution of her for the real Miss Wilmot. The sudden reversal of potential tragedy, coupled with Wilmot's recognition of his errors, provides an opportunity for the tears of exquisite joy that are the hallmark of sentimental comedy. The rhetorical strategy of the play has employed laughter to ridicule those frailties of character that needed to be attacked, and tears of joy to mark those moments of moral insight and action that we are to regard as exemplary. By pursuing this double strategy, Burney brings together the two dominant strains of English comedy in order to achieve a single dramatic effect.

The brush with tragedy raises a final critical question, which is whether this play should be considered a melodrama. Melodrama is a hybrid form in which a protagonist encounters, and eventually overcomes, an external adversary; it is often considered a less sophisticated dramatic form than either comedy or tragedy, in which the protagonist overcomes, or succumbs to, a complication arising in his or her own character or conduct. There are what appear to be melodramatic touches in The Woman-Hater, particularly the undeserved sufferings of Eleonora and the emotional excesses of Wilmot, but these touches are elements of Gothic drama, a form popular in the 1780s and 1790s, rather than melo-drama. Gothic drama, as Paula Backscheider contends, involves an "authority figure gone mad, or at least seriously obsessive and neurotically moody," a figure of particular concern to English audiences in an age when their own sovereign, George III, suffered from porphyria.[1] A first reading of *The Woman-Hater* might locate this neurotic authority figure in the vituperative Sir Roderick, but the truly Gothic character is the potential villain Wilmot, whose dark mutterings in Act IV – "I will not seek her habitation till midnight. Our interview must have no witnesses, no interruption. — Whither — whither — when it is over, shall I guide my desperate steps?" (p. 249)—may conceal a murderous intent. Wilmot is, as Backscheider says of the Gothic protagonist, "subject to cataclysmic passions, has committed or is contemplating unspeakable crimes that reek of ancient, sacred taboos, and is engaged in a magnificent struggle with himself." Similarly, Eleonora may be read as a Gothic heroine whose function is, first, to be sexually vulnerable, and then to bring out the protagonist's latent benevolence.[2] In her tragedies, also influenced by the contemporary vogue for the Gothic, Burney's heroines meet a variety of appalling fates. But *The Woman-Hater* concludes instead with Wilmot's submission to Eleonora, and Joyce's reminder that woman-hating is only an inverted recognition of female authority.

It is unfortunate that *The Woman-Hater*, like *The Witlings* and Burney's two other comedies, was never performed on stage in her lifetime. Had the plays gone into production, they would have received the final polish that only a theatrical performance can give, and the stage in turn might have recovered from them something of the comic tradition—the subtle touches of wit, the insight into character, the pleasure of wrongs set right—that theatrical audiences of the late eighteenth and early nineteenth century saw too rarely. Instead, Burney's plays were packed away with her other private manuscripts, coming to light only in 1945 after their acquisition by the Berg Collection of the New York Public

---

1   Paula Backscheider, *Spectacular Politics: Theatrical Power and Mass Culture in Early Modern England* (Baltimore: Johns Hopkins University Press, 1993) 162-63.
2   Backscheider 199-200.

Library. Since then, the plays have been the subject of a pioneering article by Joyce Hemlow, of substantial parts of biographies of Burney by Margaret Anne Doody, Kate Chisholm, Claire Harman, and Janice Thaddeus, and of a book by Barbara Darby. Separate editions of *Edwy and Elgiva*, *A Busy Day*, and *The Witlings* have been published, and *The Witlings* has also been anthologized. With the publication of *The Complete Plays of Frances Burney* in two volumes in 1995, the entire range of Burney's dramatic work became accessible to a large reading audience, making possible for the first time a fair assessment of her accomplishment.[1] Almost simultaneously, productions of two of the comedies, *A Busy Day* and *The Witlings*, took place in London and New York, followed by a new production of *A Busy Day* in Bristol and a West-End premiere at the Lyric Theatre, Shaftesbury Avenue, in 2000, and a North American premiere of *A Busy Day* in 2001.[2] Burney's plays gained her neither fame nor financial reward in her time, but, even at this late date, they may earn for her the literary reputation she most desired—that of dramatist.

---

1  See Hemlow, "Fanny Burney: Playwright (1949-50)"; Doody, *Frances Burney*, 1985; Chisholm, *Fanny Burney: Her Life, 1752-1840* (London: Chatto & Windus, 1998); Harman, *Fanny Burney: A Biography* (London: HarperCollins, 2000); Thaddeus, *Frances Burney: A Literary Life* (London: Macmillan, 2000); Darby, *Frances Burney, Dramatist: Gender, Performance, and the Late Eighteenth-Century Stage* (Lexington: University Press of Kentucky, 1997); *Edwy and Elgiva*, ed. Miriam J. Benkovitz (Hamden, CT: Shoe String Press, 1957); *A Busy Day*, ed. Tara Ghoshal Wallace (New Brunswick, NJ: Rutgers University Press, 1985); *A Busy Day*, ed. Alan Coveney (London: Oberon Books, 2000); *The Witlings*, ed. Clayton J. Delery (East Lansing, MI: Colleagues Press, 1995); *The Meridian Anthology*, ed. Rogers, 1994; *The Complete Plays of Frances Burney*, ed. Sabor *et al.*, 1995.

2  Show of Strength productions of *A Busy Day* in Bristol, 29 September-23 October 1993, and London, 29 June-30 July 1994; production of *The Witlings* at the College of Staten Island, CUNY, 9-13 November 1994; Bristol Old Vic production of *A Busy Day* at the Bristol Old Vic Theatre, 12 April-6 May 2000, and the Lyric Theatre, London, 19 June-August 2000; Chancellor High School production of *A Busy Day*, Fredericksburg, Virginia, 6-8 April, 2001.

# Frances Burney: A Brief Chronology

1752    Born in King's Lynn, Norfolk, 13 June.
1760    Family moves to Poland Street, London.
1762    Death of mother, Esther Sleepe Burney (27 September).
1767    Destroys juvenilia, including diaries, poetry, plays, and novel, "The History of Caroline Evelyn," in bonfire on birthday (13 June). Father, Dr. Charles Burney, marries Elizabeth Allen (2 October).
1768    Begins new journal (27 March).
1770    Refuses to play the "quite shocking" part of Tag in family performance of Garrick's farce *Miss in her Teens* (February).
1771    Plays Lady Easy and Lady Graveairs in family performance of scenes from Colley Cibber's comedy *The Careless Husband* (30 June). Plays Lady Truman in family performance of Addison's comedy *The Drummer* (29 September).
1774    Family moves to Newton's former house, St. Martin's Street, Leicester Square.
1777    Epilogue, probably by Burney, to John Jackson's tragedy *Gerilda: or the Siege of Harlech*, spoken by Jane Barsanti at Crow Street Theatre, Dublin (13 January), and published in *Walker's Hibernian Magazine* (January). Plays Mrs. Lovemore in elaborate family performance of Arthur Murphy's *The Way to Keep Him*, including an additional scene probably written by herself (7 April). On the same night plays Huncamunca in Fielding's *Tom Thumb*.
1778    First novel, *Evelina; or, A Young Lady's Entrance into the World*, published (29 January). Begins writing her first play, *The Witlings*.
1779    Completes first draft of *The Witlings* (4 May), encouraged by dramatists Richard Brinsley Sheridan and Arthur Murphy, as well as by Samuel Johnson, Joshua Reynolds, and Hester Thrale. After reading a revised draft of the play on 2 August, her father and family

friend Samuel Crisp urge her to suppress the play, for fear of offending the London bluestockings.

1780   Revises Act IV of *The Witlings*, with a view to showing the whole play to Sheridan (January). Plans further revisions, but is persuaded by Dr. Burney and Crisp to abandon the play.

1782   Second novel, *Cecilia; or, Memoirs of an Heiress*, published (12 July).

1786   Begins five years of service at court, as Keeper of the Robes to Queen Charlotte (17 July).

1788   Begins writing her first tragedy, *Edwy and Elgiva* (October) during period of madness of King George III.

1790   Returns to *Edwy and Elgiva* (4 April); completes first draft (August). Begins writing *Hubert De Vere* (August) and *The Siege of Pevensey*.

1791   Completes first draft of *Hubert De Vere*; begins writing *Elberta* (June). Ill health impels her to leave service of Queen (7 July); granted annual pension of 100 pounds.

1793   Meets Alexander d'Arblay, exiled Adjutant-General of the Marquis de Lafayette (January); secret courtship; marriage (28 July). *Hubert De Vere* accepted by Kemble for production at Drury Lane (5 July); later withdrawn in favour of *Edwy and Elgiva*. Pamphlet, *Brief Reflections Relative to the Emigrant French Clergy* (November); proceeds to charity.

1794   Revised version of *Edwy and Elgiva* accepted by Kemble and Sheridan for production at Drury Lane (December). Birth of son, her only child, Alexander (18 December).

1795   *Edwy and Elgiva* produced at Drury Lane, starring John Philip Kemble and Sarah Siddons, with prologue by brother Charles; withdrawn after one performance (21 March). Further revised by both Burney and d'Arblay (May-June).

1796   Third novel, *Camilla; or, A Picture of Youth*, published (12 July). Death of stepmother (20 October).

1797   Begins revising *Hubert De Vere* as a closet drama.

1798   Writes second comedy, *Love and Fashion*. May have

contributed to a farce, *The Triumphant Toadeater*, probably by her brother-in-law, Ralph Broome.

1799    *Love and Fashion* accepted for March 1800 production at Covent Garden by Thomas Harris (30 October).

1800    Death of sister Susanna (6 January) causes Burney to withdraw *Love and Fashion* from production (February). Probably begins writing *The Woman-Hater* and *A Busy Day*.

1802    Probably completes *The Woman-Hater*, intended for Drury Lane, and *A Busy Day*, intended for Covent Garden; neither produced. Burney and son follow General d'Arblay to France (April).

1811    Undergoes mastectomy for breast cancer, without anaesthetic, at home in Paris (30 September).

1812    Returns to England with son.

1814    Fourth novel, *The Wanderer; or, Female Difficulties*, published (28 March). Death of father (12 April). Works on unfinished tragedy, *Elberta*. Returns to France, leaving son at Cambridge.

1815    Moves to Belgium while d'Arblay fights in army opposing Napoleon; returns to England with husband (October).

1817    Death of favourite brother, Charles (28 December).

1818    Death of General d'Arblay (3 May) at home in Bath.

1819    Son Alexander ordained priest in Church of England (11 April).

1832    *Memoirs of Doctor Burney* published (November).

c.1836  Times readings of *Hubert De Vere*, *The Siege of Pevensey*, and *Love and Fashion* with view towards possible production.

1837    Death of Alexander (19 January).

1840    Dies in London (6 January), aged 87; buried in Wolcot Churchyard, Bath, beside husband and son.

1842–46 Niece Charlotte Barrett edits *Diary and Letters of Madame d'Arblay* (7 vols).

1889    *The Early Diary of Frances Burney 1768-1778*, ed. Annie Raine Ellis (2 vols).

1957    *Edwy and Elgiva*, ed. Miriam J. Benkovitz.

1972-84 *The Journals and Letters of Fanny Burney (Madame d'Arblay) 1791-1840*, ed. Joyce Hemlow *et al.* (12 vols).

1984 *A Busy Day*, ed. Tara Ghoshal Wallace.

1988 *The Early Journals and Letters of Fanny Burney*, ed. Lars E. Troide *et al.* (6 vols in progress).

1993 *A Busy Day* produced by the Show of Strength company at Hen and Chicken Theatre, Bedminster, Bristol (29 September-23 October).

1994 Show of Strength production of *A Busy Day* revived at King's Head Theatre, London (29 June-30 July). *The Witlings* produced at the College of Staten Island, CUNY (9-13 November).

1995 *The Complete Plays of Frances Burney*, ed. Peter Sabor *et al.* (2 vols).

2000 Bristol Old Vic production of *A Busy Day* at Bristol Old Vic Theatre (12 April-6 May) and at Lyric Theatre, Shaftesbury Avenue, London (19 June-August).

2001 Chancellor High School production of *A Busy Day*, Fredericksburg, Virginia (6-8 April).

2002 Dedication of Commemorative Window, Poets' Corner, Westminster Abbey (13 June); "Burney People," readings from the four comedies and *Elberta* during two-day conference marking Burney's 250th birthday, National Portrait Gallery (14 June).

# A Note on the Text

The texts of *The Witlings* and *The Woman-Hater* in this edition are those prepared for *The Complete Plays of Frances Burney*, 2 vols. (London: Pickering & Chatto, 1995): *The Witlings* by Peter Sabor and *The Woman-Hater* by Geoffrey Sill.

Since none of Burney's plays was printed in her lifetime, the copy-texts used here are her manuscripts, preserved in the Berg Collection of the New York Public Library. There is only one surviving manuscript of *The Witlings*, a fair copy in Burney's hand. It consists of 165 pages in five notebooks, one for each act, of which only the first two are numbered. The handwriting, in ink, is exceptionally neat; there are no illegible words. On some twenty occasions a word or passage is deleted, usually in pencil and usually with an insertion replacing the deleted material; the final version of the text is printed here. In addition to deleting material, Burney marked several passages for possible cancellation without scoring through them, using symbols similar to those in her journals and letters to indicate the potential cuts. Since those passages were not, in fact, deleted, they have been retained in this edition.

There are two surviving manuscripts of *The Woman-Hater*. The first, 486 pages sewn together into five notebooks, one for each act, together with some separate sheets, is in Burney's hand. The pages used are the backs of letters and of subscription notices for *Camilla*. It is very heavily corrected, usually in the ink used for the text but occasionally in pencil. These corrections represent two stages of revision: those made at the time of writing and those added before the second manuscript was transcribed.

The second manuscript, a fair copy in Burney's hand of 202 pages in five notebooks, one for each act, is printed here. It contains fewer revisions than the other and is much more neatly transcribed. Boxed with this copy are ninety-nine pages of autograph notes related both to *The Woman-Hater* and to Burney's other comedies, *The Witlings*, *Love and Fashion*, and *A Busy Day*. These notes show the gradual evolution of *The Woman-Hater* from its origins in *The Witlings*, as discussed in the Introduction.

In editing Burney's plays, our intention has been to produce a clear reading or acting text, while also respecting the manuscript version that she left. Burney's act and scene divisions have been followed, although these differ greatly between the two plays: *The Witlings* has acts unbroken by scene divisions, while each act of *The Woman-Hater* has a large number of scenes, in some cases with a single speech divided into two scenes. Eighteenth-century spellings have been retained, as have different spellings of the same word. Burney's habitual use of "it's" to show possession, as well as her spelling of "neither" as "niether," in the *Complete Plays of Frances Burney*, have been regularized in this edition. We have also regularized the spellings of the names of characters in the plays and corrected any obvious errors.

Certain changes, similarly, have been made to punctuation and capitalization. Periods missing from the ends of sentences have been inserted, and lower-case letters used to begin a sentence after a period have been changed to upper case. Dashes of different lengths have been regularized to the same length, and raised letters, used for abbreviations such as Mr., have been dropped. Other kinds of abbreviations have been written out in full: thus numerals are changed to words, the ampersand to "and," etc. Running quotation marks have been replaced by quotation marks at the beginning and end of the passage in question. Catchwords, ornamental letters, different sizes of capitals, and other features of the manuscript have not been reproduced.

As is customary in editing plays from manuscript, more changes have been made to the presentation of stage directions than to the dialogue. Names of speakers preceding dialogue and within stage directions have been capitalized throughout, and the directions have been printed in italics. In the manuscripts, the direction "*aside*" is often written after the passage to which it applies; in this edition it is printed before the passage, making it clear to readers that an aside has begun. We have not found it necessary to add directions indicating that an aside has given way to regular dialogue.

# THE WITLINGS

## A COMEDY

### BY A SISTER OF THE ORDER

# DRAMATIS PERSONAE

BEAUFORT.

CENSOR.

DABLER.

JACK, half Brother[1] to Beaufort.

CODGER, Father to Jack, and Father in Law[2] to Beaufort.

BOB, Son to Mrs. Voluble.

LADY SMATTER, Aunt to Beaufort.

CECILIA.

MRS. SAPIENT.[3]

MRS. VOLUBLE.

MRS. WHEEDLE, a Milliner.

MISS JENNY, her apprentice.

BETTY, Maid to Mrs. Voluble.

---

1  *half Brother*: Jack's mother's first husband was Beaufort's father; her second husband was Codger: Beaufort's father was Lady Smatter's brother.

2  *Father in Law*: stepfather.

3  *Sapient*: wise.

# ACT I

*Scene, a Milliner's Shop.*[1] *A Counter is spread with Caps, Ribbons, Fans and Band Boxes.*[2] Miss Jenny *and several young women at Work.*

*Enter* Mrs. Wheedle.

Mrs. Wheedle. So, young ladies! pray what have you done to Day? (*she examines their Work.*) Has any body been in yet?
Miss Jenny. No, ma'am, nobody to Signify;—only some people a foot.
Mrs. Wheedle. Why, Miss Sally, who is this Cap for?                    5
Miss Sally. Lady Mary Megrim,[3] ma'am.
Mrs. Wheedle. Lady Mary Megrim, Child? Lord, she'll no more wear it than I shall! why how have you done the Lappets?[4] they'll never set while it's a Cap;—one would think you had never worked in a Christian Land before. Pray, Miss    10
Jenny, set about a Cap for Lady Mary yourself.
Miss Jenny. Ma'am I can't; I'm working for Miss Stanley.
Mrs. Wheedle. O ay, for the Wedding.
Miss Sally. Am I to go on with this Cap, ma'am?
Mrs. Wheedle. Yes, to be sure, and let it be sent with the other    15
things to Mrs. Apeall in the Minories;[5] it will do well enough for the City.

*Enter a* Footman.

Footman. Is Lady Whirligig's[6] Cloak ready?

---

1  *a Milliner's Shop*: Doody notes how unusual this setting is for an eighteenth-century play (*Frances Burney*, 77). In *Evelina*, the heroine visits milliner's shops in London (27) and Bristol (328), and in *The Wanderer*, the heroine works as a milliner (chs 45-7).
2  *Band Boxes*: flimsy boxes made of cardboard or very thin wood, used for carrying hats, millinery, etc.
3  *Megrim*: ill-tempered caprice.
4  *Lappets*: streamers attached to a cap. Caps, worn indoors, were made of fine material, pleated and arranged.
5  *the Minories*: a street in the City of London, occupied by flourishing tradespeople. A woman such as Mrs. Apeall would wish to "ape," or imitate, fashionable women in the west end of London. The City, then as now the centre of trade and finance, lies to the east of Temple Bar.
6  *Whirligig*: a spinning toy; metaphorically, a woman of constant whims.

MRS. WHEEDLE. Not quite, Sir, but I'll send it in five minutes.

20 FOOTMAN. My Lady wants it immediately; it was bespoke a Week ago, and my lady says you promised to let her have it last Friday.

MRS. WHEEDLE. Sir it's just done, and I'll take care to let her Ladyship have it directly.

*Exit* FOOTMAN.

25 MISS JENNY. I don't think it's cut out yet.

MRS. WHEEDLE. I know it i'n't. Miss Sally, you shall set about it when you've done that Cap. Why Miss Polly, for goodness' sake what are you doing?

MISS POLLY. Making a Tippet,[1] ma'am, for Miss Lollop.[2]

30 MRS. WHEEDLE. Miss Lollop would as soon wear a Halter: 'twill be fit for nothing but the Window, and there the Miss Notables who work for themselves may look at it for a Pattern.

*Enter a* YOUNG WOMAN.

YOUNG WOMAN. If you please, ma'am, I should be glad to look at some Ribbons.

35 MRS. WHEEDLE. We'll shew you some presently.

*Enter* MRS. VOLUBLE.

MRS. VOLUBLE. Mrs. Wheedle, how do do? I'm vastly glad to see you. I hope all the young Ladies are well. Miss Jenny, my dear, you look pale; I hope you a'n't in Love, Child? Miss Sally, your Servant. I saw your Uncle the other Day, and he's
40 very well, and so are all the children; except, indeed, poor Tommy, and they're afraid he's going to have the Whooping Cough. I don't think I know that other young lady? O Lord yes, I do,—it's Miss Polly Dyson! I beg your pardon, my dear, but I declare I did not recollect you at first.

45 MRS. WHEEDLE. Won't you take a Chair, Mrs. Voluble?

---

1 *Tippet*: a short cape covering the shoulders.
2 *Lollop*: to lounge about.

MRS. VOLUBLE. Why yes, thank you, ma'am; but there are so many pretty things to look at in your shop, that one does not know which way to turn oneself. I declare it's the greatest treat in the World to me to spend an Hour or two here in a morning; one sees so many fine things, and so many fine folks,—Lord, who are all these sweet things here for?

MRS. WHEEDLE. Miss Stanley, Ma'am, a young lady just going to be married.

MRS. VOLUBLE. Miss Stanley? why I can tell you all about her. Mr. Dabler, who Lives in my House, makes Verses upon her.

MISS JENNY. Dear me! is that Gentleman who Dresses so smart a Poet?

MRS. VOLUBLE. A Poet? yes, my dear, he's one of the first Wits of the age. He can make Verses as fast as I can talk.

MISS JENNY. Dear me! why he's quite a fine Gentleman; I thought Poets were always as poor as Job.[1]

MRS. VOLUBLE. Why so they are, my dear, in common; your *real* Poet is all rags and atoms: but Mr. Dabler is quite another thing; he's what you may call a Poet of Fashion. He studies, sometimes, by the Hour together. O he's quite one of the great Geniusses, I assure you! I listened at his Door, once, when he was at it,—for he talks so loud when he's by himself, that we can hear him quite down Stairs: but I could make nothing out, only a heap of Words all in a Chime, as one may say,—mean, lean, Dean, wean—Lord, I can't remember half of them! At first when he came, I used to run in his Room, and ask what was the matter? but he told me I must not mind him, for it was only the *Fit* was on him, I think he called it, and so—

YOUNG WOMAN. I wish Somebody would shew me some Ribbons, I have waited this half Hour.

MRS. WHEEDLE. O, ay, I forgot; do shew this young Gentlewoman some Ribbons. (*in a low voice*) Take last year's. You shall see some just out of the loom.

MRS. VOLUBLE. Well but, Mrs. Wheedle, I was going to tell you about Miss Stanley; you must know she's a young Lady with a

---

1  *poor as Job*: proverbial; poverty was one of the many calamities that befell the patient sufferer of the Book of Job.

Fortune all in her own Hands, for she's just come of age, and she's got neither Papa nor Mama, and so —

*Enter a* FOOTMAN.

FOOTMAN. Lady Bab Vertigo desires Mrs. Wheedle will come to
85    the Coach Door.

*Exit.* MRS. WHEEDLE *goes out.*

MRS. VOLUBLE (*turning to* MISS JENNY). And so, Miss Jenny, as I was saying, this young lady came to spend the Winter in Town[1] with Lady Smatter, and so she fell in Love with my lady's Nephew, Mr. Beaufort, and Mr. Beaufort fell in Love
90    with her, and so —

*Re-enter* MRS. WHEEDLE.

MRS. WHEEDLE. Miss Jenny, take Lady Bab the new Trimming.
MRS. VOLUBLE (*turning to* MISS SALLY). And so, Miss Sally, the match is all agreed upon, and they are to be married next Week, and so, as soon as the Ceremony is over —
95 MRS. WHEEDLE. Miss Sally, put away those Ribbons.
MRS. VOLUBLE (*turning to* MISS POLLY). And so, Miss Polly, as soon as the Ceremony's over, the Bride and Bridegroom —
CENSOR (*within*). No, faith, not I! do you think I want to study the fashion of a Lady's Top knot?[2]
100 BEAUFORT. Nay, prithee, Censor, in compassion to me —

*Enter* BEAUFORT *and* CENSOR *strug'ling.*

CENSOR. Why how now, Beaufort? is not a man's person his own property? do you conclude that, because you take the liberty to expose your own to a ridiculous and unmanly situation, you may use the same freedom with your Friend's?

---

1  *Winter in Town*: the London season for the fashionable began in about November, ending with the birthday of George III on 4 June.
2  *Top knot*: a bow of ribbons, etc., in a lace cap or in a woman's hair.

BEAUFORT. Pho, prithee don't be so churlish. Pray, ma'am 105 (*advancing to* MRS. WHEEDLE), has Miss Stanley been here this Morning?

MRS. WHEEDLE. No, Sir; but I expect her every moment.

BEAUFORT. Then, if you'll give me leave, I'll wait till she comes.

CENSOR. Do as you list, but, for my part, I am gone. 110

BEAUFORT. How! will you not stay with me?

CENSOR. No, Sir; I'm a very stupid fellow,—I take no manner of delight in Tapes and Ribbons. I leave you, therefore, to the unmolested contemplation of this valuable collection of Dainties: and I doubt not but you will be equally charmed 115 and edified by the various curiosities you will behold, and the sagacious observations you will hear. Sir, I heartily wish you well entertained. (*going.*)

BEAUFORT (*holding him*). Have you no Bowels, man?

CENSOR. Yes, for *myself*, and therefore it is I leave you. 120

BEAUFORT. You sha'n't go, I swear!

CENSOR. With what Weapons will you stay me? Will you tie me to your little Finger with a piece of Ribbon, like a lady's Sparrow? or will you inthrall me in a Net of Brussel's Lace? Will you raise a Fortification of Caps? or Barricade me with 125 Furbelows?[1] Will you Fire at me a Broad Side of Pompoons?[2] or will you stop my retreat with a Fan?

MISS JENNY. Dear, how odd the Gentleman talks!

MRS. WHEEDLE. I wonder they don't ask to look at something.

MISS VOLUBLE. I fancy I know who they are. (*whispers.*) 130

BEAUFORT. Are you not as able to bear the place as I am? if you had any Grace, you would Blush to be thus out-done in forbearance.

CENSOR. But, my good friend, do you not consider that there is some little difference in our situations? I, for which I bless my 135 Stars! am a *Free* man, and therefore may be allowed to have an opinion of my own, to act with consistency, and to be guided by the light of Reason: you, for which I most heartily pity you, are a Lover, and, consequently, can have no pretensions

---

1   *Furbelows*: pleated borders of women's gowns or petticoats.
2   *Pompoons*: variant of "pompon," a band of ribbons or threads used to ornament hair, cap, or dress.

140 to similar privileges. With you, therefore, the practice of patience, the toleration of impertinence, and the Study of Nonsence, are become duties indispensable; and where can you find more ample occasion to display these acquirements, than in this Region of Foppery, Extravagance and Folly?

145 BEAUFORT. Ought you not, in justice, to acknowledge some obligation to me for introducing you to a place which abounds in such copious materials to gratify your Splenetic Humour?

CENSOR. Obligation? what, for shewing me new Scenes of the 150 absurdities of my Fellow Creatures?

BEAUFORT. Yes, since those new Scenes give fresh occasion to exert that Spirit of railing which makes the whole happiness of your Life.

CENSOR. Do you imagine, then, that, like Spencer's Strife, I *seek* 155 occasion?[1] Have I not Eyes? and can I open them without becoming a Spectator of Dissipation, Idleness, Luxury and disorder? Have I not Ears? and can I use them without becoming an Auditor of Malevolence, Envy, futility and Detraction? O Beaufort, take me where I can *avoid* occasion 160 of railing, and then, indeed, I will confess my obligation to you!

MRS. VOLUBLE (*whispering* MRS. WHEEDLE). It's the youngest that's the Bridegroom, that is to be; but I'm pretty sure I know the other too, for he comes to see Mr. Dabler; I'll speak 165 to him. (*advances to* CENSOR) Sir, your humble Servant.

CENSOR. Madam!

MRS. VOLUBLE. I beg your pardon, Sir, but I think I've had the pleasure of seeing you at my House, Sir, when you've called upon Mr. Dabler.

170 CENSOR. Mr. Dabler?—O, yes, I recollect.—Why, Beaufort, what do you mean? did you bring me hither to be food to this magpie?

BEAUFORT. Not I, upon my Honour; I never saw the Woman before. Who is she?

---

1  *like Spencer's Strife, I seek occasion*: in Edmund Spenser's *The Fairie Queene* (1590-6), the varlet Strife tells Guyon that his Lord has sent him "To seeke *Occasion,* where so she bee;/ For he is all disposd to bloudy fight" (II.iv.43, ll. 6-7). Burney makes the same allusion in *The Wanderer*, 527.

CENSOR. A Fool, a prating, intolerable Fool. Dabler Lodges at her 175
House, and whoever passes through her Hall to visit him, she
claims for her acquaintance. She will consume more Words in
an Hour than Ten Men will in a Year; she is infected with a
rage for talking, yet has nothing to say, which is a Disease of
all others the most pernicious to her fellow Creatures, since 180
the method she takes for her own relief proves their bane.
Her Tongue is as restless as Scandal, and, like that, feeds upon
nothing, yet attacks and tortures every thing; and it vies, in
rapidity of motion, with the circulation of the Blood in a
Frog's Foot.[1] 185

MISS JENNY (*to* MRS. VOLUBLE). I think the Gentleman's very
proud, ma'am, to answer you so short.

MRS. VOLUBLE. O, but he won't get off so, I can tell him! I'll
speak to him again. (*to* CENSOR) Poor Mr. Dabler, Sir, has
been troubled with a very bad Head ache lately; I tell him he 190
studies too much, but he says he can't help it; however, I think
it's a Friend's part to advise him against it, for a little caution
can do no harm, you know, Sir, if it does no good, and Mr.
Dabler's such a worthy, agreeable Gentleman, and so much
the Scholar, 'twould be a thousand pities he should come to 195
any ill. Pray, Sir, do you think he'll ever make a match of it
with Mrs. Sapient? She's ready enough, we all know, and to
be sure, for the matter of that, she's no chicken.[2] Pray, Sir, how
old do you reckon she may be?

CENSOR. Really, Madam, I have no talents for calculating the age 200
of a Lady. What a torrent of Impertinence! Upon my Honour, Beaufort, if you don't draw this Woman off, I shall
decamp.

BEAUFORT. I cannot imagine what detains Cecilia; however, I will
do any thing rather than wait with such Gossips by myself. I 205
hope, ma'am, we don't keep you standing?

MRS. VOLUBLE. O no, Sir, I was quite tired of sitting. What a
polite young Gentleman, Miss Jenny! I'm sure he deserves to
marry a Fortune. I'll speak to him about the 'Sprit[3] Party;

---

1   *circulation of the Blood in a Frog's Foot*: frogs were commonly used in anatomical experi-
    ments to demonstrate the circulation of the blood.
2   *she's no chicken*: proverbial for advancing in years.
3   *'Sprit*: i.e. *esprit*, wit.

210    he'll be quite Surprised to find how much I know of the
       matter. I think, Sir, your name's Mr. Beaufort?
       BEAUFORT. At your Service, ma'am.
       MRS. VOLUBLE. I was pretty sure it was you, sir, for I happened to
       be at my Window one morning when you called in a Coach;
215    and Mr. Dabler was out,—that is, between Friends, he was
       only at his Studies, but he said he was out, and so that's all
       one. So you gave in a card,[1] and drove off. I hope, Sir, your
       good aunt, my Lady Smatter, is well? for though I have not
       the pleasure of knowing her Ladyship myself, I know them
220    that do.
       CENSOR. Nay, when you have told me Lady Smatter is President,
       you need add Nothing more to convince me of its futility.
       Faith, Beaufort, were you my Enemy instead of my friend, I
       should scarce forbear commisserating your situation in being
225    dependant upon that Woman. I hardly know a more insuffer-
       able Being, for having, unfortunately, just *tasted the Pierian
       Spring*, she has acquired that *little knowledge*,[2] so dangerous to
       shallow understandings, which serves no other purpose than
       to stimulate a display of Ignorance.
230    MRS. VOLUBLE. I always know, Sir, when there's going to be a
       'Sprit party, for Mr. Dabler shuts himself up to study. Pray, Sir,
       did you ever see his monody[3] on the Birth of Miss Dawdle's
       Lap Dog?
       CENSOR. A monody on a Birth?
240    MRS. VOLUBLE. Yes, Sir; a monody, or Elegy, I don't exactly
       know which you call it, but I think it's one of the prettiest
       things he ever wrote; there he tells us—O dear, is not that
       Mrs. Sapient's Coach? I'm pretty sure I know the Cypher.[4]

1   *gave in a Card*: personal calling cards were left behind by visitors who found their
    intended company "not at home." Such cards could also be sent in place of a visit; see
    *Cecilia*, 63.
2   *tasted the Pierian Spring … little knowledge*: alluding to Pope's *An Essay on Criticism*
    (1711): "A *little learning* is a dang'rous thing;/Drink deep, or taste not the *Pierian
    Spring*" (ll. 215-16). The spring was sacred to the Pierides, a name for the Muses.
3   *monody*: a poem in which a mourner bewails someone's death; hence, like an elegy (a
    poem of lamentation), especially inappropriate to celebrate a lapdog's birth.
4   *Cypher*: as a sign of her social pretensions, Mrs. Sapient has her monogram printed on
    her coach.

CENSOR. Mrs. Sapient? Nay, Beaufort, if *She* is coming hither—

BEAUFORT. Patience, Man; she is one of the Set, and will divert 245
you.

CENSOR. You are mistaken; such consummate folly only makes
me melancholy. She is more weak and superficial even than
Lady Smatter, yet she has the same facility in giving herself
credit for wisdom; and there is a degree of assurance in her 250
conceit that is equally wonderful and disgusting, for as Lady
Smatter, from the shallowness of her knowledge, upon all subjects forms a *wrong* Judgement, Mrs. Sapient, from extreme
weakness of parts, is incapable of forming *any*; but, to com-
pensate for that deficiency, she retails all the opinions she 255
hears, and confidently utters them as her own. Yet, in the
most notorious of her plagiarisms, she affects a scrupulous
modesty, and apologises for troubling the Company with her
poor opinion!

BEAUFORT. She is, indeed, immeasurably wearisome. 260

CENSOR. When she utters a truth self-evident as that the Sun
shines at noon Day, she speaks it as a Discovery resulting from
her own peculiar penetration and Sagacity.

BEAUFORT. Silence! she is here.

*Enter* MRS. SAPIENT.

MRS. SAPIENT. O Mrs. Wheedle, how could you disappoint me 265
so of my short apron? I believe you make it a rule never
to keep to your Time; and I declare, for *my* part, I know
nothing so provoking as people's promising more than they
perform.

MRS. WHEEDLE. Indeed, ma'am, I beg ten thousand pardons, but 270
really, ma'am, we've been so hurried, that upon my Word,
ma'am—but you shall certainly have it this afternoon. Will
you give me leave to shew you any Caps, ma'am? I have some
exceeding pretty ones just finished.

MRS. SAPIENT (*looking at the caps*). O, for Heaven's sake, don't 275
shew me such flaunting things, for, in *my* opinion, nothing
can be really elegant that is Tawdry.

MRS. WHEEDLE. But here, ma'am, is one I'm sure you'll like; it's

in the immediate Taste,—only look at it, ma'am! what can be
280    prettier?

MRS. SAPIENT. Why yes, this is well enough, only I'm afraid it's
too young for me; don't you think it is?

MRS. WHEEDLE. Too young? dear ma'am no, I'm sure it will
become you of all things: only try it. (*Holds it over her Head*.)
285    O ma'am, you can't think how charmingly you look in it!
and it sets so sweetly! I never saw any thing so becoming in
my life.

MRS. SAPIENT. Is it? well, I think I'll have it,—if you are sure it is
not too young for me. You must know, I am mightily for
290    people's consulting their Time of Life in their choice of
Cloaths: and, in *my* opinion, there is a wide difference
between fiveteen and fifty.

CENSOR (*to* BEAUFORT). She'll certainly tell us, next, that, in *her*
opinion, a man who has but one Eye, would look rather bet-
295    ter if he had another!

MRS. WHEEDLE. I'm sure, ma'am, you'll be quite in love with
this Cap, when you see how well you look in it. Shall I shew
you some of our new Ribbons, ma'am?

MRS. SAPIENT. O, I know, now, you want to tempt me; but *I*
300    always say the best way to escape temptation is to run away
from it: however, as I *am* here—

MRS. VOLUBLE. Had not you better sit down, ma'am? (*offering a
chair*).

MRS. SAPIENT. O Mrs. Voluble, is it you? How do do? Lord, I
don't like any of these Ribbons. Pray how does Mr. Dabler
305    do?

MRS. VOLUBLE. Very well, thank you, ma'am; that is; not *very*
well, but *pretty* well considering, for to be sure, ma'am, so
much study's very bad for the Health; it's pity he don't take
more care of himself, and so I often tell him; but your great
310    Wits never mind what little folks say, if they talk never so
well, and I'm sure I've sometimes talked to him by the Hour
together about it, for I'd never spare my words to serve a
friend; however, it's all to no purpose, for he says he has a kind
of *Fury*, I think he calls it, upon him, that makes him write
315    whether he will or not. And, to be sure, he does write most

charmingly! and he has such a collection of Miniscrips! Lord, I question if a pastry Cook or a Cheesemonger could use them in a Year![1] for he says he never destroyed a Line he ever wrote in his life. All that he don't like, he tells me he Keeps by him for his Postimus works, as he calls them, and I've some notion he intends soon to print them.

MRS. WHEEDLE. Do, ma'am, pray let me put this Cloak up for you, and I'll make you a Hat for it immediately.

MRS. SAPIENT. Well, then, take great care how you put in the Ribbon, for you know I won't keep it if it does not please me. Mr. Beaufort!—Lord bless me, how long have you been here? O Heavens! is that Mr. Censor? I can scarce believe my Eyes! Mr. Censor in a Milliner's Shop! Well, this does, indeed, justify an observation I have often made, that the greatest Geniusses sometimes do the oddest things.

CENSOR. Your surprise, madam, at seeing me here to-Day will bear no comparison to what I must myself experience, should you ever see me here again.

MRS. SAPIENT. O, I know well how much you must despise all this sort of Business, and, I assure you, I am equally averse to it myself: indeed I often think what pity it is so much Time should be given to mere shew;—for what are we the better to-morrow for what we have worn to Day? No Time, in *my* opinion, turns to so little account as that which we spend in Dress.

CENSOR (*to* BEAUFORT). Did you ever hear such an impudent falsehood?

MRS. SAPIENT. For *my* part, I always wear just what the Milliner and Mantua-maker[2] please to send me; for I have a kind of maxim upon this Subject which has some weight with *me*, though I don't know if any body else ever suggested it: but it is, that the real value of a Person springs from the *Mind*, not from the outside appearance. So I never trouble myself to look at anything till the moment I put it on. Be sure (*turning*

---

1   *pastry Cook or a Cheesemonger … in a Year.* a joke of long standing. Waste paper was used for such purposes as lining pastry dishes and wrapping cheese.

2   *Mantua-maker.* dressmakers were so named, even after the mantua itself, a woman's gown, ceased to be fashionable.

*quick to the Milliners*), you take care how you trim the Hat! I
sha'n't wear it else.

CENSOR. Prithee, Beaufort, how long will you give a man to
decide which is greatest, her folly, or her Conceit?

MRS. SAPIENT. Gentlemen, good morning; Mrs. Voluble, you
355    may give my Compliments to Mr. Dabler. Mrs. Wheedle,
pray send the things in Time, for, to *me*, nothing is more disagreeable than to be disappointed.

*As she is going out,* JACK *enters abruptly, and brushes past her.*

MRS. SAPIENT. O Heavens!

JACK. Lord, ma'am, I beg you a thousand pardons! I did not see
360    you, I declare. I hope I did not hurt you?

MRS. SAPIENT. No, Sir, no; but you a little alarmed me,—and
really an alarm, when one does not know how to account for
it, gives one a rather odd Sensation,—at least *I* find it so.

JACK. Upon my Word, ma'am, I'm very sorry,—I'm sure if I'd
365    seen you—but I was in such monstrous haste, I had no Time
to look about me.

MRS. SAPIENT. O, Sir, 'tis of no consequence; yet, allow me to
observe that, in *my* opinion, too much haste generally defeats
its own purpose. Sir, good morning.

*Exit.*

370  BEAUFORT. Why Jack, won't you see her to her Coach?

JACK. O ay, true, so I must!

*follows her.*

CENSOR. This Brother of yours, Beaufort, is a most ingenious
youth.

BEAUFORT. He has foibles which you, I am sure, will not spare;
375    but he means well, and is extremely good-natured.

CENSOR. Nay, but I am serious, for, without ingenuity, no man, I
think, could continue to be always in a hurry, who is never
employed.

*Re-enter* JACK.

JACK. Plague take it, Brother, how unlucky it was that you made me go after her! in running up to her, my duced spurs caught hold of some of her falaldrums,[1] and in my haste to disengage myself, I tore off half her trimming. She went off in a very ill-humour, telling me that, in *her* opinion, a disagreeable accident was very — very — very disagreeable, I think, or something to that purpose. 380 385

BEAUFORT. But, for Heaven's Sake, Jack, what is the occasion of all this furious haste?

JACK. Why Lord, you know I'm always in a hurry; I've no notion of Dreaming away Life: how the Deuce is any thing to be done without a little spirit? 390

BEAUFORT. Pho, prithee, Jack, give up this idle humour.

JACK. Idle? nay, Brother, call me what else you please, but you can never charge me with idleness.

BEAUFORT. Why, with all your boasted activity, I question if there is a man in England who would be more embarrassed how to give any account of his Time. 395

JACK. Well, well, I can't stay now to discourse upon these matters,— I have too many things to *do,* to stand here talking.

BEAUFORT. Nay, don't go till you tell us what you have to do this morning? 400

JACK. Why, more things than either of you would do in a month, but I can't stop now to tell you any of them, for I have three friends waiting for me in Hyde Park,[2] and twenty places to call at in my way. (*going.*)

MRS. WHEEDLE. (*following him*). Sir would you not chuse to look at some Ruffles?[3] 405

JACK. O, ay,— have you any thing new? what do you call these?

MRS. WHEEDLE. O pray, Sir, take care! they are so delicate they'll hardly bear to be touched.

JACK. I don't like them at all! shew me some others. 410

---

1 *falaldrums*: a variant of "falderal," a gewgaw, trifle, useless ornament.
2 *Hyde Park*: the largest of the London parks, extending from Bayswater Road in the north to Knightsbridge in the south, merging with Kensington Gardens to the west.
3 *Ruffles*: delicate lace frills, worn around the wrist, breast, or neck.

MRS. WHEEDLE. Why, sir, only see! you have quite Spoilt this pair.

JACK. Have I? well, then, you must put them up for me. But pray have you got no better?

415 MRS. WHEEDLE. I'll look some directly, Sir,—but, dear sir, pray don't put your Switch upon the Caps! I hope you'll excuse me, Sir, but the set is all in all in these little tasty things.

CENSOR. And pray, Jack, are all your hurries equally important, and equally necessary as those of this morning?

420 JACK. Lord, you grave fellows, who plod on from Day to Day without any notion of Life and Spirit, spend half your Lives in asking people questions they don't know how to answer.

CENSOR. And we might consume the other half to as little pur- pose, if we waited to find out questions which such people *do*

425 know how to answer.

JACK. Severe, very severe, that! however, I have not Time, now, for Repartee, but I shall give you a Rowland for your Oliver when we meet again.[1] (*going.*)

MRS. WHEEDLE. Sir I've got the Ruffles,—won't you look at

430 them?

JACK. O, the Ruffles! well, I'm glad you've found them, but I can't stay to look at them now. Keep them in the way against I call again.

*Exit.*

MRS. WHEEDLE. Miss Jenny, put these Ruffles up again. That

435 Gentleman never knows his own mind.

MISS JENNY. I'm sure he's tumbled and tossed the things about like mad.

CENSOR. 'Tis to be much regretted, Beaufort, that such a youth as this was not an Elder Brother.

440 BEAUFORT. Why so?

CENSOR. Because the next Heir might so easily get rid of him; for, if he was knocked down, I believe he would think it loss of Time to get up again, and if he were pushed into a River, I

---

1  *give you a Rowland for your Oliver:* proverbial for a blow for a blow, tit for tat. Roland and Oliver, two of the paladins of Charlemagne, were equally matched in combat.

question if he would not be Drowned, ere he could persuade himself to swim long enough in the same Direction to save himself. 445

BEAUFORT. He is young, and I hope this ridiculous humour will wear away.

CENSOR. But how came *you* so wholly to escape its infection? I find not, in you, any portion of this inordinate desire of 450 action, to which all power of thinking must be sacrificed.

BEAUFORT. —Why we are but half Brothers, and our Educations were as different as our Fathers, for my mother's Second Husband was no more like her first, than am *I to Hercules*;[1]— though Jack, indeed, has no resemblance even to his own 455 Father.

CENSOR. Resemblance? an Hare and a Tortoise are not more different; for Jack is always running, without knowing what he pursues, and his Father is always pondering, without knowing what he thinks of. 460

BEAUFORT. The Truth is, Mr. Codger's humour of perpetual deliberation so early sickened his Son, that the fear of inheriting any share of it, made him rush into the opposite extreme, and determine to avoid the censure of inactive meditation, by executing every plan he could form at the very moment of 465 Projection.

CENSOR. And pray, Sir,—if such a Question will not endanger a challenge,— what think you, by this Time, of the punctuality of your Mistress?

BEAUFORT. Why,— to own the truth—I fear I must have made 470 some mistake.

CENSOR. Bravo, Beaufort! ever doubt your own Senses, in preference to suspecting your mistress of negligence or Caprice.

BEAUFORT. She is much too noble minded, too just in her sentiments, and too uniform in her conduct, to be guilty of either. 475

CENSOR. Bravissimo, Beaufort! I commend your patience, and, this Time twelvemonth I'll ask you how it wears! In the mean Time, however, I would not upon any account interrupt your contemplations either upon her Excellencies, or

---

1 *I to Hercules*: alluding to Shakespeare's *Hamlet*, in which Hamlet describes his uncle Claudius as "no more like my father/Than I to Hercules" (I.ii.152-3).

480 your own mistakes, but, as I expect no advantage from the one, you must excuse my any longer suffering from the other: and, ere you again entangle me in such a wilderness of frippery, I shall take the liberty more closely to investigate the accuracy of your appointments.

*Exit.*

485 BEAUFORT. My Situation begins to grow as ridiculous as it is disagreeable; Surely Cecilia cannot have forgotten me!

MRS. VOLUBLE (*advancing to him*). To be sure, Sir, it's vastly incommodious to be kept waiting so, but, sir, if I might put in a Word, I think—

*Enter* JACK *running.*

490 JACK. Lord, Brother, I quite forgot to tell you Miss Stanley's message.

BEAUFORT. Message! what message?

JACK. I declare I had got half way to Hyde Park, before I ever thought of it.

495 BEAUFORT. Upon my Honour, Jack, this is too much!

JACK. Why I ran back the moment I recollected it, and what could I do more? I would not even stop to tell Will. Scamper what was the matter, so he has been calling and bawling after me all the way I came. I gave him the slip when I got to

500 the shop,—but I'll just step and see if he's in the street. (*going.*)

BEAUFORT. Jack, you'll provoke me to more anger than you are prepared for! what was the message? tell me quickly!

JACK. O ay, true! why she said she could not come.

BEAUFORT. Not come? but *why*? I'm sure she told you *why*?

505 JACK. O yes, she told me a long story about it,—but I've forgot what it was.

BEAUFORT (*warmly*). Recollect, then!

JACK. Why so I will. O, it was all your aunt Smatter's fault,—

---

1   *Ranelagh Songs*: Ranelagh Gardens in Chelsea, opened in 1742, contained a rococo rotunda, at which orchestral and vocal music was played. The concerts featured well-

somebody came in with the new Ranelagh Songs,[1] so she
stayed at Home to study them; and Miss Stanley bid me say $_{510}$
she was very sorry, but she could not come by herself.

BEAUFORT. And why might I not have been told this sooner?

JACK. Why she desired me to come and tell you of it an Hour or
two ago, but I had so many places to stop at by the way, I
could not possibly get here sooner: and when I came, my $_{515}$
Head was so full of my own appointments, that I never once
thought of her message. However, I must run back to Will.
Scamper, or he'll think me crazy.

BEAUFORT. Hear me, Jack! if you do not take pains to correct this
absurd rage to attempt every thing, while you execute noth- $_{520}$
ing, you will render yourself as contemptible to the World, as
you are useless or mischievous to your Family.

*Exit.*

JACK. What a passion he's in! I've a good mind to run to Miss
Stanley, and beg her to intercede for me. (*going.*)

MRS. WHEEDLE. Sir, won't you please to look at the Ruffles? $_{525}$

JACK. O ay, true,— where are they?

MRS. WHEEDLE. Here, Sir. Miss Jenny, give me those Ruffles
again.

JACK. O if they a'n't ready, I can't stay.

*Exit.*

MRS. VOLUBLE. Well, Mrs. Wheedle, I'm sure you've a pleasant $_{530}$
life of it here, in seeing so much of the World. I'd a great
mind to have spoke to that young Gentleman, for I'm pretty
sure I've seen him before, though I can't tell where. But he
was in such a violent hurry, I could not get in a word. He's a
fine lively young Gentleman, to be sure. But now, Mrs. $_{535}$
Wheedle, when will you come and Drink a snug dish of Tea
with me? you, and Miss Jenny, and any of the young ladies
that can be spared? I'm sure if you can *all* come—

known singers and newly-composed songs. Ranelagh is mentioned in *Evelina*, p. 24,
and *Cecilia*, p. 286.

*Enter* BOB.

BOB. I ask pardon, Ladies and Gentlemen, but pray is my mother
540    here?
MRS. VOLUBLE. What's that to you, sirrah? who gave you leave to
    follow me? get Home, directly, you dirty figure you! go, go, I
    say!
BOB. Why Lord, mother, you've been out all the morning, and
545    never told Betty what was for Dinner!
MRS. VOLUBLE. Why you great, Tall, greedy, gormondising, lub-
    berly Cub, you, what signifies whether you have any Dinner
    or no? go, get away, you idle, good for nothing, dirty, greasy,
    hulking, tormenting—(*she drives him off, and the scene closes*).

# ACT II

*Scene, a Drawing Room at* LADY SMATTER's.

LADY SMATTER *and* CECILIA

LADY SMATTER. Yes, yes, this song is certainly Mr. Dabler's, I am not to be deceived in his style. What say you, my dear Miss Stanley, don't you think I have found him out.

CECILIA. Indeed I am too little acquainted with his Poems to be able to judge. 5

LADY SMATTER. Your indifference surprises me! for my part, I am never at rest till I have discovered the authors of every thing that comes out;[1] and, indeed, I commonly hit upon them in a moment. I declare I sometimes wonder at myself, when I think how lucky I am in my guesses. 10

CECILIA. Your Ladyship devotes so much Time to these researches, that it would be strange if they were unsuccessful.

LADY SMATTER. Yes, I do indeed devote my Time to them; I own it without blushing, for how, as a certain author Says, can Time be better employed than in cultivating intellectual 15 accomplishments? And I am often Surprised, my dear Miss Stanley, that a young lady of your good sense should not be more warmly engaged in the same pursuit.

CECILIA. My pursuits, whatever they may be, are too unimportant to deserve being made public. 20

LADY SMATTER. Well to be sure, we are all Born with sentiments of our own, as I read in a Book I can't just now recollect the name of, so I ought not to wonder that yours and mine do not coincide; for, I declare, if my pursuits were not made public, I should not have any at all, for where can be the pleasure 25 of reading Books, and studying authors, if one is not to have the credit of talking of them?

CECILIA. Your Ladyship's desire of celebrity is too well known for your motives to be doubted.

---

1 *discovered the authors of every thing that comes out*: since many eighteenth-century works (including Burney's novels) were published anonymously, guessing authorship was a common pursuit.

30 LADY SMATTER. Well but, my dear Miss Stanley, I have been thinking for some Time past of your becoming a member of our Esprit Party: Shall I put up your name?

CECILIA. By no means; my ambition aspires not at an Honour for which I feel myself so little qualified.

35 LADY SMATTER. Nay, but you are too modest; you can't suppose how much you may profit by coming among us. I'll tell you some of our regulations. The principal persons of our party are Authors and Critics; the authors always bring us something new of their own, and the Critics regale us with manu-
40 script notes upon something old.

CECILIA. And in what class is your Ladyship?

LADY SMATTER. O, I am among the Critics. I love criticism passionately, though it is really laborious Work, for it obliges one to read with a vast deal of attention. I declare I am sometimes
45 so immensely fatigued with the toil of studying for faults and objections, that I am ready to fling all my Books behind the Fire.

CECILIA. And what authors have you chiefly criticised?

LADY SMATTER. Pope and Shakespeare. I have found more errors
50 in those[1] than in any other.

CECILIA. I hope, however, for the sake of readers less fastidious, your Ladyship has also left them some beauties.

LADY SMATTER. O yes, I have not cut them up regularly through; indeed I have not, yet, read above half their Works, so how
55 they will fare as I go on, I can't determine. O, here's Beaufort.

*Enter* BEAUFORT.

BEAUFORT. Your Ladyship's most obedient.

CECILIA. Mr. Beaufort, I am quite ashamed to see You! yet the disappointment I occasioned you was as involuntary on my part, as it could possibly be disagreeable on yours. Your
60 Brother, I hope, prevented your waiting long?

---

1 *Pope and Shakespeare ... errors in those*: there were precedents for Lady Smatter's iconoclasm. In his *Essay on the Writings and Genius of Pope* (vol. I, 1756; vol. II not published until 1782), Joseph Warton declared that Pope belonged only to the second rank of poets. Many critics, including Samuel Johnson in his edition of 1765, made stringent criticisms of Shakespeare.

BEAUFORT. That you meant he should is sufficient reparation for my loss of Time; but what must be the disappointment that an apology from you would not soften?

LADY SMATTER (*reading*). O lovely, charming, beauteous maid,—I wish this Song was not so difficult to get by Heart,—but I am always beginning one Line for another. After all, Study is a most fatiguing thing! O how little does the World suspect, when we are figuring in all the brilliancy of Conversation, the private hardships, and secret labours of a Belle Esprit!¹

*Enter a* SERVANT.

SERVANT. Mr. Codger, my lady.

*Enter* MR. CODGER.

LADY SMATTER. Mr. Codger, your Servant. I hope I see you well?

CODGER. Your Ladyship's most humble. Not so well, indeed, as I could wish, yet, perhaps, better than I deserve to be.

LADY SMATTER. How is my friend Jack?

CODGER. I can't directly say, madam; I have not seen him these two Hours, and poor Jack is but a harem scarem young man; many things may have happened to him in the space of two Hours.

LADY SMATTER. And what, my good Sir, can you apprehend?

CODGER. To enumerate all the Casualties I apprehend might, perhaps, be tedious, I will, therefore, only mention the Heads. In the first place, he may be thrown from his Horse; in the second place, he may be run over while on Foot; in the third place —

LADY SMATTER. O pray *place* him no more in situations so horrible. Have you heard lately from our friends in the north?

CODGER. Not very lately, madam: the last Letter I received was Dated the sixteenth of February, and that, you know, madam, was five Weeks last Thursday.

LADY SMATTER. I hope you had good news?

---

1   *Belle Esprit*: fine wit.

CODGER. Why, madam, yes; at least, none bad. My Sister Deborah acquainted me with many curious little pieces of History that have happened in her neighbourhood: would it be agreeable
95  to your Ladyship to hear them?

LADY SMATTER. O no, I would not take up so much of your Time.

CODGER. I cannot, madam, employ my Time more agreeably. Let me see,—in the first place—no, that was not first,—let me
100  recollect!

BEAUFORT. Pray, Sir, was any mention made of Tom?

CODGER. Yes; but don't be impatient; I shall speak of him in his turn.

BEAUFORT. I beg your pardon, Sir, but I enquired from hearing
105  he was not well.

CODGER. I shall explain whence that report arose in a few minutes; in the mean Time, I must beg you not to interrupt me, for I am trying to arrange a chain of anecdotes for the satisfaction of Lady Smatter.

110  LADY SMATTER. Bless me, Mr. Codger, I did not mean to give you so much trouble.

CODGER. It will be no trouble in the World, if your Ladyship will, for a while, forbear speaking to me, though the loss upon the occasion will be all mine. (*He retires to the Side Scene.*[1])

115  LADY SMATTER. What a formal old Fogrum[2] the man grows! Beaufort, have you seen this Song?

BEAUFORT. I believe not, madam.

LADY SMATTER. O, it's the prettiest thing! but I don't think you have a true taste for Poetry; I never observed you to be enrap-
120  tured, lost in Extacy, or hurried as it were out of yourself, when I have been reading to you. But *my* enthusiasm for poetry may, perhaps, carry me too far; come now, my dear Miss Stanley, be sincere with me, don't you think I indulge this propensity too much?

125  CECILIA. I should be sorry to have your Ladyship suppose me

---

1  *Side Scene*: the wing, as opposed to the main part of the stage. Burney very rarely provides technical stage-directions of this kind.

2  *Fogrum*: an antiquated or old-fashioned person, a fogy. The word was a favourite pejorative of Burney's father and of her friend Samuel Crisp; see *Camilla*, 46, and note.

quite insensible to the elegance of Literary pursuits, though I neither claim any Title, nor profess any ability to judge of them.

LADY SMATTER. O You'll do very well in a few Years. But, as you observe, I own I think there is something rather elegant in a Taste for these sort of amusements: otherwise, indeed, I should not have taken so much pains to acquire it, for, to confess the truth, I had from Nature quite an aversion to reading,—I remember the Time when the very Sight of a Book was disgustful to me! 130 135

CODGER. (*coming forward*). I believe, madam, I can now satisfy your enquiries.

LADY SMATTER. What enquiries?

CODGER. Those your Ladyship made in relation to my Letter from our Friends in Yorkshire. In the first place, my Sister Deborah writes me Word that the new Barn which, you may remember, was begun last Summer, is pretty nearly finished. And here, in my Pocket Book,[1] I have gotten the Dimensions of it. It is fifteen Feet by— 140

LADY SMATTER. O, for Heaven's Sake, Mr. Codger, don't trouble yourself to be so circumstantial. 145

CODGER. The trouble, madam, is inconsiderable, or, if it were otherwise, for the information of your Ladyship I would most readily go through with it. It is fifteen Feet by thirty. And pray does your Ladyship remember the Old Dog Kennel at the Parsonage House? 150

LADY SMATTER. No, Sir; I never look at Dog Kennels.

CODGER. Well, madam, my Sister Deborah writes me Word—

*Enter* SERVANT.

SERVANT. Mr. Dabler, my lady.

*Enter* MR. DABLER.

LADY SMATTER. Mr. Dabler, you are the man in the World I most wished to see. 155

---

1   *Pocket Book*: a small, book-like case, with compartments for papers, etc.

DABLER. Your Ladyship is Beneficence itself!

LADY SMATTER. A visit from you, Mr. Dabler, is the greatest of favours, since your Time is not only precious to yourself, but to the World.

DABLER. It is, indeed, precious to myself, madam, when I devote it to the Service of your Ladyship. Miss Stanley, may I hope you are as well as you look? if so, your Health must indeed be in a State of perfection; if not, never before did Sickness wear so fair a Mask.

LADY SMATTER. 'Tis a thousand pities, Mr. Dabler, to throw away such poetical thoughts and Imagery in common Conversation.

DABLER. Why, ma'am, the truth is, something a little out of the usual path is expected from a Man whom the World has been pleased to style a Poet;—though I protest I never knew why!

LADY SMATTER. How true is it that Modesty, as Pope, or Swift, I forget which, has it, is the constant attendant upon Merit!

DABLER. If Merit, madam, were but the constant attendant upon Modesty, then, indeed, I might hope to attain no little share! Faith, I'll set that down. (*He takes out his Tablets.*[1])

CODGER. And so, madam, my Sister Deborah writes me Word—

LADY SMATTER. O dear, Mr. Codger, I merely wanted to know if all our friends were well.

CODGER. Nay, if your Ladyship does not want to hear about the Dog Kennel—

LADY SMATTER. Not in the least! I hate Kennels, and Dogs too.

CODGER. As you please, madam! (*aside*) She has given me the trouble of ten minutes recollection, and now she won't hear me!

LADY SMATTER. Mr. Dabler, I believe I've had the pleasure of seeing something of yours this morning.

DABLER. Of mine? you alarm me beyond measure!

LADY SMATTER. Nay, nay, 'tis in Print, so don't be frightened.

DABLER. Your Ladyship relieves me: but, really, people are so little delicate in taking Copies of my foolish manuscripts, that I protest I go into no House without the fear of meeting something of my own. But what may it be?

---

1  *Tablets*: a notebook made of stiff sheets fastened together, used for memoranda.

LADY SMATTER. Why I'll repeat it.

    O Sweetest, Softest, gentlest maid—        195

DABLER. No, ma'am, no;— you mistake,—

    O lovely, beauteous, charming maid,—

is it not so?

LADY SMATTER. Yes, yes, that's it. O what a vile memory is mine! after all my studying to make such a mistake! I declare I for-    200 get as fast as I learn. I shall begin to fancy myself a Wit by and by.

DABLER. Then will your Ladyship for *the first* time be the *last* to learn Some thing. (*aside*) 'Gad, I'll put that into an Epigram!

LADY SMATTER. I was reading, the other Day, that the memory of    205 a Poet should be short, that his Works may be original.

DABLER. Heavens, madam, where did you meet with that?

LADY SMATTER. I can't exactly say, but either in Pope or Swift.

DABLER. O curse it, how unlucky!

LADY SMATTER. Why so?          210

DABLER. Why, madam, 'tis my own thought! I've just finished an Epigram upon that very Subject! I protest I shall grow more and more sick of Books every Day, for I can never look into any, but I'm sure of popping upon something of my own.

LADY SMATTER. Well but, dear Sir, pray let's hear your Epigram.    215

DABLER. Why, if your Ladyship insists upon it —(*reads*)

    Ye gentle Gods, O hear me plead,

    And kindly grant this little loan;

    Make me forget whate'er I read

    That what I write may be my own.        220

LADY SMATTER. O charming! very clever indeed.

BEAUFORT. But pray, Sir, if such is your wish, why should you read at all?

DABLER. Why, sir, one must read; one's reputation requires it; for it would be cruelly confusing to be asked after such or such    225 an author, and never to have looked into him, especially to a person who passes for having some little knowledge in these matters.

BEAUFORT (*aside*). What a shallow Coxcomb!

LADY SMATTER. You must positively let me have a Copy of that    230 Epigram, Mr. Dabler. Don't you think it charming, Mr. Codger?

CODGER. Madam, I never take any thing in at first hearing; if Mr. Dabler will let me have it in my own Hand, I will give your Ladyship my opinion of it, after I have read it over two or three Times.

DABLER. Sir it is much at your Service; but I must insist upon it that you don't get it by Heart.

CODGER. Bless me, Sir, I should not do that in half a year! I have no turn for such sort of things.

LADY SMATTER. I know not in what Mr. Dabler most excells, Epigrams, Sonnets, Odes or Elegies.

DABLER. Dear ma'am, mere nonsense! but I believe your Ladyship forgets my little Lampoons?

LADY SMATTER. O no, that I never can! there you are indeed perfect.

DABLER. Your Ladyship far over-rates my poor abilities;—my Writings are mere trifles, and I believe the World would be never the worse, if they were all committed to the Flames.

BEAUFORT (aside). I would I could try the Experiment!

LADY SMATTER. Your Talents are Universal.

DABLER. O ma'am, you quite over-power me! but now you are pleased to mention the Word *Universal*,—did your Ladyship ever meet with my little attempt in the Epic way?[1]

LADY SMATTER. O no, you sly Creature! but I shall now suspect you of every thing.

DABLER. Your Ladyship is but too partial. I have, indeed, some little facility in Stringing Rhymes, but I should suppose there's nothing very extraordinary in that: every body, I believe, has some little Talent,—mine happens to be for Poetry, but it's all a chance! nobody can chuse for himself, and really, to be candid, I don't know if some other things are not of equal consequence.

LADY SMATTER. There, Mr. Dabler, I must indeed differ from you! what in the Universe can be put in competition with Poetry?

---

1  *Universal … Epic way*: in the eighteenth century, the epic or heroic poem was considered the noblest and most universal of all the literary genres. Dabler, however, fails to distinguish between epics and lowly lampoons in applying the adjective "little" to each genre.

DABLER. Your Ladyship's enthusiasm for the fine arts —

*Enter a* SERVANT.

SERVANT. Mrs. Sapient, Madam.

LADY SMATTER. Lord, how tiresome! She'll talk us to Death!

*Enter* MRS. SAPIENT.

Dear Mrs. Sapient, this is vastly good of you!                    270

DABLER. Your arrival, madam, is particularly critical at this Time, for we are engaged in a literary Controversy; and to whom can we so properly apply to enlighten our Doubts by the Sun Beams of her Counsel, as to Mrs. Sapient?

LADY SMATTER. What a sweet speech! (*aside*) I wonder how he     275
could make it to that stupid woman!

MRS. SAPIENT. You do me too much Honour, Sir. But what is the Subject I have been so unfortunate as to interrupt? for though I shall be ashamed to offer my Sentiments before such a Company as this, I yet have rather a peculiar way of think-  280
ing upon this subject.

DABLER. As how, ma'am?

MRS. SAPIENT. Why, Sir, it seems to *me* that a proper degree of Courage is preferable to a superfluous excess of modesty.

DABLER. Excellent! extremely right, madam. The present       285
question is upon Poetry. We were considering whether, impartially Speaking, some other things are not of equal importance?

MRS. SAPIENT. I am unwilling, Sir, to decide upon so delicate a point; yet, were I to offer my humble opinion, it would be,   290
that though to *me* nothing is more delightful than poetry, I yet fancy there may be other things of greater utility in common Life.

DABLER. Pray, Mr. Codger, what is your opinion?

CODGER. Sir I am so intently employed in considering this Epi-  295
gram, that I cannot, just now, maturely weigh your Question; and indeed, Sir, to acknowledge the truth, I could have excused your interrupting me.

DABLER. Sir you do my foolish Epigram much Honour. (*aside*)
That Man has twice the Sense one would suppose from his
look. I'll shew him my new Sonnet.

MRS. SAPIENT. How much was I surprised, Mr. Beaufort, at seeing Mr. Censor this morning in a Milliner's shop!

CECILIA. I rejoice to hear you had such a Companion; and yet,
perhaps, I ought rather to regret it, since the Sting of his
rallery might but inflame your disappointment and vexation.

BEAUFORT. The Sting of a professed Satirest only proves poiso-
nous to fresh Subjects; those who have often felt it are merely
tickled by the Wound.

DABLER (*aside*). How the Deuce shall I introduce the Sonnet?
Pray, Ladies and Gentlemen, you who so often visit the
Muses, is there any thing new in the Poetical way?

LADY SMATTER. Who, Mr. Dabler, can so properly answer that
Question as you,— you, to whom all their Haunts are open?

DABLER. O dear ma'am, Such Compositions as mine are the
merest Baubles in the World! I dare say there are people who
would even be ashamed to set their Names to them.

BEAUFORT (*aside*). I hope there is but one Person who would not!

MRS. SAPIENT. How much more amiable in *my* Eyes is Genius
when joined with Diffidence, than with conceit!

CODGER (*returning the Epigram*). Sir I give you my thanks: and I
think, Sir, your wish is some what uncommon.

DABLER. I am much pleased, Sir, that you approve of it. (*aside*)
This man does not want Understanding, with all his formali-
ty. He'll be prodigiously struck with my sonnet.

MRS. SAPIENT. What, is that something new of Mr. Dabler's?
surely, Sir, you must write Night and Day.

DABLER. O dear no, ma'am, for I compose with a facility that is
really surprising. Yet, sometimes, to be sure, I have been pretty hard worked; in the Charade Season I protest I hardly Slept
a Wink! I spent whole Days in looking over Dictionaries for
Words of double meaning: and really I made some not amiss.
But 'twas too easy; I soon grew sick of it. Yet I never quite
gave it up till, accidentally, I heard a House maid say to a scullion My first, is yourself; my Second, holds good chear; and

my third, is my own office;—and, 'Gad, the Word was scrubbing!¹

CODGER. With respect, Sir, to that point concerning which you consulted me, I am inclined to think—

DABLER. Sir! 340

CODGER. You were speaking to me, Sir, respecting the utility of Poetry; I am inclined to think—

DABLER. O, apropos, now I think of it, I have a little sonnet here that is quite pat to the subject, and—

CODGER. What subject, good Sir? 345

DABLER. What subject?—why—this subject, you know.

CODGER. As yet, Sir, we are talking of no subject; I was going—

DABLER. Well but—ha! ha!—it puts me so in mind of this little sonnet we were speaking of, that—

CODGER. But, Sir, you have not heard what I was going to say.— 350

DABLER. True, Sir, true;—I'll put the Poem away for the present,—unless, indeed, you very much wish to see it?

CODGER. Another Time will do as well, Sir. I don't rightly comprehend what I read before Company.

DABLER. Dear Sir, such trifles as these are hardly worth your serious study; however, if you'll promise not to take a Copy, I think I'll venture to trust you with the manuscript,—but you must be sure not to shew it a single Soul,—and pray take great care of it. 355

CODGER. Good Sir, I don't mean to take it at all. 360

DABLER. Sir!

CODGER. I have no Time for reading; and I hold that these sort of things only turn one's Head from matters of more importance.

DABLER. O very well, sir,—if you don't want to see it—(*aside*) what a tasteless old Dolt! curse me if I shall hardly be civil to him when I meet him next! 365

CODGER. Notwithstanding which, Sir, if I should find an odd Hour or two in the course of the Winter, I will let you know, and you may send it to me. 370

---

1  *scrub-bing*: a "scrub" is a lowly person, such as a scullion, or washer of dishes and pots; a "bing" is a wine bin, holding "good chear."

DABLER. Dear Sir, you do me a vast favour! (*aside*) The fellow's a perfect Driveler!

LADY SMATTER. I declare, Mr. Codger, had we known you were so indifferent to the charms of Poetry, we should never have admitted you of our Party.

CODGER. Madam I was only moved to enter it in order to oblige your Ladyship; but I shall hardly attend it above once more,— or twice at the utmost.

*Enter* JACK.

JACK (*to Lady Smatter*). Ma'am your Servant. Where's Miss Stanley? I'm so out of Breath I can hardly Speak. Miss Stanley, I'm come on purpose to tell you some news.

CECILIA. It ought to be of some importance by your haste.

BEAUFORT. Not a whit the more for that! his haste indicates nothing, for it accompanies him in every thing.

JACK. Nay, if you won't hear me at once, I'm gone!

CODGER. And pray, Son Jack, whither may you be going?

JACK. Lord, Sir, to an hundred places at least. I shall be all over the Town in less than half an Hour.

CODGER. Nevertheless it is well known, you have no manner of Business over any part of it. I am much afraid, Son Jack, you will be a Blockhead all your life.

LADY SMATTER. For shame, Mr. Codger! Jack, you were voted into our Esprit Party last meeting; and if you come to night, you will be admitted.

JACK. I'll come with the greatest pleasure, ma'am, if I can but get away from Will. Scamper, but we are upon a frolic to night, so it's ten to one if I can make off.

MRS. SAPIENT. If I might take the liberty, Sir, to offer *my* advice upon this occasion, I should say that useful friends were more improving than frivolous companions, for, in *my* opinion, it is pity to waste Time.

JACK. Why, ma'am, that's just my way of thinking! I like to be always getting forward, always doing something. Why I am going now as far as Fleet Street, to a Print shop, where I left

Tom Whiffle. I met him in my way from Cornhill,[1] and promised to be back with him in half an Hour.    405

BEAUFORT. Cornhill? you said you were going to Hyde Park.

JACK. Yes, but I met Kit Filligree, and he hauled me into the City. But, now you put me in mind of it, I believe I had best run there first, and see who's waiting.    410

BEAUFORT. But what, in the mean Time, is to become of Tom Whiffle?

JACK. O, hang him, he can wait.

CODGER. In truth, Son Jack, you Scandalise me! I have even apprehensions for your Head; you appear to me to be *non*    415 *compos mentis.*[2]

BEAUFORT. 'Tis pity, Jack, you cannot change situations with a running Footman.[3]

JACK. Ay, ay, good folks, I know you all love to cut me up, so pray amuse yourselves your own way,—only don't expect me to    420 stay and hear you. (*going.*)

CODGER. Son Jack, return. Pray answer me to the following Question.

JACK. Dear Sir, pray be quick, for I'm in a horrid hurry.

CODGER. A little more patience, Son, would become you better;    425 you should consider that you are but a Boy, and that I am your Father.

JACK. Yes, Sir, I do. Was that all, Sir?

CODGER. All? why I have said nothing.

JACK. Very true, Sir.    430

CODGER. You ought, also, to keep it constantly in your Head that I am not merely Older, but Wiser than yourself.

JACK. Yes, Sir. (*aside*) Demme, though, if I believe that!

CODGER. You would do well, also, to remember, that such haste to quit my presence, looks as if you took no pleasure in my    435 Company.

---

1   *Fleet Street … Cornhill*: Fleet Street, a major thoroughfare in the City of London, was the site of numerous printshops. Cornhill, another major City thoroughfare, was the site of the Royal Exchange.

2   *non compos mentis*: Latin for "not master of one's mind"; the legal term for insanity.

3   *running Footman*: a servant who runs before his master's carriage.

JACK. It does so, Sir. (*aside*) Plague take it, I sha'n't get away this age.

CODGER. Son Jack, I insist upon your minding what I say.

440 JACK. I will, Sir. (*going*.)

CODGER. Why you are running away without hearing my Question.

JACK (*aside*). O dem it, I shall never get off! Pray, Sir, what is it?

CODGER. Don't Speak so quick, Jack, there's no understanding a
445 Word you say. One would think you supposed I was going to take the trouble of asking a Question that was not of sufficient importance to deserve an answer.

JACK. True, Sir: but do pray be so good to make haste.

CODGER. Son, once again, don't put yourself in such a fury; you
450 hurry me so, you have almost made me forget what I wanted to ask you; let me see,—O, now I recollect; pray do you know if the Fish was sent Home before you came out?

JACK. Lord no, Sir, I know nothing of the matter! (*aside*) How plaguy tiresome! to keep me all this Time for such a Ques-
455 tion as that.

CODGER. Son Jack, you know nothing! I am concerned to say it, but you know nothing!

LADY SMATTER. Don't judge him hastily. Mr. Dabler, you seem lost in thought.

460 DABLER. Do I, ma'am? I protest I did not know it.

LADY SMATTER. O you are a sly Creature! Planning some Poem, I dare Say.

JACK. I'll e'en take French leave.[1] (*going*.)

CECILIA (*following him*). You are destined to be tormented this
465 morning, for I cannot suffer you to escape till we come to an explanation: you said you had news for me?

JACK. O ay, true; I'll tell you what it was. While I was upon 'change[2] this morning—but hold, I believe I'd best tell Lady Smatter first.

470 CECILIA. Why So?

JACK. Because perhaps you'll be frightened.

---

1  *take French leave*: depart without permission, from the custom in France of departing from a reception without taking leave of the host or hostess. The earliest citation in *OED* is from Smollett's *Humphry Clinker* (1771).

2  *'change*: the Royal Exchange in the City, where merchants conducted business.

CECILIA. Frightened? at what?

JACK. Why it's very bad news.

CECILIA. Good God, what can this mean?

BEAUFORT. Nothing, I dare be sworn.                                    475

JACK. Very well, Brother! I wish you may think it nothing when
you've heard it.

CECILIA. Don't keep me in suspense, I beseech you.

BEAUFORT. Jack, what is it you mean by alarming Miss Stanley
thus.                                                                  480

JACK. Plague take it, I wish I had not spoke at all! I shall have him
fly into another passion!

CECILIA. Why will you not explain yourself?

JACK. Why, ma'am, if you please, I'll call on you in the afternoon.

CECILIA. No, no, you do but encrease my apprehensions by this         485
delay.

BEAUFORT. Upon my Honour, Jack, this is insufferable!

JACK. Why Lord, Brother, don't be so angry.

LADY SMATTER. Nay, now Jack, you are really provoking.

MRS. SAPIENT. Why yes, I must needs own I am, myself, of opin-        490
ion that it is rather disagreeable to wait long for bad news.

CODGER. In truth, Jack, you are no better than a Booby.

JACK. Well, if you will have it, you will! but I tell you before hand
you won't like it. You know Stipend, the Banker?

CECILIA. Good Heaven, know him? yes,—what of him?                     495

JACK. Why—now, upon my Word, I'd rather not speak.

CECILIA. You sicken me with apprehension!

JACK. Well,—had you much money in his Hands?

CECILIA. Every thing I am worth in the World!

JACK. Had you faith?                                                  500

CECILIA. You terrify me to Death!—what would you say?

BEAUFORT. No matter what,—Jack, I could murder you!

JACK. There, now, I said how it would be! now would not any
body suppose the man broke through my fault?

CECILIA. Broke?—O Heaven, I am ruined!                               505

BEAUFORT. No, my dearest Cecilia, your Safety is wrapt in mine,
and, to my Heart's last sigh, they shall be inseparable.

LADY SMATTER. Broke?—what can this mean?

MRS. SAPIENT. Broke? who is broke? I am quite alarmed.

CODGER. In truth, this has the appearance of a Serious Business.
CECILIA. Mr. Beaufort, let me pass—I can stand this no longer.
BEAUFORT. Allow me to conduct you to your own Room; this
torrent will else over-power you. Jack, wait till I return.

*he leads* CECILIA *out.*

JACK. No, no, Brother, you'll excuse me there!—I've stayed too
515 long already. (*going.*)
LADY SMATTER. Hold, Jack. I have ten thousand Questions to ask
you. Explain to me what all this means. It is of the utmost
consequence I should know immediately.
MRS. SAPIENT. I, too, am greatly terrified: I know not but I may
520 be myself concerned in this transaction; and really the
thought of losing one's money is extremely serious, for, as far
as *I* have seen of the World, there's no living without it.
CODGER. In truth, Son Jack, you have put us all into tribula-
tion—
525 MRS. SAPIENT. What, Sir, did you say was the Banker's name?
JACK (*aside*). Lord, how they worry me! Stipend, ma'am.
MRS. SAPIENT. Stipend? I protest he has concerns with half my
acquaintance! Lady Smatter, I am in the utmost consternation
at this intelligence; I think one hears some bad news or other
530 every Day,—half the people one knows are ruined![1] I wish
your Ladyship good morning: upon my word, in *my* opinion,
a Bankruptcy is no pleasant thing!

*Exit.*

LADY SMATTER. Pray, Jack, satisfy me more clearly how this affair
stands; tell me all you know of it?
530 JACK (*aside*). Lord, I sha'n't get away till midnight! Why ma'am,
the man's broke, that's all.
LADY SMATTER. But *how*? is there no prospect his affairs may be
made up?

---

1  *half the people one knows are ruined*: heavy stock-market speculation brought about an
economic crisis in the late 1770s, resulting in a large number of bankruptcies. Burney
takes up the subject in *Cecilia* (1782), depicting the financial collapse (and suicide) of a
man of fashion, Mr. Harrel.

JACK. None; they say upon 'change there won't be a shilling in the Pound.[1]

LADY SMATTER. What an unexpected blow! Poor Miss Stanley!

DABLER. 'Tis a shocking circumstance indeed. (aside) I think it will make a pretty good Elegy, though!

LADY SMATTER. I can't think what the poor Girl will do! for here is an End of our marrying her!

DABLER. 'Tis very hard upon her indeed. (aside) 'Twill be the most pathetic thing I ever wrote! Ma'am, your Ladyship's most obedient. (aside) I'll to Work while the subject is warm,—nobody will read it with dry Eyes!

*Exit.*

LADY SMATTER. I have the greatest regard in the World for Miss Stanley,—nobody can esteem her more; but I can't think of letting Beaufort marry without money.

CODGER. Pray, madam, how came Miss Stanley to have such very large concerns with Mr. Stipend?

LADY SMATTER. Why he was not only her Banker, but her Guardian, and her whole Fortune was in his Hands. She is a pretty sort of Girl,—I am really grieved for her.

JACK. Lord, here's my Brother! I wish I could make off.

*Re-enter* BEAUFORT.

BEAUFORT. Stay, Sir! one word, and you will be most welcome to go. Whence had you the intelligence you so humanely communicated to Miss Stanley?

JACK. I had it upon 'change. Every body was talking of it.

BEAUFORT. Enough. I have no desire to detain you any longer.

JACK. Why now, Brother, perhaps you think I am not sorry for Miss Stanley, because of my coming in such a hurry? but I do assure you it was out of mere good nature, for I made a point of running all the way, for fear she should hear it from a stranger.

---

1   *a shilling in the Pound*: i.e., Stipend's creditors could expect to receive less than 5 per cent of the money he owes them.

BEAUFORT. I desire you will leave me: my mind is occupied with
570     other matters than attending to your defence.
JACK. Very well, Brother. Plague take it, I wish I had gone to
    Hyde Park at once!

*Exit.*

CODGER. In truth, Son Beaufort, I must confess Jack has been
    somewhat abrupt; but, nevertheless, I must hint to you that,
575     when I am by, I think you might as well refer the due reproof
    to be given by me. Jack is not every body's son, although he
    be mine.
BEAUFORT. I am sorry I have offended you, Sir, but—
CODGER. Madam, as your House seems in some little perturba-
580     tion, I hope you will excuse the shortness of my visit if I take
    leave now. Your Ladyship's most humble servant. Jack is a
    good Lad at the bottom, although he be somewhat wanting
    in solidity.

*Exit.*

BEAUFORT. At length, thank Heaven, the House is cleared. O
585     madam, will you not go to Miss Stanley? I have left her in an
    agony of mind which I had no ability to mitigate.
LADY SMATTER. Poor thing! I am really in great pain for her.
BEAUFORT. Your Ladyship alone has power to soothe her,—a
    power which, I hope, you will instantly exert.
590 LADY SMATTER. I will go to her presently—or send for her here.
BEAUFORT. Surely your Ladyship will go to *her*?—at such a Time
    as this, the smallest failure in respect—
LADY SMATTER. As to that, Beaufort,—but I am thinking what
    the poor Girl had best do; I really don't know what to advise.
595 BEAUFORT. If I may be honoured with your powerful interces-
    sion, I hope to prevail with her to be mine immediately.
LADY SMATTER. Pho, pho, don't talk so idly.
BEAUFORT. Madam!
LADY SMATTER. Be quiet a few minutes, and let me consider
600     what can be done.

BEAUFORT. But, while we are both absent, what may not the sweet Sufferer imagine?

LADY SMATTER. Suppose we get her into the Country?—yet I know not what she can do when she is there; she can't Live on Green Trees. 605

BEAUFORT. What does your Ladyship mean?

LADY SMATTER. Nothing is so difficult as disposing of a poor Girl of Fashion.

BEAUFORT. Madam!

LADY SMATTER. She has been brought up to nothing,—if she 610 can make a Cap, 'tis as much as she can do,—and, in such a case, when a Girl is reduced to a Penny, what is to be done?

BEAUFORT. Good Heaven, madam, will Miss Stanley ever be reduced to a Penny, while I live in affluence?

LADY SMATTER. Beaufort,—to cut the matter short, you must 615 give her up.

BEAUFORT. Give her up?

LADY SMATTER. Certainly; you can never suppose I shall consent to your marrying a Girl who has lost all her Fortune. While the match seemed suitable to your expectations, and to my 620 intentions towards you, I readily countenanced it, but now, it is quite a different thing,—all is changed, and—

BEAUFORT. No, madam, no, all is not changed, for the Heart of Beaufort is unalterable! I loved Miss Stanley in prosperity,— in adversity, I adore her! I solicited her favour when she was 625 surrounded by my Rivals, and I will still supplicate it, though she should be deserted by all the World besides. Her distress shall encrease my tenderness, her poverty shall redouble my Respect, and her misfortunes shall render her more dear to me than ever! 630

LADY SMATTER. Beaufort, you offend me extremely. I have as high notions of Sentiment and delicacy as you can have, for the study of the fine arts, as Pope justly says, greatly enlarges the mind; but, for all that, if you would still have me regard you as a Son, you must pay me the obedience due to a moth- 635 er, and never suppose I adopted you to marry you to a Beg- gar.

BEAUFORT. A Beggar?—Indignation Choaks me!—I must leave

you, madam,—the submission I pay you as a Nephew, and
640 the obedience I owe you as an adopted Son, will else both
give way to feelings I know not how to stifle!

*Exit.*

LADY SMATTER *alone.*

LADY SMATTER. This is really an unfortunate affair. I am quite
distressed how to act, for the Eyes of all the World will be
upon me! I will see the Girl, however, and give her a hint
645 about Beaufort;—William!

*Enter a* SERVANT.

Tell Miss Stanley I beg to speak to her.

*Exit* SERVANT.

I protest I wish she was fairly out of the House! I never cor-
dially liked her,—she has not a grain of Taste, and her Compliments are so cold, one has no pleasure in receiving them,—
650 she is a most insipid thing! I sha'n't be sorry to have done
with her.

*Enter* CECILIA.

Miss Stanley, my dear, your Servant.
CECILIA. Oh madam!
LADY SMATTER. Take courage; don't be so downcast,—a noble
655 mind, as I was reading the other Day, is always superior to
misfortune.
CECILIA. Alas, madam, in the first moments of sorrow and disappointment, Philosophy and Rhetoric offer their aid in vain!
Affliction may, indeed, be alleviated, but it must first be felt.
660 LADY SMATTER. I did not expect, Miss Stanley, you would have
disputed this point with *me*; I thought, after so long studying
matters of this sort, I might be allowed to be a better Judge

than a Young Person who has not studied them at all.

CECILIA. Good Heaven, madam, are you offended?

LADY SMATTER. Whether I am or not, we'll not talk of it now; it 665
would be illiberal to take offence at a Person in distress.

CECILIA. Madam!

LADY SMATTER. Do you think Jack may have been misinformed?

CECILIA. Alas no! I have just received this melancholy confirmation of his intelligence. (*Gives* LADY SMATTER *a Letter.*) 670

LADY SMATTER. Upon my Word 'tis a sad thing! a sad stroke
upon my Word! however, you have good friends, and such as,
I dare say, will take care of you.

CECILIA. Take care of me, madam?

LADY SMATTER. Yes, my dear, *I* will for one. And you should 675
consider how much harder such a Blow would have been to
many other poor Girls, who have not your resources.

CECILIA. My resources? I don't understand you?

LADY SMATTER. Nay, my dear, I only mean to comfort you, and
to assure you of my continued regard; and if you can think of 680
any thing in which I can serve you, I am quite at your Command; nobody can wish you better. My House, too, shall
always be open to you. I should scorn to desert you because
you are in distress. A mind, indeed, cultivated and informed,
as Shakespeare has it, will ever be above a mean action. 685

CECILIA. I am quite confounded!

LADY SMATTER. In short, my dear, you will find *me* quite at your
disposal, and as much your Friend as in the sunshine of your
prosperity: — but as to Beaufort —

CECILIA. Hold, madam! I now begin to understand your Lady- 690
ship perfectly.

LADY SMATTER. Don't be hasty, my dear. I say as to Beaufort, he
is but a young man, and young men, you know, are mighty
apt to be rash; but when they have no independance, and are
of no profession, they should be very cautious how they dis- 695
oblige their Friends. Besides, it always happens that, when
they are drawn in to their own ruin, they involve —

CECILIA. No more, I beseech you, madam! I know not how to
brook such terms, or to endure such indignity. I shall leave
your Ladyship's House instantly, nor, while any other will 700

receive me, shall I re-enter it! Pardon me, madam, but I am yet young in the school of adversity, and my spirit is not yet tamed down to that abject submission to unmerited mortifications which Time and long suffering can alone render sup-
705    portable.

LADY SMATTER. You quite surprise me, my dear! I can't imagine what you mean. However, when your mind is more composed, I beg you will follow me to my own Room. Till then, I will leave you to your meditations, for, as Swift has well said,
710    'tis vain to reason with a Person in a passion.

*Exit.*

CECILIA *alone.*

CECILIA. Follow you? no, no, I will converse with you no more. Cruel, unfeeling Woman! I will quit your inhospitable Roof, I will seek shelter—alas where?—without fortune, destitute of Friends, ruined in circumstances, yet proud of Heart,—
715    where can the poor Cecilia seek shelter, peace or protection? Oh Beaufort! 'tis thine alone to console me; thy sympathy shall soften my calamities, and thy fidelity shall instruct me to support them. Yet fly I must!—Insult ought not to be borne, and those who twice risk, the third time deserve it.

# ACT III

*Scene a Dressing Room at* LADY SMATTER'S.

*Enter* LADY SMATTER, *followed by* BEAUFORT.

BEAUFORT. Madam you distract me! 'tis impossible her intentions should be unknown to you,—tell me, I beseech you, whither she is gone? what are her designs? and why she deigned not to acquaint me with her resolution?

LADY SMATTER. Why will you, Beaufort, eternally forget that it is 5 the duty of every wise man, as Swift has admirably said, to keep his passions to himself?

BEAUFORT. She must have been *driven* to this Step,—it could never have occurred to her without provocation, relieve me then, madam, from a suspence insupportable, and tell me, at 10 least, to what asylum she has flown?

LADY SMATTER. Beaufort, you make me Blush for you!—Who would suppose that a Scholar, a man of cultivated talents, could behave so childishly? Do you remember what Pope has said upon this Subject? 15

BEAUFORT. This is past endurance!—no, madam, no!—at such a Time as this, his very name is disgustful to me.

LADY SMATTER. How!—did I hear right?—the name of Pope disgustful?—

BEAUFORT. Yes, madam,—Pope, Swift, Shakespeare himself, and 20 every other name you can mention but that of Cecilia Stanley, is hateful to my Ear, and detestable to my remembrance.

LADY SMATTER. I am thunderstruck!—this is downright blasphemy.

BEAUFORT. Good Heaven, madam, is this a Time to talk of Books 25 and Authors?—however, if your Ladyship is cruelly determined to give me no satisfaction, I must endeavour to procure intelligence elsewhere.

LADY SMATTER. I protest to you she went away without speaking to me; she sent for a Chair,[1] and did not even let the Servants 30 hear whither she ordered it.

---

1   *a Chair*: sedan chairs, like hackney carriages, were licensed to carry passengers in London.

BEAUFORT. Perhaps, then, she left a Letter for you?—O I am sure she did! her just sense of propriety would never suffer her to quit your Ladyship's House with an abruptness so unaccount-
35 able.
LADY SMATTER. Well, well, whether she writ or not is nothing to the purpose; she has acted a very prudent part in going away, and, once again I repeat, you must give her up.
BEAUFORT. No, madam, never!—never while Life is lent me will
40 I give up the tie that renders it most dear to me.
LADY SMATTER. Well, Sir, I have only this to Say,—one must be given up, she or me,—the decision is in your own Hands.
BEAUFORT. Deign then, madam, to hear my final answer, and to hear it, if possible, with lenity. That your favour, upon every
45 account, is valuable to me, there can be no occasion to assert, and I have endeavoured to prove my sense of the goodness you have so long shewn me, by all the gratitude I have been able to manifest: you have a claim undoubted to my utmost respect, and humblest deference; but there is yet another claim
50 upon me,—a sacred, an irresistable claim,—Honour! And this were I to forego, not all your Ladyship's most unbounded liberality and munificence would prove adequate reparation for so dreadful, so attrocious a sacrifice!

*Enter* SERVANT.

SERVANT. Mr. Censor, my lady.
55 LADY SMATTER. Beg him to walk up Stairs. I will put this affair into his Hands; (*aside*) he is a sour, morose, ill-tempered Wretch, and will give Beaufort no Quarter.

*Enter* CENSOR.

Mr. Censor I am very glad to see you.
CENSOR. I thank your Ladyship. Where is Miss Stanley?
60 LADY SMATTER. Why not at Home. O Mr. Censor, we have the saddest thing to tell you!—we are all in the greatest afflic-tion,—poor Miss Stanley has met with the cruellist misfor-tune you can conceive.

CENSOR. I have heard the whole affair.

LADY SMATTER. I am vastly glad you came, for I want to have a little rational consultation with you. Alas, Mr. Censor, what an unexpected stroke! You can't imagine how unhappy it makes me. 65

CENSOR. Possibly not; for my Imagination is no reveller,—it seldom deviates from the Bounds of probability. 70

LADY SMATTER. Surely you don't doubt me?

CENSOR. No, madam, not in the least!

LADY SMATTER. I am happy to hear you say so.

CENSOR (aside). You have but little reason if you understood me. When does your Ladyship expect Miss Stanley's return? 75

LADY SMATTER. Why, really, I can't exactly say, for she left the House in a sort of hurry. I would fain have dissuaded her, but all my Rhetoric was ineffectual,—Shakespeare himself would have pleaded in vain! To say the truth, her Temper is none of the most flexible; however, poor Thing, great allowance ought to be made for her unhappy situation, for, as the Poet has it, misfortune renders every body unamiable. 80

CENSOR. What Poet?

LADY SMATTER. Bless me, don't you know? Well, I shall now grow proud indeed if I can boast of making a Quotation that is new to the learned Mr. Censor. My present Author, Sir, is Swift. 85

CENSOR. Swift?—you have, then, some private Edition of his Works?

LADY SMATTER. Well, well, I won't be possitive as to Swift,— perhaps it was Pope. 'Tis impracticable for any body that reads so much as I do to be always exact as to an Author. Why now, how many Volumes do you think I can run through in one year's reading? 90

CENSOR. More than would require seven years to digest. 95

LADY SMATTER. Pho, pho, but I study besides, and when I am preparing a Criticism, I sometimes give a whole Day to poring over only one Line. However, let us, for the present, quit these abstruse points, and, as Parnel says, "e'en talk a little like folks of this world." 100

CENSOR. Parnel?—you have, then, made a discovery with

which you should oblige the public, for that Line passes for Prior's.[1]

LADY SMATTER. Prior?—O, very true, so it is. Bless me, into
105 what errors does extensive reading lead us! But to Business,—
this poor Girl must, some way or other, be provided for, and
my opinion is she had best return to her Friends in the
Country. London is a dangerous place for Girls who have no
Fortune. Suppose you go to her, and reason with her upon
110 the subject?

BEAUFORT. You *do* know her Direction,[2] then?

LADY SMATTER. No matter; I will not have *you* go to her, whoever does. Would you believe it, Mr. Censor, this unthinking
young man would actually marry the Girl without a Penny?
115 However, it behoves me to prevent him, if only for example's
Sake. That, indeed, is the chief motive which Governs me, for
such is my *fatal pre-eminence*, as Addison calls it,[3] that, should I
give way, my name will be quoted for a Licence to indiscreet
marriages for Ages yet to come.

120 CENSOR. I hope, madam, the gratitude of the World will be adequate to the obligations it owes you.

LADY SMATTER. Well, Mr. Censor, I will commit the affair to
your management. This paper will tell you where Miss Stanley is to be met with, and pray tell the poor Thing she may
125 always depend upon my protection, and that I feel for her
most extremely; but, above all things, let her know she must
think no more of Beaufort, for why should the poor Girl be
fed with false hopes? It would be barbarous to trifle with her

---

1   *that Line passes for Prior's*: Lady Smatter has confused Thomas Parnell (1679-1718), a
    friend of Pope and Swift and fellow member of the Scriblerus Club, with his near con-
    temporary, Matthew Prior (1664-1721). The line is from Prior's poem "A Better
    Answer" (1718): "Let Us e'en talk a little like Folks of this World" (l. 4). Prior himself is
    alluding to Falstaff's words to Pistol in Shakespeare's *Henry IV, Part 2*: "I pray thee now,
    deliver them like a man of this world" (V.iii.95).
2   *Direction*: the common term for address.
3   *fatal pre-eminence, as Addison calls it*: misquoting Joseph Addison's *Cato* (1713), in which
    the hero demands:
         Am I distinguish'd from you but by toils,
         Superior toils, and heavier weight of cares!
         Painful pre-eminence! (III.v.21-3)
    See also *The Woman-Hater*, p. 208, note 1.

expectations. I declare I should hate myself were I capable of such cruelty. Tell her so, Mr. Censor, and tell her— 130

BEAUFORT. Oh madam, forbear!—Heavens, what a Message for Miss Stanley! Dishonour not yourself by sending it. Is she not the same Miss Stanley who was so lately respected, carressed, and admired? whose esteem you sought? whose favour you solicited?—whose alliance you coveted?—Can a few 135 moments have obliterated all remembrance of her merit? Shall *we* be treacherous, because *she* is unfortunate? must *we* lose our integrity, because *she* has lost her Fortune? Oh madam, reflect, while it is yet Time, that the judgement of the World at large is always impartial, and let us not, by with- 140 holding protection from Her, draw universal contempt and reproach upon Ourselves!

LADY SMATTER. Beaufort, you offend me extremely. Do you suppose I have laboured so long at the fine arts, and studied so deeply the intricacies of Literature, to be taught, at last, the 145 right rule of conduct by my Nephew? O Mr. Censor, how well has Shakespeare said rash and inconsiderate is Youth!— but I must wave a further discussion of this point at present, as I have some notes to prepare for our Esprit Party of to night. But remember, Beaufort, that if you make any attempt to see 150 or write to Miss Stanley, I will dis-own and disinherit you. Mr. Censor, you will enforce this Doctrine, and pray tell him, it was a maxim with Pope,—or Swift, I am not sure which,— that resolution, in a cultivated Mind, is unchangeable.

*Exit.*

BEAUFORT *and* CENSOR.

BEAUFORT. By Heaven, Censor, with all your apathy and misan- 155 thropy, I had believed you incapable of listening to such inhumanity without concern.

CENSOR. Know you not, Beaufort, that though we can all see the Surface of a River, its depth is only to be fathomed by Experiment? Had my concern been shallow, it might have 160 babbled without impediment, but, as it was Strong and violent, I restrained it, lest a torrent of indignation should have overflowed your future hopes, and laid waste my future influence.

165 BEAUFORT. Shew me, I beseech you, the Paper, that I may hasten to the lovely, injured Writer, and endeavour, by my fidelity and simpathy to make her forget my connections.

CENSOR. Not so fast, Beaufort. When a man has to deal with a Lover, he must think a little of himself, for he may be sure the
170 Innamorato will think only of his Mistress.

BEAUFORT. Surely you do not mean to refuse me her Direction?

CENSOR. Indeed I do, unless you can instruct me how to sustain the assault that will follow my surrendering it.

BEAUFORT. Why will you trifle with me thus? What, to you, is
175 the resentment of Lady Smatter?

CENSOR. How gloriously inconsistent is the conduct of a professed Lover! while to his Mistress he is all tame submission and abject servility, to the rest of the World he is commanding, selfish and obstinate; every thing is to give way to him, no
180 convenience is to be consulted, no objections are to be attended to in opposition to his wishes. It seems as if he thought it the sole business of the rest of mankind to study his single Interest,—in order, perhaps, to recompence him for pretending to his Mistress that he has no Will but hers.

185 BEAUFORT. Shew me the address,—then rail at your leisure.

CENSOR. You think nothing, then, of the disgrace I must incur with this literary Phenomenon if I disregard her injunctions? Will she not exclude me for-ever from the purlieus of Parnassus?[1]—Stun me with the names of Authors she has never
190 read?—and pester me with flimsy Sentences[2] which she has the assurance to call Quotations?—

BEAUFORT. Well, well, well!—

CENSOR. Will she not tell me that Pope brands a breach of Trust as dishonourable?—that Shakespeare stigmatises the mean-
195 ness of Treachery?—And recollect having read in Swift— that Fortitude is one of the cardinal virtues?—

---

1  *purlieus of Parnassus*: the realm of literature, from the mountain in Greece held sacred to Apollo and the Muses.

2  *Sentences*: pithy sayings, maxims, or proverbs. Censor here describes precisely Lady Smatter's manner of attributing such "sentences" to standard authors.

BEAUFORT. Stuff and folly!—does it matter what she says?—the Paper!—the Direction!—

CENSOR. Heavens, that a Woman whose utmost natural capacity will hardly enable her to understand the History of Tom Thumb,[1] and whose comprehensive faculties would be absolutely baffled by the Lives of the seven Champions of Christendom,[2] should dare blaspheme the names of our noblest Poets with Words that convey no ideas, and Sentences of which the Sound listens in vain for the Sense![3]—, she is insufferable!

BEAUFORT. How unseasonable a discussion! yet you seem to be more irritated at her folly about Books, than at her want of feeling to the sweetest of her Sex.

CENSOR. True; but the reason is obvious,—Folly torments because it gives present disturbance,—as to want of feeling,—'tis a thing of Course. The moment I heard that Miss Stanley had lost her Fortune, I was certain of all that would follow.

BEAUFORT. Can you, then, see such treachery without rage or emotion?

CENSOR. No, not without *emotion,* for base actions always excite contempt,—but *rage* must be stimulated by surprise: no man is much moved by events that merely answer his expectations.

BEAUFORT. Censor, will you give me the direction? I have neither Time nor patience for further uninteresting discussions. If you are determined to refuse it, say so; I have other resources, and I have a Spirit resolute to essay them all.

CENSOR. It is no news to me, Beaufort, that a man may find more ways than one to ruin himself; yet, whatever pleasure may attend putting them in practice, I believe it seldom happens when he is irreparably undone, that he piques himself upon his Success.

BEAUFORT. I will trouble you no longer,—your Servant. (*going.*)

---

1  *the History of Tom Thumb*: a folk-tale, popular since the sixteenth century. Children learning to read would begin with stories such as this.

2  *Lives of the seven Champions of Christendom*: a romance by Richard Johnson (1596-7), later rewritten in chapbook form and a favourite with children.

3  *the Sound listens in vain for the Sense*: alluding to Pope's *An Essay on Criticism*: "The *Sound* must seem an *Echo* to the *Sense*" (l. 365).

CENSOR. Hold, Beaufort! Forget, for a few moments, the Lover, and listen to me, not with passion but understanding. Miss Stanley, you find, has now no dependence but upon you;—you have none but upon Lady Smatter,—what follows?

BEAUFORT. Distraction, I believe,—I have nothing else before me!

CENSOR. If, instantly and wildly, you oppose her in the first heat of her determination, you will have served a ten years' Apprenticeship to her caprices, without any other payment than the pleasure of having endured them. She will regard your disobedience as rebellion to her Judgement, and resent it with acrimony.

BEAUFORT. Oh misery of Dependance!—the heaviest toil, the hardest labour, fatigue the most intense,—what are they compared to the corroding servility of discontented Dependance?

CENSOR. Nothing, I grant, is so painful to endure, but nothing is so difficult to shake off; and therefore, as you are now situated, there is but one thing in the World can excuse your seeking Miss Stanley.

BEAUFORT. Whatever it may be, I shall agree to it with transport. Name it.

CENSOR. Insanity.

BEAUFORT. Censor, at such a Time as this, rallery is unpardonable.

CENSOR. Attend to me, then, in sober sadness. You must give up all thoughts of quitting this House, till the ferocity of your learned Aunt is abated.

BEAUFORT. Impossible!

CENSOR. Nay, prithee, Beaufort, act not as a Lunatic while you disclaim Insanity. I will go to Miss Stanley myself, and bring you an account of her situation.

BEAUFORT. Would you have me, then, submit to this Tyrant?

CENSOR. Would I have a Farmer, after sewing a Field, not wait to reap the Harvest?

BEAUFORT. I will endeavour, then, to yield to your counsel; but, remember Censor, my yielding is not merely reluctant,—it must also be transitory; for if I do not speedily find the good effects of my Self-denial, I will boldly and firmly give up forever all hopes of precarious advantage, for the certain, the greater, the nobler blessing of claiming my lovely Cecilia,— 270 though at the hazard of ruin and destruction!

CENSOR. And do you, Beaufort, remember in turn, that had I believed you capable of a different conduct, I had never ranked you as my Friend.

BEAUFORT. Oh Censor, how soothing to my anxiety is your 275 hard-earned, but most flattering approbation! Hasten, then, to the sweet Sufferer,— tell her my Heart bleeds at her unmerited distresses,— tell her that, with her fugitive Self, peace and Happiness both flew this mansion,— tell her that, when we meet — 280

CENSOR. All these messages may be given!—but not till then, believe me! Do you suppose I can find no better topic for Conversation, than making Soft Speeches by proxy?

BEAUFORT. Tell her, at least, how much —

CENSOR. My good Friend, I am not ignorant that Lovers, Fops, 285 fine Ladies and Chambermaids have all charters for talking nonsense; it is, therefore, a part of their business, and they deem it indispensable; but I never yet heard of any order of Men so unfortunate as to be under a necessity of listening to them. 290

*Exit.*

BEAUFORT *alone.*

BEAUFORT. Dear, injured Cecilia! why cannot I be myself the Bearer of the faith I have plighted thee? — prostrate myself at thy feet, mitigate thy Sorrows, and share, or redress thy Wrongs! Even while I submit to captivity, I disdain the chains that bind me,— but alas, I rattle them in vain! O happy Those 295 who to their own industry owe their subsistence, and to their own fatigue and hardships their succeeding rest, and rewarding affluence! Now, indeed, do I feel the weight of Bondage,

since it teaches me to envy even the toiling Husbandman, and
laborious mechanic.[1]

300

*The Scene changes to an apartment at* MRS. VOLUBLE'S;
DABLER *is discovered Writing.*

DABLER. *The pensive maid, with saddest sorrow sad,*—no, hang it,
that won't do!—*saddest sad* will never do. With,—with—
with *mildest,*—ay that' it!—*The pensive maid with mildest sorrow
sad,*—I should like, now, to hear a man mend that line!—I
shall never get another equal to it.—Let's see,—sad, bad,
Lad, Dad,—curse it, there's never a Rhyme will do!—
Where's the art of Poetry?[2]—, here,—now we shall have it;
(*reads*) Add,—hold, that will do at once,—*with mildest sorrow
sad, shed Crystal Tears, and Sigh to Sigh did add.* Admirable!
admirable by all that's good. Now let's try the first Stanza
(*reads*),
  Ye gentle Nymphs, whose Heart's are prone to love,
  Ah, hear my Song, and ah! my Song approve;
  And ye, ye glorious, mighty Sons of Fame,
  Ye mighty Warriors—
How's this, two *mightys?*—hang it, that won't do!—let's
see,—ye *glorious* Warriors,—no, there's *glorious* before,—
curse it, now I've got it all to do over again! just as I thought I
had finished it!—ye *fighting,*—no,—ye *towering,* no;—ye,—
ye—ye—I have it, by Apollo!—

305

310

315

*Enter* BETTY.

BETTY. Sir, here's a person below who—
DABLER (*starting up in a rage*). Now curse me if this is not too
much! What do you mean by interrupting me at my studies?
how often have I given orders not to be disturbed?
BETTY. I'm sure, Sir, I thought there was no harm in just telling
you—

320

325

---

1 *Husbandman … mechanic:* farmer; workman.
2 *art of Poetry:* Edward Bysshe's *The Art of English Poetry* (1702) contained a rhyming dictionary, as well as "Rules for making English Verse" and a poetical commonplace book.
 It went through nine editions between 1702 and 1762.

DABLER. Tell me nothing!—get out of the Room directly!—
and take care you never break in upon me again,—no, not if
the House be on Fire!—Go, I say!

BETTY. Yes, Sir. (aside) Lord, how masters and *Misisses* do love
scolding! 330

*Exit.*

DABLER *alone.*

DABLER. What a provoking intrusion! just as I had Worked
myself into the true Spirit of Poetry!—I sha'n't recover my
ideas this half Hour. 'Tis a most barbarous thing that a man's
retirement cannot be sacred. (*Sits down to write.*) Ye *fighting,*—
no, that was not it,—ye—ye—ye—curse it (*stamping*), if I 335
have not forgot all I was going to say! That unfeeling, impen-
etrable Fool has lost me more ideas than would have made a
fresh man's reputation. I'd rather have given one hundred
Guineas[1] than have seen her. I protest, I was upon the point
of making as good a Poem as any in the Language,—my 340
numbers flowed,—my thoughts were ready,—my Words
glided,—but now, all is gone!—all gone and evaporated!
(*claps his Hand on his Forehead*) here's nothing left! nothing in
the World!—What shall I do to compose myself? Suppose I
read?—why where the Deuce are all the things gone? (*look-* 345
*ing over his Papers*) O, here,—I wonder how my Epigram will
read to Day,—I think I'll shew it to Censor,—he has seen
nothing like it of late;—I'll pass it off for some Dead Poet's,
or he'll never do it justice;—let's see, suppose Pope?—no, it's
too smart for Pope,—Pope never wrote any thing like it!— 350
well then, suppose—

*Enter* MRS. VOLUBLE.

O curse it, another interruption!

MRS. VOLUBLE. I hope, Sir, I don't disturb you?—I'm sure I
would not disturb you for the World, for I know nothing's so

---

1   *one hundred Guineas*: £105; a guinea was worth 21 shillings.

troublesome; and I know you Gentlemen Writers dislike it of all things; but I only just wanted to know if the Windows were Shut, for fear of the Rain, for I asked Betty if she had been in to see about them, but she said—

DABLER. They'll do very well,—pray leave them alone,—I am extremely busy;—(aside) I must leave these Lodgings, I see!

MRS. VOLUBLE. O Sir, I would not stay upon any account, but only sometimes there are such sudden showers, that if the Windows are left open, half one's things may be spoilt, before one knows any thing of the matter. And if so much as a paper of yours was to be damaged, I should never forgive myself, for I'd rather all the Poets in the World should be Burnt in one great Bon fire, than lose so much as the most miniken bit of your Writing, though no bigger than my Nail.

DABLER. My dear Mrs. Voluble, you are very obliging. (aside) She's a mighty good sort of Woman,—I've a great mind to read her that Song: —no, this will be better. —Mrs. Voluble, do you think you can keep a Secret?

MRS. VOLUBLE. O Dear Sir, I'll defy any body to excell me in that! I am more particular Scrupulous about Secrets than any body.

DABLER. Well, then, I'll read you a little thing I've just been com-posing, and you shall tell me your opinion of it. (reads) *on a young lady blinded by Lightning.*

> Fair Cloris, now depriv'd of Sight,
>     To Error ow'd her fate uneven;
> Her Eyes were so refulgent bright
> The blundering Lightning thought them Heaven.

What do you think of it, Mrs. Voluble?

MRS. VOLUBLE. O, I think it the prettiest, most moving thing I ever heard in my life.

DABLER. Do you indeed? —pray sit down, Mrs. Voluble, I protest I never observed you were standing.

MRS. VOLUBLE. Dear Sir, you're vastly polite. (*seats herself.*)

DABLER. So you really think it's pretty good, do you?

MRS. VOLUBLE. O dear yes, Sir; I never heard any thing I liked so well in my life. It's prodigious fine, indeed!

DABLER. Pray don't sit so near the Door, Mrs. Voluble; I'm afraid you will take Cold. (*aside*) 'Tis amazing to me where this Woman picked up so much Taste!

MRS. VOLUBLE. But I hope, Sir, my being here is of no hindrance to you, because, if it is, I'm sure— 395

DABLER. No, Mrs. Voluble (*looking at his Watch*), I am obliged to go out myself now. I leave my Room in your charge; let care be taken that no human Being enters it in my absence, and don't let one of my Papers be touched or moved upon any account. 400

MRS. VOLUBLE. Sir I shall lock the Door, and put the key in my Pocket. No body shall so much as know there's a paper in the House.

*Exit* DABLER.

MRS. VOLUBLE *alone*.

I believe it's almost a Week since I've had a good rummage of them myself. Let's see, is not this 'Sprit Night? yes; and he won't come Home till very late, so I think I may as well give them a fair look over at once. (*seats herself at the Table*) Well, now, how nice and snug this is! What's here? (*takes up a Paper.*) 405

*Enter* BOB.

BOB. Mother, here's Miss Jenny, the Milliner maker. 410

MRS. VOLUBLE. Is there? ask her to come up.

BOB. Lord, mother, why you would not have her come into Mr. Dabler's Room? why if he—

MRS. VOLUBLE. What's that to you? do you suppose I don't know what I'm about? you're never easy but when you're a talking,—always prate, prate, prate about something or other. Go and ask her to come up, I say. 415

BOB. Lord, one can't speak a Word!—

*Exit.*

Mrs. Voluble. Have done, will you? mutter, mutter, mutter;—
420 It will be a prodigious treat to Miss Jenny to come into this
Room.

*Enter* Miss Jenny.

Miss Jenny, how do do, my dear? this is very obliging of you.
Do you know whose Room you are in?

Miss Jenny. No, ma'am.

425 Mrs. Voluble. Mr. Dabler's own Room, I assure you! And
here's all his Papers; these are what he calls his *miniscrips.*

Miss Jenny. Well, what a heap of them!

Mrs. Voluble. And he's got five or six Boxes brimful besides.

Miss Jenny. Dear me! well, I could not do so much if I was to
430 have the Indies![1]

Mrs. Voluble. Now if you'll promise not to tell a living Soul a
Word of the matter, I'll read you some of them: but be sure,
now, you don't tell.

Miss Jenny. Dear no, I would not for ever so much.

435 Mrs. Voluble. Well, then, let's see,—what's this? (*takes up a
Paper.*) *Elegy on the Slaughter of a Lamb.*

Miss Jenny. O, pray let's have that.

Mrs. Voluble. I'll put it aside, and look out some more. *A Dialogue between a Tear and a Sigh,—verses on a young lady's fainting
440 away—*

Miss Jenny. That must be pretty indeed! I dare say it will make
us cry.

Mrs. Voluble. *An Epitaph on a Fly killed by a Spider; an—*

*Enter* Bob.

Bob. Mother, here's a young Gentlewoman wants you.

445 Mrs. Voluble. A young Gentlewoman?—who can it be?

Bob. I never see her before. She's a deal smarter than Miss Jenny.

---

1   *have the Indies*: possess the wealth of the west and the east Indies.

MISS JENNY. I'm sure I'd have come more Dressed, if I'd known of seeing any body.

MRS. VOLUBLE. Well, I can't imagine who it is. I'm sure I'm in a sad pickle. Ask her into the Parlour. 450

MISS JENNY. Dear ma'am, you'd better by half see her here; all the fine folks have their Company up Stairs,[1] for I see a deal of the Quality, by carrying Things Home.

MRS. VOLUBLE. Well then, ask her to come up.

BOB. But suppose Mr. Dabler— 455

MRS. VOLUBLE. Mind your own Business, Sir, and don't think to teach me. Go and ask her up this minute.

BOB. I'm going, a'n't I?

*Exit.*

MRS. VOLUBLE. I do verily believe that Boy has no equal for prating; I never saw the like of him,—his Tongue's always a 460 running.

*Re-enter* BOB, *followed by* CECILIA.

BOB. Mother, here's the young Gentlewoman.

CECILIA. I presume, ma'am, you are Mrs. Voluble?

MRS. VOLUBLE. Yes, ma'am.

CECILIA. I hope you will excuse this intrusion; and I must beg 465 the favour of a few minutes private Conversation with you.

MRS. VOLUBLE. To be sure, ma'am. Bobby, get the lady a Chair. I hope, ma'am, you'll excuse Bobby's coming in before you; he's a sad rude Boy for manners.

BOB. Why the young Gentlewoman bid me herself; 'twas no fault 470 of mine.

MRS. VOLUBLE. Be quiet, will you? Jabber, jabber, jabber,— there's no making you hold your Tongue a minute. Pray, ma'am, do sit down.

---

1 *Company up Stairs*: Miss Jenny is right. The parlour, downstairs, was used as a family sitting-room; company was properly received in a drawing-room, which would normally be upstairs. See *Evelina*, ed. Sir Frank D. MacKinnon (Oxford: Clarendon Press, 1930), 535, 538.

CECILIA. I thank you, I had rather stand. I have but a few Words to say to you, and will not detain you five minutes.

MISS JENNY. Suppose Master Bobby and I go down Stairs till the lady has done? (*apart to* MRS. VOLUBLE) Why Lord, Mrs. Voluble, I know who that lady is as well as I know you! why it's Miss Stanley, that we've been making such a heap of things for.

MRS. VOLUBLE. Why you don't say so! what, the Bride?

MISS JENNY. Yes.

MRS. VOLUBLE. Well, I protest I thought I'd seen her some where before. (*to* CECILIA) Ma'am, I'm quite ashamed of not recollecting you sooner, but I hope your goodness will excuse it. I hope, ma'am, the good lady your Aunt is well?—that is, your aunt that is to be?

CECILIA. If you mean Lady Smatter,—I believe she is well.—

MRS. VOLUBLE. I'm sure, ma'am, I've the greatest respect in the World for her Ladyship, though I have not the pleasure to know her; but I hear all about her from Mrs. Hobbins,—to be sure, ma'am, you know Mrs. Hobbins, my lady's House-Keeper?

CECILIA. Certainly: it was by her Direction I came hither.

MRS. VOLUBLE. That was very obliging of her, I'm sure, and I take your coming as a very particular favour. I hope, ma'am, all the rest of the Family's well? And Mrs. Simper, my lady's Woman? But I beg pardon for my ill manners, ma'am, for to be sure, I ought first to have asked for Mr. Beaufort. I hope he's well, ma'am?

CECILIA. I—I don't know—I believe,—I fancy he is.—

MRS. VOLUBLE. Well, he's a most agreeable Gentleman indeed, ma'am, and I think—

CECILIA. If it is inconvenient for me to speak to you now.

MRS. VOLUBLE. Not at all, ma'am; Miss Jenny and Bobby can as well divert themselves in the Parlour.

MISS JENNY. Dear me yes, I'll go directly.

BOB. And I'll go and sit in the Kitchen, and look at the clock, and when it's five minutes, I'll tell Miss Jenny.

MISS JENNY. Come, then, Master Bobby. (*aside*) She's very melancholic, I think, for a young lady just going to be married.

*Exit with* BOB.

CECILIA. The motive which has induced me to give you this trouble, Mrs. Voluble—

MRS. VOLUBLE. Dear ma'am, pray don't talk of trouble, for I'm 515 sure I think it none. I take it quite as a favour to receive a visit from such a young lady as you. But pray, ma'am, sit down; I'm quite ashamed to see you standing,—it's enough to tire you to Death.

CECILIA. It is not of the least consequence. A very unexpected 520 and unhappy Event has obliged me, most abruptly, to quit the House of Lady Smatter, and if—

MRS. VOLUBLE. Dear ma'am, you surprise me! but I hope you have not parted upon account of any disagreement?

CECILIA. I must beg you to hear me. I have, at present, insupera- 525 ble objections to visiting any of my Friends; and Mrs. Hobbins, who advised me to apply to you, said she believed you would be able to recommend me to some place where I can be properly accommodated till my affairs are settled.

MRS. VOLUBLE. To be sure, ma'am, I can. But pray, ma'am, may I 530 make bold to ask the reason of your parting?

CECILIA. I am not, at present, at liberty to tell it. Do you recollect any place that—

MRS. VOLUBLE. O dear yes, ma'am, I know many. Let's see,— there's one in King Street,—and there's one in Charles 535 Street,[1]—and there's another in—Lord, I dare say I know an Hundred! only I shall be very cautious of what I recommend, for it is not every place will do for such a lady as you. But pray, ma'am, where may Mr. Beaufort be? I hope he has no Hand in this affair? 540

CECILIA. Pray ask me no Questions!

MRS. VOLUBLE. I'm sure, ma'am, I don't mean to be troublesome; and as to asking Questions, I make a point not to do it, for I think that curiosity is the most impertinent thing in the World. I suppose, ma'am, he knows of your being here? 545

CECILIA. No, no,—he knows nothing about me.

---

1 *King Street … Charles Street*: several London streets with these names existed in the 1770s.

MRS. VOLUBLE. Well, that's quite surprising, upon my word! To be sure, poor Gentleman, it must give him a deal of concern, that's but natural, and besides —

550 CECILIA. Can you name no place to me, Mrs. Voluble, that you think will be eligible?

MRS. VOLUBLE. Yes sure, I can, ma'am. I know a lady in the very next street, who has very genteel apartments, that will come to about five or six Guineas a Week,[1] for, to be sure, a young

555 lady of your Fortune would not chuse to give less.

CECILIA. Alas!

MRS. VOLUBLE. Dear ma'am, don't vex so; I dare say my lady will think better of it; besides, it's for her Interest, for though, to be sure, Mr. Beaufort will have a fine Income, yet young

560 Ladies of forty thousand Pounds Fortune a'n't to be met with every Day; and the folks say, ma'am, that yours will be full that.

CECILIA. I must entreat you, Mrs. Voluble, not to speak of my affairs at present; my mind is greatly disordered, and I cannot

565 bear the Subject.

MRS. VOLUBLE. Dear ma'am, I won't say another word. To be sure, nothing's so improper as talking of private affairs,—it's a thing I never do, for really —

*Enter* MISS JENNY *and* BOB.

MISS JENNY. May we come in?

570 MRS. VOLUBLE. Lord no; why I ha'n't heard one single thing yet.

BOB. It's a great deal past the five minutes. I've been looking at the clock all the Time.

MISS JENNY. Well, then, shall we go again?

CECILIA. No, it is not necessary. Mrs. Voluble, you can be so

575 good as to answer my Question, without troubling any body to leave the Room.

MISS JENNY. Then we'll keep at this side, and we sha'n't hear what you say. (MISS JENNY *and* BOB *walk aside.*)

---

1   *five or six Guineas a Week*: a very high price; a pound was a common weekly rate for lodgings.

Mrs. Voluble. What think you, ma'am, of that place I mentioned? 580

Cecilia. I mean to be quite private, and should wish for a situation less expensive.

Mrs. Voluble. Why sure, ma'am, you would not think of giving less than five Guineas a Week? That's just nothing out of such a Fortune as yours. 585

Cecilia. Talk to me no more of my Fortune, I beseech you,—I have none!—I have lost it all!—

Mrs. Voluble. Dear ma'am, why you put me quite in a cold Sweat! lost all your Fortune?

Cecilia. I know not what I say!—I can talk no longer;—pray 590 excuse my incoherence;—and if you can allow me to remain here for half an Hour, I may, in that Time perhaps hear from my Friends, and know better how to guide myself.

Mrs. Voluble. Yes, sure, ma'am, I shall be quite proud of your Company. But I hope, ma'am, you was not in earnest about 595 losing Fortune?

Cecilia. Let nothing I have said be mentioned, I beseech you; converse with your Friends as if I was not here, and suffer me to recover my composure in silence. (*Walks away.*) (*aside*) Oh Beaufort, my only hope and refuge! hasten to my support, ere 600 my spirits wholly sink under the pressure of distressful suspence.

Mrs. Voluble. Well, this is quite what I call a *nigma*! Miss Jenny my dear, come here; I'll tell you how it is,—do you know she's come away from Lady Smatter's? 605

Miss Jenny. Dear me!

Mrs. Voluble. Yes; and what's worse, she says she's lost all her Fortune.

Miss Jenny. Lost all her Fortune? Lack a dasy! why then whose to pay for all our things? why we've got such a heap as will 610 come to a matter of I don't know how much.

Mrs. Voluble. Well, to be sure it's a sad thing; but you're to know I don't much believe it, for she said it in a sort of a pet; and my notion is she has been falling out with her Sweatheart, and if so may be her Head's a little touched. Them 615 things often happens in the Quarrels of Lovers.

*Enter* BETTY.

BETTY. Ma'am here's a Gentleman wants the young lady.
CECILIA (*starting*). 'Tis surely Beaufort!—Beg him to walk up
    Stairs.—Mrs. Voluble, will you excuse this liberty?
620 MRS. VOLUBLE. Yes, sure, ma'am.

*Exit* BETTY.

CECILIA (*aside*). Dear, constant Beaufort!—how grateful to my
    Heart is this generous alacrity!
MRS. VOLUBLE (*aside to Miss Jenny*). I dare say this is her Sweet-
    heart.
625 MISS JENNY. Dear me, how nice! we shall hear all they say!

*Enter* CENSOR.

CECILIA. Mr. Censor!—good Heaven!
CENSOR. Miss Stanley I will not say I rejoice,—for, in truth, in
    this place I grieve to see you.
MRS. VOLUBLE. Pray, sir, won't you sit down?
630 CENSOR. I thank you, madam, I had rather stand—Miss Stanley I
    must beg the Honour of speaking to you alone.
MRS. VOLUBLE. O Sir, if you like it, I'm sure we'll go.
CENSOR. Ay, pray do.
MRS. VOLUBLE (*aside to Miss Jenny*). This Gentleman is by no
635     means what I call a polite person. Sir, I hope you'll put the
    young lady in better Spirits; she has been very low indeed
    since she came; and, Sir, if you should want for any thing, I
    beg—
CENSOR. Do, good madam, be quick. I am in haste.
640 MRS. VOLUBLE. We're going directly, Sir. Come, Miss Jenny.
    Bobby, you great oaf, what do you stand gaping there for?
    why don't you go?
BOBBY. Why you would not have me go faster than I can, would
    you?

*Exit.*

MRS. VOLUBLE. I would have you hold your Tongue, Mr. prate- 645
apace! always wrangling and wrangling. Come, Miss Jenny!

*Exit.*

MISS JENNY. I don't see why we might not as well have stayed
here.

*Exit.*

CECILIA *and* CENSOR.

CECILIA. By what means, sir, have you discovered me?—have
you been at Lady Smatter's?—does any body there know 650
where I am, except her Ladyship?
CENSOR. First let me ask you what possible allurement could
draw you under this Roof? did you mean, by the volubility
of folly, to over-power the sadness of recollection? did you
imagine that nonsence has the same oblivious quality as the 655
Waters of Lethe?[1] and flatter yourself that, by swallowing large
Draughts, you should annihilate all remembrance of your
misfortunes?
CECILIA. No, no! I came hither by the dire guidance of necessity.
I wish to absent myself from my Friends till the real state of 660
my affairs is better known to me. I have sent my Servant into
the City, whence I expect speedy intelligence. Lady Smatter's
Housekeeper assured me that the character of this Woman
was unblemished, and I was interested in no other enquiry.
But tell me, I beseech you, whence you had your information 665
of the calamity that has befallen me? and who directed you
hither? and whether my Letter has been shewn or con-
cealed?—and what I am to infer from *your* being the first to
seek me?
CENSOR. Pray go on! 670
CECILIA. Sir!
CENSOR. Nay, if you ask forty more Questions without waiting

---

1 *Waters of Lethe*: in Greek myth, drinking water from the river Lethe in Hades produced
forgetfulness of the past.

for an answer, I have messages that will more than keep pace with your enquiries; therefore ask on, and spare not!

675 CECILIA (*disconcerted*). No, Sir, I have done!

CENSOR. How! have I, then, discovered the art of silencing a Lover? Hasten to me, ye wearied Guardians of pining youth, I will tell ye a Secret precious to ye as repose! fly hither, ye sad and solemn Confidents of the love-lorn tribe, for I can point
680 out relief to exhausted Patience!

CECILIA. Spare this rallery, I beseech you;—and keep me not in suspence as to the motive of your visit.

CENSOR. My first motive is the desire of seeing,—my second of serving you; if indeed, the ill-usage you have experienced
685 from one Banker, will not intimidate you from trusting in another.

CECILIA. How am I to understand you?

CENSOR. As an honest man! or, in other Words, as a man to whose Friendship distressed Innocence has a claim indis-
690 putable.

CECILIA. You amaze me!

CENSOR. It must be some Time ere your affairs can be settled, and the loss of Wealth will speedily, and roughly make you know its value. Consider me, therefore, as your Banker, and
695 draw upon me without reserve. Your present situation will teach you many Lessons you are ill prepared to learn; but Experience is an unfeeling master, whose severity is neither to be baffled by youth, nor softened by Innocence. Suppose we open our account to Day?—(*presenting a Paper*) this may
700 serve for a beginning; I will call again to-morrow for fresh orders. (*going.*)

CECILIA. Stay, stay Mr. Censor!—amazement has, indeed, silenced me, but it must not make me forget myself. Take back, I entreat you, this paper—

705 CENSOR. Probably you suspect my motives? and, if you do, I am the last man whom your doubts will offend; they are autho-rised by the baseness of mankind, and, in fact, suspicion, in Worldly transactions, is but another Word for common sense.

CECILIA. Is it, then, possible you can think so ill of all others, and
710 yet be so generous, so benevolent yourself?

CENSOR. Will any man follow an Example he abhors to look at? Will you, for instance, because you see most Women less handsome than yourself, ape deformity in order to resemble them?

CECILIA. O how little are you known, and how unjustly are you 715 judged! For my own part, I even regarded you as my Enemy, and imagined that, if you thought of me at all, it was with ill-will.

CENSOR. In truth, madam, my character will rather encrease than diminish your surprise as you become more acquainted with 720 it. You will, indeed, find me an odd fellow; a fellow who can wish you well without loving you, and, without any sinister view, be active in your Service; a fellow, in short, unmoved by Beauty, yet susceptible of pity,—invulnerable to Love, yet zealous in the cause of distress. If you accept my good offices, 725 I shall ever be your Debtor for the esteem your acceptance will manifest,—if you reject them, I shall but conclude you have the same Indignant apprehensions of the depravity of your fellow Creatures that I harbour in my own Breast.

CECILIA. If, hitherto I have escaped misanthropy, think you, Sir, 730 an action such as this will teach it me? no; I am charmed with your generous offer, and shall henceforward know better how to value you; but I must beg you to take back this paper (*returns it*). I have at present no occasion for assistance, and I hope—but tell me, for uncertainty is torture, have you, or 735 have you not been at Lady Smatter's?

CENSOR. I have; and I come hither loaded with as many messages as ever abigail[1] was charged with for the milliner of a fantastic Bride. The little Sense, however, comprised in their many Words, is briefly this; Lady Smatter offers you her protec- 740 tion,—which is commonly the first Step towards the inso-lence of avowed superiority: and Beaufort—

CECILIA. Beaufort?—Good Heaven!—did Mr. Beaufort know whither you were coming?

CENSOR. He did; and charged me with as many vows, supplica- 745

---

1   abigail: a lady's maid, so named after the resourceful wife and "handmaid" of King David (1 Samuel 25) and the name of the waiting gentlewoman in Beaumont and Fletcher's play *The Scornful Lady* (1610).

tions, promises, and tender nonsences, as if he took my memory for some empty habitation that his Fancy might furnish at its pleasure. He Commissioned me—

CECILIA. Oh Heaven! (*weeps.*)

750 CENSOR. Why how now? he commissioned me, I say—

CECILIA. Oh faithless Beaufort! lost, lost Cecilia!

CENSOR. To sue for him,—Kneel for him,—

CECILIA. Leave me, leave me, Mr. Censor!—I can hear no more.

CENSOR. Nay, prithee, madam, listen to his message.

755 CECILIA. No, Sir, never! at such a Time as this, a message is an Insult! He must know I was easily to be found, or he would not have sent it, and, knowing that, whose was it to have sought me?—Go, go, hasten to your Friend,—tell him I heard all that it became me to hear, and that I understood

760 him too well to hear more: tell him that I will save both him and myself the disgrace of a further explanation,—tell him, in short, that I renounce him for ever!

CENSOR. Faith, madam, this is all beyond my comprehension.

CECILIA. To desert me at such a Time as this! to know my abode,

765 yet fail to seek it! to suffer my wounded Heart, bleeding in all the anguish of recent calamity, to doubt his Faith, and suspect his tenderness!

CENSOR. I am so totally unacquainted with the Laws and maxims necessary to be observed by fine Ladies, that it would ill

770 become me to prescribe the limits to which their use of reason ought to be contracted; I can only—

CECILIA. Once more, Mr. Censor, I must beg you to leave me. Pardon my impatience, but I cannot converse at present. Ere long, perhaps, indignation may teach me to suppress my Sor-

775 row, and Time and Reason may restore my tranquility.

CENSOR. Time, indeed, may possibly stand your Friend, because Time will be regardless of your impetuosity, but Faith, madam, I know not what right you have to expect Succour from Reason, if you are determined not to hear it. Beaufort, I

780 say—

CECILIA. Why will you thus persecute me? nothing can extenuate the coldness, the neglect, the insensibility of his conduct. Tell him that it admits no palliation, and that henceforth— no, tell him nothing,—I will send him no message,—I will

receive none from him,—I will tear his Image from my 785
Heart,—I will forget, if possible, that there I cherished it!—

*Enter* MRS. VOLUBLE.

MRS. VOLUBLE. I hope I don't disturb you, Sir? Pray, ma'am,
don't let me be any hindrance to you; I only just come to ask
if you would not have a bit of Fire, for I think it's grown quite
cold. What say you, Sir? pray make free if you like it. I'm sure 790
I would have had one before if I had known of having such
company; but really the Weather's so changeable at this Time
of the year, that there's no knowing what to do. Why this
morning I declare it was quite hot. We Breakfasted with both
the Windows open. As to Bobby, I verily thought he'd have 795
caught his Death, for he would not so much as put his Coat
on.
CENSOR. Intolerable! the man who could stand this, would Sing
in the Stocks, and Laugh in the Pillory!—Will you, Miss
Stanley, allow me five minutes conversation to explain— 800
MRS. VOLUBLE. I beg that my being here may not be any stop to
you, for I'll go directly if I'm in the way. I've no notion of
prying into other people's affairs,—indeed, I quite make it a
rule not to do it, for I'm sure I've business enough of my
own, without minding other Peoples. Why now, Sir, how 805
many things do you think I've got to do before night? Why
I've got to—
CENSOR. O pray, good madam, don't make your complaints to
me,—I am hard of Heart, and shall be apt to hear them without the least compassion. Miss Stanley— 810
MRS. VOLUBLE. Nay, Sir, I was only going—
CENSOR. Do prithee, good Woman, give me leave to speak. Miss
Stanley, I say—
MRS. VOLUBLE. Good Woman! I assure you, Sir, I'm not used to
be spoke to in such a way as that. 815
CENSOR. If I have called you by an apellation opposite to your
character, I beg your pardon; but—
MRS. VOLUBLE. I can tell you, Sir, whatever you may think of it, I
was never called so before; besides,—
CENSOR. Miss Stanley, some other Time— 820

Mrs. Voluble. Besides, Sir, I say, I think in one's own House it's very hard if—

Censor. Intolerable! Surely this Woman was sent to satirize the use of Speech! once more—

825 Mrs. Voluble. I say, Sir, I think it's very hard if—

Censor. Miss Stanley, your most obedient!

*Exit abruptly.*

Mrs. Voluble. Well, I must needs say, I think this is the rudest fine Gentleman among all my acquaintance. Good Woman, indeed! I wonder what he could see in me to make use of
830 such a Word as that! I won't so much as go down Stairs to open the Street Door for him,—yes I will, too, for I want to ask him about—

*Exit talking.*

Cecilia *alone.*

Cecilia. Hast thou not, Fortune, exhausted, now, thy utmost severity?—reduced to Poverty,—abandoned by the World,—
835 betrayed by Beaufort,—what more can I fear?—Beaufort, on whose constancy I relied,—Beaufort, from whose simpathy I expected consolation,—Beaufort, on whose Honour, delicacy and Worth I founded Hopes of sweetest tranquility, of lasting happiness, of affection unalterable! Oh hopes for-ever
840 blighted! Oh Expectations eternally destroyed! Oh fair and lovely tranquility—thou hast flown this Bosom, never, never more to revisit it!

*Re-enter* Mrs. Voluble.

Mrs. Voluble. I could not overtake him all that ever I could do, and yet I went as fast as—Lord, ma'am, sure you a'n't a cry-
845 ing?

Cecilia. Loss of Fortune I could have borne with patience,— change of situation I could have suffered with fortitude,—but such a Stroke as this!—

Mrs. Voluble. Poor young lady!—I declare I don't know what to think of to entertain her. 850

Cecilia. Oh Beaufort! had our situations been reversed, would such have been my conduct?

Mrs. Voluble. Come, dear ma'am, what signifies all this fretting? If you'll take my advice—

*Enter* Betty.

Betty. Do pray, ma'am, Speak to master Bobby,—he's a turning 855 the House out of Windows,[1] as a body may say.

Mrs. Voluble. Well, if I don't believe that Boy will be the Death of me at last!—only think, ma'am, what a plague he is to me! I'm sure I have my misfortunes as well as other people, so you see, ma'am, you a'n't the only person in trouble.— 860 Why ma'am, I say!—did not you hear Betty? She Says that Bobby—

Cecilia. O for a little repose!—leave me to myself, I beseech you! I can neither speak or listen to you;—pray go,—pray— alas, I know not what I say!—I forget that this House is 865 yours, and that I have no right even to the shelter its Roof affords me.

Mrs. Voluble. Dear ma'am, pray take a little comfort,—

Cecilia. Have you, madam, any Room which for a few Hours you can allow me to call my own?—where, unmolested and 870 alone, I may endeavour to calm my mind, and settle some plan for my future conduct?

Mrs. Voluble. Why, ma'am, the Room over-head is just such another as this, and if it's agreeable—

Cecilia. Pray shew it me,—I'm sure it will do. 875

Mrs. Voluble. I only wish, ma'am, it was better for your sake; however, I'll make it as comfortable as ever I can, and as soon—

*Exit, talking, with* Cecilia.

---

1 *turning the House out of Windows*: proverbial for putting everything into confusion.

BETTY *alone.*

BETTY. I'll be Hanged, now, if it is not enough to provoke a
880 Stork[1] to live in such a House as this! one may clean and
clean for-ever, and things look never the better for it. As to
Master Bobby, he does more mischief than his Head's worth;
and as to my *Mississ*, if she can but keep talk, talk, talk, she
don't care a pin's point for nothing else.

*Re-enter* MRS. VOLUBLE.

885 MRS. VOLUBLE. Why Betty, what do you stand there for?—Do
you think I keep you to look at?
BETTY. You won't keep me for nothing long.

*Exit* BETTY.

MRS. VOLUBLE *alone.*

MRS. VOLUBLE. There, now, that's the way with all of them! if
one does but say the least thing in the World, they're ready to
890 give one Warning. I declare Servants are the plague of one's
Lives. I've got a good mind to—Lord, I've got so many
things to do, I don't know what to set about first! Let me see
(*seats herself*), now I'll count them over. In the first place, I
must see after a Porter to carry the lady's message;—then I
895 must get the best Plates ready against Mrs. Wheedle
comes;—after that, I must put Mr. Dabler's papers in order,
for fear of a Surprise;—then I must get in a little bit of something nice for Supper;—then—Oh Lord, if I had not forgot
that 'scape Grace Bobby!

*runs off.*

---

1   *provoke a Stork*: presumably Betty's error for "Stoic"; see p. 126, note 1.

# ACT IV

*A Library at* Lady Smatter's. Lady Smatter, Mrs. Sapient, Dabler *and* Codger, *Seated at a round Table covered with Books.*

Lady Smatter. Now before we begin our Literary Subjects, allow me to remind you of the rule established at our last meeting, That every one is to speak his real sentiments, and no flattery is to taint our discussions.

All. Agreed. 5

Lady Smatter. This is the smallest assembly we have had yet; some or other of our members fail us every Time.

Dabler. But where such luminaries are seen as Lady Smatter and Mrs. Sapient, all other could only appear to be Eclipsed.

Lady Smatter. What have you brought to regale us with to 10 night, Mr. Dabler?

Dabler. Me? dear ma'am, nothing!

Lady Smatter. Oh barbarous!

Mrs. Sapient. Surely you cannot have been so cruel? for, in *my* opinion, to give pain causelessly is rather disobliging. 15

Dabler. Dear Ladies, you know you may command me; but, I protest, I don't think I have any thing worth your hearing.

Lady Smatter. Let us judge for ourselves. Bless me, Mr. Codger, how insensible you are! why do you not join in our entreaties? 20

Codger. For what, madam?

Lady Smatter. For a Poem, to be sure.

Codger. Madam, I understood Mr. Dabler he had nothing worth your hearing.

Lady Smatter. But surely you did not believe him? 25

Codger. I knew no reason, madam, to doubt him.

Lady Smatter. O you Goth![1] come, dear Mr. Dabler, produce something at once, if only to shame him.

Dabler. Your Ladyship has but to Speak. (*Takes a Paper from his Pocket Book, and reads*)

On a certain Party of Beaux Esprits. 30

---

1  *Goth*: barbarian.

Learning, here, doth pitch her Tent,
Science,[1] here, her Seeds doth Scatter;
Learning, in form of Sapient,
Science, in guise of heav'nly Smatter.

35 LADY SMATTER. O charming! beautiful Lines indeed.

MRS. SAPIENT. Elegant and poignant to a degree!

LADY SMATTER. What do *you* think, Mr. Codger, of this Poem? to be sure (*whispering him*), the compliment to Mrs. Sapient is preposterously overstrained, but, otherwise, nothing can be
40 more perfect.

MRS. SAPIENT. Mr. Dabler has, indeed, the happiest turn in the World at easy elegance. Why, Mr. Codger, you don't speak a Word? Pray, between friends (*whispering him*), what say you to the notion of making Lady Smatter represent Science? don't
45 you think he has been rather unskilful in his Choice?

CODGER. Why, madam, you give me no Time to think at all.

LADY SMATTER. Well, now to other matters. I have a little observation to offer upon a Line of Pope; he says

Most Women have no Character at all;[2]

50 Now I should be glad to know, if this was true in the Time of Pope why People should complain so much of the depravity of the present age?

DABLER. Your Ladyship has asked a Question that might perplex a Solomon.[3]

55 MRS. SAPIENT. It is, indeed, surprisingly ingenious.

DABLER. Yes, and it reminds me of a little foolish thing which I composed some Time ago.

LADY SMATTER. O pray let us hear it.

DABLER. Your Ladyship's commands —

60 The lovely Iris, young and fair,
Possess'd each charm of Face and air

---

1 *Science*: investigative knowledge, as opposed to the knowledge of classical languages implied by "learning." Both terms, of course, are inappropriate to Sapient and Smatter.

2 *Most Women have no Character at all*: misquoting line two of Pope's *Moral Essays* (1731-5), Epistle II, "To a Lady: Of the Characters of Women." Lady Smatter misinterprets the line, as Codger tries in vain to tell her, by reading "Character" (reputation) for Pope's "Characters."

3 *perplex a Solomon*: the biblical king Solomon was proverbial for his wisdom.

That with the Cyprian[1] might compare;
So sweet her Face, so soft her mind,
So mild she speaks,—she looks so kind,—
To hear—might melt!—to see,—might blind!     65
LADY SMATTER. O elegant! enchanting! delicious!
    (*together*)
MRS. SAPIENT. O delightful! pathetic! delicate!
LADY SMATTER. Why Mr. Codger, have you no Soul? is it possible you can be unmoved by such poetry as this?
CODGER. I was considering, madam, what might be the allusion   70
to which Mr. Dabler referred, when he said he was reminded of this little foolish thing, as he was pleased to call it himself.
DABLER (*aside*). I should like to toss that old fellow in a Blanket!
CODGER. Now, Sir, be so good as to gratify me by relating what may be the connection between your Song, and the fore-   75
going Conversation?
DABLER (*Pettishly*). Sir, I only meant to read it to the Ladies.
LADY SMATTER. I'm sure you did us great honour. Mrs. Sapient, the next proposition is yours.
MRS. SAPIENT. Pray did your Ladyship ever read Dryden?   80
LADY SMATTER. Dryden? O yes!—but I don't just now recollect him;—let's see, what has he writ?
DABLER. Cymon and Iphigenia.[2]
LADY SMATTER. O ay, so he did; and really for the Time of Day I think it's mighty pretty.   85
DABLER. Why yes, it's well enough; but it would not do now.
MRS. SAPIENT. Pray what does your Ladyship think of the Spectator?
LADY SMATTER. O, I like it vastly. I've just read it.
CODGER (*to* LADY SMATTER). In regard, madam, to those Verses   90
of Mr. Dabler, the chief fault I have to find with them, is—
DABLER. Why, Sir, we are upon another Subject now! (*aside*)

---

1  *the Cyprian*: the goddess Aphrodite or Venus, called Cyprian because, having been born in the sea, she went to the Island of Cyprus.

2  *Cymon and Iphigenia*: in his *Fables Ancient and Modern* (1700), Dryden translated this into verse from the prose of Boccaccio's *Decameron*. Since the *Fables* were more highly regarded in the eighteenth century than today, it is not surprising that this particular piece by Dryden should come to Dabler's mind.

What an old Curmudgeon! he has been pondering all this
Time only to find fault!

95　MRS. SAPIENT. For *my* part, I have always thought that the best
papers in the Spectator are those of Addison.[1]

LADY SMATTER. Very justly observed!

DABLER. Charmingly said! exactly my own opinion.

MRS. SAPIENT. Nay, I may be mistaken; I only offer it as my pri-
100　vate Sentiment.

DABLER. I can but wish, Madam, that poor Addison had Lived to
hear such praise.

LADY SMATTER. Next to Mr. Dabler, my favourite Poets are Pope
and Swift.

105　MRS. SAPIENT. Well, after all, I must confess I think there are as
many pretty things in old Shakespeare as in any body.

LADY SMATTER. Yes, but he is too common; *every* body can speak
well of Shakespeare!

DABLER. I vow I am quite sick of his Name.

110　CODGER. Madam, to the best of my apprehension, I conceive
your Ladyship hath totally mistaken that Line of Pope which
says
　　　Most Women have no Character at all.

LADY SMATTER. Mistaken? how so, sir? This is curious enough!
115　(*aside to* DABLER) I begin to think the poor Creature is
Superannuated.

DABLER. So do I, ma'am; I have observed it for some Time.

CODGER. By *no* Character, madam, he only means —

LADY SMATTER. A *bad* Character, to be sure!

120　CODGER. There, madam, lieth your Ladyship's mistake; he means,
I say —

LADY SMATTER. O dear Sir, don't trouble yourself to tell *me* his
meaning;—I dare say I shall be able to make it out.

MRS. SAPIENT (*aside to* DABLER). How irritable is her Temper!

125　DABLER. O, intolerably!

---

1　*those of Addison*: Joseph Addison and Richard Steele together edited *The Spectator* for
555 issues between March 1711 and December 1712, each writing 251 numbers. Addison's contributions were the more highly regarded, and his reputation eclipsed that of
Steele throughout the century; Mrs. Sapient's observation is a truism.

CODGER. Your Ladyship, madam, will not hear me. I was going—

LADY SMATTER. If you please, Sir, we'll drop the subject, for I rather fancy you will give me no very new information concerning it,—do you think he will, Mr. Dabler? 130

CODGER. Mr. Dabler, Madam, is not a competent Judge of the case, as—

DABLER (*rising*). Not a Judge, Sir? not a Judge of Poetry?

CODGER. Not in the present circumstance, Sir, because, as I was going to Say— 135

DABLER. Nay then, Sir, I'm sure I'm a Judge of nothing!

CODGER. That may be, Sir, but is not to the present purpose; I was going—

DABLER. Suppose, Sir, we refer to the Ladies? Pray, now, Ladies, which do *you* think the most adequate Judge of Poetry, Mr. 140 Codger, or your humble Servant? Speak sincerely, for I hate flattery.

MRS. SAPIENT. I would by no means be so ill bred as to determine for Mr. Dabler in the presence of Mr. Codger, because *I* have always thought that a preference of one person implies 145 less approbation of another; yet—

CODGER. Pray, madam, let me speak; the reason, I say—

MRS. SAPIENT. Yet the well-known skill of Mr. Dabler in this delightful art—

CODGER. Madam, this interruption is somewhat injudicious, 150 since it prevents my explaining—

MRS. SAPIENT (*rising*). Injudicious, Sir? I am sorry, indeed, if I have merited such an accusation: there is nothing I have more scrupulously endeavoured to avoid, for, in *my* opinion, to be injudicious is no mark of an extraordinary understanding. 155

LADY SMATTER (*aside to* DABLER). How soon she's hurt!

DABLER. O most unreasonably!

CODGER. Madam you will never hear me out; you prevent my explaining the reason, I say, why Mr. Dabler cannot decide upon Lady Smatter's error in judgement— 160

LADY SMATTER (*rising*). Error in judgement? really this is very diverting!

CODGER. I say, madam—

LADY SMATTER. Nay, Sir, 'tis no great matter; and yet, I must con-
165    fess, it's rather a hard case that, after so many years of intense
Study, and most laborious reading, I am not allowed to criti-
cise a silly line of Pope.

DABLER. And if I, who, from infancy have devoted all my Time
to the practice of Poetry, am now thought to know nothing
170    of the matter,—I should be glad to be informed who has a
better Title?

MRS. SAPIENT. And if I, who, during my whole life, have made
propriety my peculiar Study, am now found to be deficient in
it,—I must really take the liberty to observe that I must have
175    thrown away a great deal of Time to very little purpose.

LADY SMATTER. And as to this line of Pope—

*Enter a* SERVANT.

SERVANT. Mr. Censor, my lady, begs to speak to your Ladyship
for only two minutes upon Business of consequence.

DABLER. Censor? Suppose we admit him?—(*aside*) 'twill be an
180    admirable opportunity to shew him my Epigram.

LADY SMATTER. Admit him? what, to ask his opinion of Mr.
Codger's critical annotations?

CODGER. My doubt, madam, is, if you will give him Time to
speak it.

185 LADY SMATTER. Well, is it agreeable to ye all that Mr. Censor
should have admittance? I know it is contrary to rule, yet, as
he is one of the Wits, and therefore ought to be among us,
suppose we indulge him?

CODGER. Madam I vote against it.

190 DABLER (*aside to* LADY SMATTER). I see he's afraid of him,—let's
have him by all means.

LADY SMATTER. Without doubt. Pray, Mr. Codger, why are you
against it?

CODGER. Because, madam, there are already so many talkers that I
195    cannot be heard myself.

DABLER (*aside to* LADY SMATTER). You see how it is?

LADY SMATTER. Yes, and enjoy it of all things. Desire Mr. Censor to Walk up stairs.

*Exit Servant.*

To be sure this is rather a deviation from the maxims of the society, but great minds, as a favourite author of mine 200 observes, are above being governed by common prejudices.[1]

CODGER. I am thinking, madam,—

*Enter* CENSOR.

LADY SMATTER. Mr. Censor, your Entrance is most critically fortunate; give me leave to present you to our society.

CENSOR. I expected to have seen your Ladyship alone. 205

LADY SMATTER. Yes, but I have obtained a dispensation for your admittance to our Esprit Party. But let us not waste our Time in common conversation. You must know we are at present discussing a very knotty point, and I should be glad of your opinion upon the merits of the cause. 210

DABLER. Yes; and as soon as that is decided, I have a little choice piece of Literature to communicate to you which I think you will allow to be tolerable.

MRS. SAPIENT. And I, too, Sir, must take the liberty to appeal to your Judgement concerning— 215

CENSOR. Ay, ay, Speak all at a Time, and then one hearing may do.

LADY SMATTER. Mr. Censor, when a point of the last importance is in agitation, such levity as this—

CENSOR. Why, madam, the Business which brings me hither— 220

DABLER. Business? O name not the Word in this Region of Fancy and Felicity.

MRS. SAPIENT. That's finely said, Mr. Dabler, and corroborates with an opinion of mine which I have long formed,—that Business and Fancy should be regarded as two things. 225

---

1  *great minds ... prejudices*: alluding to Swift's *Cadenus and Vanessa* (1726): "That common Forms were not design'd / Directors to a noble Mind" (ll. 612-13).

CENSOR. Why, madam, and with one of mine which I hold to be equally singular.

MRS. SAPIENT. What is it, sir?

CENSOR. That London and Paris should be regarded as two
230 Places.

MRS. SAPIENT. Pshaw!

CODGER (to LADY SMATTER). I say, madam, I am thinking—

CENSOR. Then, Sir, you are most worthily employed; and this good Company desire nothing less than to impede the pro-
235 gress of your thoughts, by troubling you to relate them.

DABLER. Very true; suppose, therefore, we change the subject. O, apropos, have you seen the new verses that run about?

CENSOR. No. Give me leave, madam (turning to LADY SMATTER), to acquaint you with the motive of my present visit. —
240 LADY SMATTER. You would not be such a Goth as to interrupt our literary Discussions?—besides, I must positively have your sentiments upon an argument I have just had with Mr. Codger upon this Line of Pope
Most Women—
245 CENSOR. Hold, madam; I am no Quixote, and therefore en-counter not danger where there is no prospect of reward;[1] nor shall I, till I emulate the fate of Orpheus,[2] ever argue about Women—in their presence.

DABLER. Ha, Ha! mighty well said. But I was going to tell you,
250 Mr. Censor, that if you have any desire to look at those Verses I was speaking of, I believe I have a Copy of them in my Pocket. Let's see,— yes, here they are; how lucky that I should happen to have them about me! (gives them to CENSOR.) (aside) I think they will surprise him.
255 CENSOR (reading). That passion which we strongest feel
We all agree to disapprove;
Yet feebly, feebly we conceal—

DABLER (pettishly). Sir you read without any spirit,—

---

1  Quixote ... prospect of reward: Burney alludes frequently to Don Quixote, hero of Cervantes' novel (1605, 1615), in her novels. Censor, unlike Quixote, is no knight errant.

2  the fate of Orpheus: the legendary poet Orpheus was torn to pieces by women: in one version, by Thracians jealous of his love for Eurydice; in another, by maenads for his failure to honour their god Dionysus.

Yet feebly,—feebly we conceal
You should drop your Voice at the Second feebly, or you lose    260
all the effect. (*aside*) It puts me in a Fever to hear such fine
lines murdered.

CENSOR (*reading*).We all are bound slaves to self love.

DABLER (*snatching the Paper*). Why you give it neither emphasis
nor expression! you read as if you were asleep. (*reading*)    265
That passion which—

CENSOR. O no more, no more of it. Pray who is the Author?

DABLER. Why really I—I don't absolutely know,—but, by what I
have heard, I should take it to be somebody very—very
clever.    270

CENSOR. You should?

DABLER. Yes: and, indeed, to own the truth, I have heard it whis-
pered that it is a posthumous Work of—of—O, of Gay,[1]—
ay, of Gay.

CENSOR. Of Gay?    275

DABLER. Yes; found in a little corner of his private Bureau.

CENSOR. And pray who has the impudence to make such an
assertion?

DABLER. Who?—O, as to that, really I don't know who in particular,—but I assure you not *me*,—though, by the way, do    280
you really think it very bad?

CENSOR. Despicable beyond abuse. Are you not of the same
opinion?

DABLER. Me?—why, really, as to that—I—I can't exactly say,—
that is, I have hardly read it.—What a Crabbed fellow! there    285
is not an ounce of Taste in his whole composition. Curse me,
if I was Nature, if I should not blush to have made him. Hold,
my Tablets! a good thought that! I'll turn it into a Lampoon,
and drop it at Stapleton's.[2] (*walks aside and writes in his Tablets.*)

---

1  *a posthumous Work of … Gay*: the reputation of John Gay (1685-1732) reached a peak in
   the 1770s. William Henry Irving notes that "there were at least ten editions of the
   *Poems* or the *Plays* during that decade" (*John Gay: Favorite of the Wits* [Durham, North
   Carolina: Duke University Press, 1940], 311).

2  *Stapleton's*: in a letter of 29 June 1777, Horace Walpole refers to "the club at Stapleton's," where a mysterious anonymous letter directed to "L.S.D." had been sent. The
   club has not otherwise been identified (*Yale Edition of Horace Walpole's Correspondence*,
   ed. W.S. Lewis *et al.* [New Haven: Yale University Press, 1937-83], XXXII, 361).

290   CENSOR (*to* LADY SMATTER). I have seen Miss Stanley, madam,
      and—

LADY SMATTER. Did you find her at Mrs. Voluble's?

CENSOR. Yes. (*they whisper.*)

MRS. SAPIENT (*listening*). (*aside*) So, so, she's at Mrs. Voluble's!—
295       there must certainly be some design upon Dabler.

CENSOR. But hear me, madam. I have something to communi-
      cate to you which—

LADY SMATTER. Not now, I can attend to nothing now. These
      Evenings, Sir, which I devote to the fine arts, must not be
300       contaminated with common affairs.

MRS. SAPIENT (*aside*). I sha'n't rest till I have dived into this mat-
      ter. I am much chagrined, madam, at the disagreeable necessi-
      ty I am under of breaking abruptly from this learned and
      ingenious assembly, but I am called hence by an appointment
305       which I cannot give up without extreme rudeness; and I must
      confess I should be rather sorry to be guilty of that, as I have
      long been of opinion that a breach of good manners—is no
      great sign of Politeness.

LADY SMATTER. I am quite sorry to lose you so soon.

*Exit* MRS. SAPIENT.

310       What a tiresome Creature! how glad I am she's gone!

CODGER. Notwithstanding the rebuff I have just met with,
      madam, I must say I cannot help thinking that—

CENSOR. Do you mean, Sir, to satirize the whole Company, that
      you thus repeatedly profess thinking among those who have
315       no other aim than talking?

CODGER. Sir when a man has been pondering upon a Subject for
      a considerable Time, and assorting his ideas in order to
      explain himself, it is an exceedingly uncivil thing to interrupt
      him.

320 LADY SMATTER. Mr. Dabler, what are you writing?

DABLER. Only a little memorandum, ma'am, about business;
      nothing more.

CODGER (*aside*). I find I can never get in two Words at a Time.

*Enter* JACK.

JACK. Ma'am your Ladyship's most obedient.

LADY SMATTER. Why did not you come sooner, Jack?—we are 325
just broke up.

JACK. I could not help it, upon my word. I came away now just as
my Tea was poured out at the Coffee House, because I would
not stay to Drink it.

CODGER (*aside*). I'm glad Jack's come; I think, at least, I shall make 330
him listen to me.

JACK. I have been in such a hurry the whole Day, that I have
never known what I have been about. I believe I have been
to sixteen places since Dinner.[1] You good folks who sit here
talking by the Hour together, must lead strange dull Lives; I 335
wonder you don't lose the use of your Limbs.

CODGER. Son Jack, when you have finished your Speech, please
to hear one of mine.

JACK. I hope it won't be a long one, Sir.

CODGER. Why do you hope that, Son, before you know how 340
well it may entertain you?

JACK. Lord, Sir, I never think of being entertained with speeches.

CODGER. What, Jack, not with your own Father's?

JACK. Lord no, Sir.

CODGER. No, Sir? and pray, Sir, Why? 345

JACK. Because I'm always tired before they're half done.

CODGER. Son Jack, 'tis these loose Companions that you keep
that teach you all this profligacy. Tired of hearing me speak!
one would think the poor Lad was an Ideot.

JACK. So this is your Club Room, where you all meet to talk? 350

CENSOR. Yes; and the principal maxim of the learned members is
That no one shall listen to what is said by his neighbour.

LADY SMATTER. Fie, Mr. Censor, I'm sure we're all attention—

CENSOR. Yes, to sieze the next opportunity of speaking.

LADY SMATTER. Never mind what Mr. Censor says, Jack, for you 355
know he is a professed Stoic.

---

1   *since Dinner*: i.e, since mid-afternoon, when dinner, the main meal of the day, was nor-
    mally served. Among the fashionable, dinner could be served as late as 6 p.m.

CENSOR. Stoic? pray what does your Ladyship mean?

LADY SMATTER. Well, well, Cynic,[1] then, if you like it better.

CENSOR. You hold, then, that their signification is the same?

360 LADY SMATTER. Mercy, Mr. Censor, do you expect me to define the exact meaning of every word I make use of?

CENSOR. No, madam, not unless I could limit your Ladyship's Language to the Contents of a Primer.[2]

LADY SMATTER. O horrid! did you ever hear any thing so sple-
365 netic? Mr. Dabler, what are you Writing? Suppose, in compli-ment to our new member, you were to indulge us with a few Lines?

DABLER. Does your Ladyship mean an Extempore?

LADY SMATTER. The thing in the World I should like best.

370 DABLER. Really, ma'am, I wish for nothing upon Earth so much as the honour of your Ladyship's Commands,—but as to an Extempore—the amazing difficulty,—the genius requisite,—the masterly freedom,—the—the—the things of that sort it requires make me half afraid of so bold an Undertaking.

375 CENSOR. Sir, your Exordium[3] is of sufficient length.

DABLER. I shall but collect my thoughts, and be ready in a moment. In the mean Time, I beg I may not interrupt the Conversation; it will be no manner of disturbance to me to hear you all talking; we Poets, ma'am, can easily detach our-
380 selves from the Company. (*Walks apart.*)

CENSOR. I should be glad if your Ladyship would inform me what Time, according to the established regulations of your Society, you allow for the *Study* of extemporary Verses?

LADY SMATTER. I think we have no fixed rule; some are quick,
385 and some are slow,—'tis just as it happens.

CENSOR (*aside*). What unconscious absurdity!

*While they are speaking,* DABLER *privately looks at a paper, which he accidentally drops instead of putting in his pocket.*

---

1 *Stoic ... Cynic*: the ancient Greek Stoics sought to achieve willing acquiescence in their fates; Cynics, in contrast, emphasized the importance of self-sufficiency. Lady Smatter, of course, seems unfamiliar with both schools.

2 *Contents of a Primer*: an elementary school-book by which children were taught to read.

3 *Exordium*: the introductory part of a discourse.

DABLER (*advancing*). I hope I have not detained you long?

LADY SMATTER. Is it possible you can be ready so soon?

DABLER. O dear yes, ma'am; these little things are done in a
moment; they cost *us* nothing.                                        390

    In one sole point agree we all,

    Both Rich and Poor, and Saint and Sinner,

    Proud or Humble, Short or Tall,—

    And that's—a taste for a good Dinner.[1]

LADY SMATTER. O charming! I never heard any thing so satirical   395
in my Life.

CENSOR. And so, Sir, you composed these lines just now?

DABLER. This very moment.

CENSOR. It seems, then, you can favour your Friends whenever
they call upon you?                                                    400

DABLER. O yes, Sir, with the utmost pleasure.

CENSOR. I should be obliged to you, then, Sir, for something
more.

DABLER. Sir you do me honour. I will but take an Instant for
consideration, and endeavour to obey you. So, so!—I            405
thought I should bring him round at last! (*walking away.*)

CENSOR. Stay, Sir. As you make these Verses with so much facility, you can have no objection, I presume, to my chusing you a
Subject?

DABLER. Sir!                                                           410

CENSOR. And then with firmer courage your Friends may
counter-act the scepticism of the Envious, and boldly affirm
that they are your own, and unstudied.

DABLER. Really, Sir, as to that, I can't say I very much mind what
those sort of people say; we authors, Sir, are so much inured    415
to illiberal attacks, that we regard them as nothing,—mere
marks, Sir, of celebrity, and hear them without the least emotion.

CENSOR. You are averse, then, to my proposal?

DABLER. O dear no, Sir!—not at all,—not in the least, I assure   420

---

1  *a good Dinner*: this epigram, although made up of clichés, is Dabler's own invention. In
her *Fanny Burney* (London: Macmillan, 1987), Judy Simons describes it as "an obscure
couplet of Pope's" (127). It is, however, neither a couplet nor by Pope.

you, Sir! (*aside*) I wish he was in the Deserts of Lybia[1] with all my Heart!

CENSOR. The readiness of your compliance, Sir, proves the promptness of your Wit. I shall name a subject which, I believe, you will find no difficulty to dilate upon,—self-sufficiency.[2]

DABLER. Sir?

CENSOR. Self-sufficiency,—don't you understand me?

DABLER. Really, Sir, in regard to that, I don't exactly know whether I do or not, but I assure you if you imagine that *I* am self-sufficient, you are most prodigiously mistaken; I defy any body to charge me with that, for though I have written so many things that have pleased every body else, I have always made it a rule to keep my own opinion to myself. Even Mr. Codger must, in this point, do me justice. Will you not, sir?

CODGER. Sir, I shall say nothing. (*folds his arms, and leans upon the Table.*)

CENSOR. Well, Sir, I will give you another Subject, then, for of this, I must own, you might long since have been weary. I will not affront you by naming so hackneyed a theme as Love, but give us, if you please, a spirited Couplet upon War.

DABLER. Upon War?—hum—let's see,—upon War,—ay,—but hold! don't you think, Sir, that War is rather a disagreeable Subject where there are Ladies? For *myself* I can certainly have no objection, but, I must confess, I am rather in doubt whether it will be quite polite to Lady Smatter.

JACK. Why Lord, Mr. Dabler, a man might ride Ten Times round Hyde Park, before you are ready to begin.

DABLER. Sir you don't know what you talk of; things of this importance are not to be settled rashly.

CENSOR. Mr. Dabler I will give you an opportunity of taking your revenge; let your Verses be upon the use and abuse of Time, and address them, if you please, to that Gentleman.

JACK. Ay, with all my Heart. He may address what he will to me, so as he will not keep me long to hear him.

DABLER. Time, did you say?—the use and the abuse of Time?—

---

1  *the Deserts of Lybia*: the Sahara desert.
2  *self-sufficiency*: excessive conceit, rather than independence.

ay, very good, a very good subject,—Time?—yes, a very
good idea, indeed!—the use and the abuse of Time,—
(*Pauses*) But pray, Sir, pray, Mr. Censor, let me Speak a word
to you; are you not of opinion—now don't imagine this is
any objection of *mine*, no, I like the Subject of all things,—it   460
is just what I wished,—but don't you think that poor Mr.
Codger, here, may think it is meant as a sneer at him?
CENSOR. How so, Sir?
DABLER. Why, Sir, on account of his being so slow. And really,
notwithstanding his old fashioned ways, one would not wish   465
to affront him, poor man, for he means no harm. Besides, Sir,
his age!—consider that; we ought all to make allowances for
the infirmities of age. I'm sure *I* do,—poor old Soul!
CENSOR. Well, Sir, I shall name but one subject more, and to that
if you object, you must give me leave to draw my own infer-   470
ence from your backwardness, and to report it accordingly.
DABLER. Sir I shall be very—I shall be extremely—that is, Sir, I
shall be quite at your Service. (*aside*) What a malignant fellow!
CENSOR. What say you, Sir, to an Epigram on slander?   475
DABLER. On slander?
CENSOR. Yes, Sir; what objection can you devise to that?
DABLER. An illiberal Subject, Sir! a most illiberal subject,—I will
have nothing to do with it.
CENSOR. The best way to manifest your contempt will be to sati-   480
rize it.
DABLER. Why, as you say,—there's something in that;—satirize
it?—ay, Satirize slander,—ha! ha! a good hit enough!
CENSOR. Then, Sir, you will favour us without further delay.
DABLER. Sir I should be extremely happy to obey you,—nothing   485
could give me greater pleasure, only that just now I am so
particularly pressed for Time, that I am obliged to run away.
Lady Smatter, I have the honour to wish your Ladyship good
night. (*going.*)
JACK (*stopping him*). Fair play, fair play! you sha'n't go till you have   490
made the Verses; or, if you do, I swear I'll run after you.
DABLER. Upon my word, Sir—
CODGER. Prithee, Jack, don't detain him. This anecdote, you

know (*affecting to whisper*), will *Tell* as well without the Verses
495 as with them.

DABLER (*aside*). That fellow is a mere compound of spite and envy.

LADY SMATTER. Come, Mr. Dabler, I see you relent.

DABLER. Why,—hem!—if—if your Ladyship insists—pray, Mr.
500 Censor, what is this same subject you have been talking of?

CENSOR. O, Sir, 'tis no matter; if you are so much hurried, why should you stay? we are all pretty well convinced of the alacrity of your wit already.

DABLER. Slander, I think it was?—but suppose, sir, for slander we
505 substitute Fashion?—I have a notion I could do something upon Fashion.

CENSOR. Probably, Sir, you *have* done something upon Fashion; entertain us, therefore, upon the given subject, or else be a better nomenclator to your verses than to call them extempo-
510 rary.

DABLER. Well, Sir, well!—(*aside and walking away*) a surly fellow!

JACK. Pray has your Ladyship heard the queer Story about the Miss Sippets?

LADY SMATTER. No; what is it?

515 JACK. Why I heard it just now at Mrs. Gabble's. Sir Harry Frisk, you know, last Winter paid his addresses to the Eldest Sister, but this Winter, to make what variety he could without quitting the Family, he deserted to the Youngest; and this morning they were to have been married.

520 LADY SMATTER. Well, and were they not?

JACK. Upon my Word I don't know.

LADY SMATTER. Don't know? what do you mean?

JACK. Why I had not Time to enquire.

LADY SMATTER. Pho, prithee, Jack, don't be so ridiculous.

525 DABLER (*holding his Hand before his Eyes, and walking about*). Not one thought,—not one thought to save me from ruin!

CENSOR. Why, Mr. Codger, what are you about? is it not rather melancholy to sit by yourself at the Table, and not join at all in the conversation.

530 CODGER (*raising his head*). Perhaps, Sir, I may conceive myself to be somewhat Slighted.

LADY SMATTER. Nay, nay, prithee, my good friend, don't be so captious.

CODGER. Madam I presume, at least, I have as good a right to be affronted as another man; for which reason— 535

DABLER (*pettishly*). Upon my Word, if you all keep talking so incessantly, it is not possible for a man to know what he is about.

CODGER. I have not spoken before for this half Hour, and yet I am as good as bid to hold my Tongue! (*leans again on the* 540 *Table.*)

JACK. O but, ma'am, I forgot to tell your Ladyship the very best part of the Story; the poor Eldest Sister was quite driven to despair, so last night, to avoid, at least, Dancing bare-foot at her Sister's Wedding,[1] she made an appointment with a young Haberdasher in the neighbourhood to set off for Scot- 545 land.[2]

LADY SMATTER. Well?

JACK. Well, and when she got into the post chaise,[3] instead of her new Lover the young Haberdasher, who do you think was waiting to receive her? 550

LADY SMATTER. Nay, nay, tell me at once.

JACK. But who do you guess?

LADY SMATTER. Pho, pho, don't be so tiresome. Who was it?

JACK. Why that I am not certain myself.

LADY SMATTER. Not certain yourself? 555

JACK. No, for I had not Time to stay till Mrs. Gabble came to the Name.

LADY SMATTER. How absurd!

CODGER (*again raising his Head*). Madam if I might be allowed,— or, rather, to speak more properly, if I could get Time to give 560 my opinion of this matter, I should say—

---

1 *Dancing bare-foot at her Sister's Wedding*: proverbially said of a woman whose younger sister is married before her.

2 *set off for Scotland*: since 1753, Lord Hardwicke's Marriage Act had required the consent of parents or guardians for the marriage of persons under 21. Runaway couples would thus head for Scotland, where marriages could be readily obtained. In *Camilla* (pp. 800-801), Eugenia Tyrold elopes with "Alphonso Bellamy" and is married at Gretna Green, close to the Scottish border.

3 *post chaise*: a small hired carriage.

LADY SMATTER. My good friend, we should all be extremely happy to hear you, if you were not so long in coming to the point;—that's all the fault we find with you; is it not, Jack?

565 JACK. To be sure, ma'am. Why sometimes, do you know, I have made a Journey to Bath and back again,[1] while he has been considering whether his next Wig should be a Bob, or a full-bottom.[2]

CODGER. Son Jack, this is very unseemly discourse, and I desire—

570 LADY SMATTER. Nay, pray don't scold him. Jack, when shall you hear any more of Miss Sippet's adventure?

JACK. Why, ma'am, either to-morrow or Friday, I don't know which.

CODGER (aside, and reclining as before). I verily believe they'd rather

575 hear Jack than me!

JACK. Why Lord, Mr. Dabler, I believe you are Dreaming. Will you never be ready?

DABLER. Sir this is really unconscionable! I was just upon the point of finishing,—and now you have put it all out of my

580 Head!

CENSOR. Well, Mr. Dabler, we release you, now, from all further trouble, since you have sufficiently satisfied us that your extemporary verses are upon a new construction.

DABLER. O, Sir, as to that, making verses is no sort of *trouble* to

585 me, I assure you,—however, if you don't chuse to hear these which I have been composing—

LADY SMATTER. O but *I* do, so pray—

JACK. Pho, pho, he has not got them ready.

DABLER. You are mistaken, Sir, these are quite ready,—entirely

590 finished,—and lodged here (*pointing to his Head*);—but as Mr. Censor—

CENSOR. Nay, if they are ready, you may as well repeat them.

DABLER. No, Sir, no, since you declined hearing them at first, I am above compelling you to hear them at all. Lady Smatter,

---

1   *a Journey to Bath and back again*: a round-trip of over two hundred miles, and so normally a journey of several days.

2   *Wig … full-bottom*: the Bob was a short wig without a queue, associated with the merchant classes. Bobwigs are worn by Briggs in *Cecilia* (94) and by a coachman in *Camilla* (264). The longer full-bottom wig was becoming *passé* by the 1770s.

the next Time I have the honour of seeing your Ladyship, I <sub>595</sub> shall be proud to have your opinion of them.

*Exit hastily.*

CENSOR. Poor Wretch! 'Glad of a Quarrel strait he shuts the Door,'[1]—what's this? *(picks up the Paper dropt by Dabler)*,—so! so! so!—

*Enter* BEAUFORT.

BEAUFORT *(to* LADY SMATTER*)*. Pardon me, madam, if I interrupt <sub>600</sub> you, I am come but for a moment. Censor *(apart to* CEN-SOR*)*,—have you no heart? are you totally divested of humanity?

CENSOR. Why what's the matter?

BEAUFORT. The matter? You have kept me on the Rack,—you <sub>605</sub> have wantonly tortured me with the most intolerable suspence that the mind of Man is capable of enduring. Where is Cecilia?—have you given her my message?—have you brought me any answer?—why am I kept in ignorance of every thing I wish or desire to know? <sub>610</sub>

CENSOR. Is your Harangue finished?

BEAUFORT. No, Sir, it is hardly begun! This unfeeling propensity to raillery upon occasions of serious distress, is cruel, is unjustifiable, is insupportable. No Man could practice it, whose Heart was not hardened against pity, Friendship, Sor- <sub>615</sub> row,—and every kind, every endearing tie by which the Bonds of Society are united.

CENSOR. At least, my good friend, object not to rallery in me, till you learn to check railing in yourself. I would fain know by what Law or what Title you Gentlemen of the Sighing Tribe <sub>620</sub> assume the exclusive privelege of appropriating all severities of Speech to yourselves.

LADY SMATTER. Beaufort, your behaviour involves me in the ut-

---

1  *Glad of a Quarrel strait he shuts the Door.* from Pope's "An Epistle to Dr. Arbuthnot" (1735): "Glad of a quarrel, strait I clapt the door" (l. 67).

most confusion. After an Education such as I have bestowed upon you, this weak anxiety about mere private affairs is unpardonable;—especially in the presence of people of learning.

BEAUFORT. I waited, madam, till Mrs. Sapient and Mr. Dabler were gone,—had I waited longer, patience must have degenerated into insensibility. From your Ladyship and from Mr. Codger, my anxiety has some claim to indulgence, since its cause is but too well known to you both.

JACK (*aside*). Not a word of me! I'll e'en sneak away before he finds me out. (*going.*)

CODGER. Son Jack, please to Stop.

JACK. Sir I can't; my Time's expired.

CODGER. Son, if I conceive aright, your Time, properly Speaking, ought to be mine.

JACK. Lord, Sir, only look at my Watch; it's just eight o'clock, and I promised Billy Skip to call on him before seven to go to the Play.

CODGER. Son Jack, it is by no means a dutiful principle you are proceeding upon, to be fonder of the Company of Billy Skip than of your own father.

BEAUFORT. For mercy's sake, Sir, debate this point some other Time. Censor, why will you thus deny me all information.

CODGER. So it is continually! whenever I speak you are all sure to be in a hurry! Jack, come hither and sit by me; *you* may hear me, I think, if nobody else will. Sit down, I say.

JACK. Lord, Sir—

CODGER. Sit down when I bid you, and listen to what I am going to tell you. (*Makes* JACK *seat himself at the Table, and talks to him.*)

LADY SMATTER. Beaufort, let *me* speak to Mr. Censor. What have you done, Sir, about this poor Girl? did you give her my message?

CENSOR. She had too much Sense, too much Spirit, too much dignity to hear it.

LADY SMATTER. Indeed?

CENSOR. Yes; and therefore I should propose—

LADY SMATTER. Sir, I must beg you not to interfere in this transaction; it is not that I mean to doubt either your knowledge or your learning, far from it,—but nevertheless I must presume that I am myself as competent a Judge of the matter as you can be, since I have reason to believe—you'll excuse me, sir,—that I have read as many Books as you have.  665

BEAUFORT. O those eternal Books! what, madam, in the name of reason, and of common Sense, can Books have to do in such an affair as this?

LADY SMATTER. How? do you mean to depreciate Books? to doubt their general utility, and universal influence? Beaufort, I  670 shall Blush to own you for my Pupil! Blush to recollect the fruitless efforts with which I have laboured, as Shakespeare finely says,

       To teach the young idea how to shoot. —

CENSOR. Shakespeare?—then what a Thief was Thompson![1]  675

LADY SMATTER. Thompson? O, ay, true, now I recollect, so it was.

CENSOR. Nay, madam, it little matters which, since both, you know, were Authors.

BEAUFORT. Unfeeling Censor! is this a Time to divert yourself with satirical dryness? defer, I conjure you, these useless, idle,  680 ludicrous disquisitions, and, for a few moments, suffer affairs of real interest and importance to be heard and understood.

LADY SMATTER. Beaufort, you expose yourself more and more every Word you utter; disquisitions which relate to Books and Authors ought never to be deferred. Authors, Sir, are the  685 noblest of human Beings, and Books—

BEAUFORT. Would to Heaven there were not one in the World!

LADY SMATTER. O monstrous!

BEAUFORT. Once again, Madam, I entreat, I conjure—

LADY SMATTER. I will not hear a Word more. Wish there was not  690 a Book in the World? Monstrous, shocking, and horrible! Beaufort, you are a lost Wretch! I tremble for your Intellects, and if you do not speedily conquer this degenerate passion, I shall abandon you without remorse to that Ignorance and Depravity to which I see you are plunging.  695

*Exit.*

---

1  *what a Thief was Thompson*: the line is from "Spring", part one of James Thomson's *The Seasons* (1730), l. 1153.

BEAUFORT *and* CENSOR. CODGER *and* JACK *at the Table.*

BEAUFORT. Hard-Hearted, vain, ostentatious Woman! Go, then, and leave me to that Independance which not all your smiles could make me cease to regret! Censor, I am weary of this contention; what is Life, if the Present must continually be
700    sacrificed to the Future? I will fly to Cecilia, and I will tear myself from her no more. If, without Her, I can receive no happiness, why, with Her, should I be apprehensive of misery?

CENSOR. Know you not, Beaufort, that if you sap the foundation of a Structure, 'tis madness to expect the Sides and the top
705    will stand self-supported? Is not security from want the Basis of all Happiness? and if you undermine that, do you not lose all possibility of enjoyment? Will the presence of Cecilia soften the hardships of Penury? Will her Smiles teach you to forget the pangs of Famine? Will her Society make you insensi-
710    ble to the severities of an Houseless Winter?

BEAUFORT. Well, well, tell me where I can find her, and she shall direct my future conduct herself.

CENSOR. I have a Scheme upon Lady Smatter to communicate to you, which, I think, has some chance of succeeding.

715 BEAUFORT. Till I have seen Cecilia, I can attend to nothing; once more, tell me where she is.

CENSOR. Where ever she is, she has more wisdom than her Lover, for she charged me to command your absence.

BEAUFORT. My absence?

720 CENSOR. Nay, nay, I mean not seriously to suppose the Girl is wise enough to wish it; however, if she pretends to desire it, you have a sufficient excuse for non-attendance.

BEAUFORT. I don't understand you. — Is Cecilia offended?

CENSOR. Yes, and most marvellously, for neither herself nor her
725    Neighbours know why.

BEAUFORT. I will not stay another minute! — I will find other methods to discover her abode. (*going.*)

CENSOR. Prithee, Beaufort, be less absurd. My scheme upon Lady Smatter —

730 BEAUFORT. I will not hear it! I disdain Lady Smatter, and her

future smiles or displeasure shall be equally indifferent to me. Too long, already, have I been governed by motives and Views which level me with her narrow-minded self; it is Time to shake off the yoke,—assert the freedom to which I was Born,—and dare to be Poor, that I may learn to be Happy! 735

*Exit.*

CENSOR. Shall this noble fellow be suffered to ruin himself? no! the World has too few like him. Jack, a word with you,— Jack, I say!—are you asleep, man?
CODGER. Asleep? Surely not.
CENSOR. If you're awake, answer! 740
JACK (*yawning*). Why, what's the matter?
CENSOR. Wake, man, wake and I'll tell you.
CODGER. How, asleep? pray, Son Jack, what's the reason of your going to Sleep when I'm talking to you?
JACK. Why, Sir, I have so little Time for Sleep, that I thought I 745 might as well take the opportunity.
CODGER. Son Jack, Son Jack, you are verily an Ignoramus!
CENSOR. Come hither, Jack. I have something to propose to you—
CODGER. Sir I have not yet done with him myself. Whereabouts 750 was I, Son, when you fell asleep?
JACK. Why there, Sir, where you are now.
CODGER. Son you are always answering like a Blockhead; I mean whereabouts was I in my Story?
JACK. What story, Sir? 755
CODGER. How? did you not hear my story about your aunt Deborah's Poultry?
JACK. Lord, no, Sir.
CODGER. Not hear it? why what were you thinking of?
JACK. Me, Sir? why how many places I've got to go to to-night. 760
CODGER. This is the most indecorous behaviour I ever saw. You don't deserve ever to hear me tell a story again. Pray, Mr. Censor, did *you* hear it?
CENSOR. No.

765 CODGER. Well, then, as it's a very good Story, I think I'll e'en take the trouble to tell it once more. You must know, then, my Sister Deborah, this silly Lad's aunt—

CENSOR. Mr. Codger I am too much engaged to hear you now,—I have Business that calls me away.

770 CODGER. This is always the Case! I don't think I ever Spoke to three Persons in my Life that did not make some pretence for leaving me before I had done!

CENSOR. Jack, are you willing to serve your Brother?

JACK. That I am! I would ride to York to see what's O'Clock[1] for 775 him.

CENSOR. I will put you in a way to assist him with less trouble, though upon a matter of at least equal importance. You, too, Mr. Codger, have, I believe, a good regard for him?

CODGER. Sir I shall beg leave to decline making any answer.

780 CENSOR. Why so, Sir?

CODGER. Because, Sir, I never intend to utter a Word more in this Room; but, on the contrary, it is my intention to abandon the Club from this Time forward.

CENSOR. But is that any reason why you should not answer me?

785 CODGER. Sir I shall quit the place directly; for I think it an extremely hard thing to be made speak when one has nothing to say, and hold one's Tongue when one has got a speech ready.

*Exit.*

JACK. Is he gone? huzza! I was never so tired in my life. (*going.*)

790 CENSOR. Hold! I have something to say to you.

JACK. Can't possibly stay to hear you.

CENSOR. Prithee, Jack, how many Duels do you fight in a year?

JACK. Me? Lord, not one.

CENSOR. How many Times, then, do you beg pardon to escape a 795 Caning?

---

1 *ride to York to see what's O'Clock*: alluding to stories about highwaymen such as John Nevison and Dick Turpin, who rode from London to York (nearly two hundred miles) at great speed. By arriving at York before the clock struck a certain hour, they could establish an alibi.

JACK. A Caning?

CENSOR. Yes; or do you imagine the very wildness and inattention by which you offend, are competent to make your apology?

JACK. Lord, Mr. Censor, you are never easy but when you are ask-   800
ing some queer Question! But I don't much mind you. You
odd sort of People, who do nothing all Day but *muz*[1] yourselves with thinking, are always coming out with these sort of
trimmers;[2] however, I know you so well, that they make no
impression on me.   805

*Exit.*

CENSOR. Through what a multiplicity of Channels does Folly
glide! its Streams, alternately turgid, calm, rapid and lazy, take
their several Directions from the peculiarities of the minds
whence they Spring,—frequently varying in their Courses,—
but ever similar in their Shallowness!   810

---

1   *muz*: colloquial for studying too intently.
2   *trimmers*: stiff rebukes or retorts.

# ACT V

*Scene a Parlour at* Mrs. Voluble's. Mrs. Voluble,
Mrs. Wheedle, Miss Jenny *and* Bob *are seated at a round Table
at Supper;* Betty *is waiting.*

Mrs. Voluble. Well, this is a sad thing indeed!—Betty, give me
some Beer. Come, Miss Jenny, here's your Love and mine.
(*Drinks.*)

Mrs. Wheedle. I do believe there's more misfortunes in our
way of Business than in any in the World; the fine Ladies have
5    no more conscience than a Jew,—they keep ordering and
ordering, and think no more of paying than if one could Live
upon a Needle and Thread.

Mrs. Voluble. Ah, the Times are very bad! very bad, indeed!—
all the Gentlefolk breaking,—why, Betty, the meat i'n't half
10    done!—poor Mr. Mite,¹ the rich cheesemonger at the Corner is quite knocked up.²

Mrs. Wheedle. You don't say so?

Mrs. Voluble. Very true, indeed.

Mrs. Wheedle. Well, who'd have thought of that? Pray, Mrs.
15    Betty, give me some Bread.

Miss Jenny. Why it is but a Week ago that I met him a driving
his own Whiskey.³

Mrs. Voluble. Ah, this is a sad World! a very sad World, indeed!
nothing but ruination going forward from one end of the
20    Town to the other. My dear Mrs. Wheedle, you don't Eat;
pray let me help you to a little Slice more.

Mrs. Wheedle. O, I shall do very well; I only wish you'd take
care of yourself.

Mrs. Voluble. There, that little bit can't hurt you, I'm sure. As
25    to Miss Jenny, she's quite like a Crocodile, for she Lives upon
air.⁴

---

1   *Mr. Mite*: "mite" was slang for a cheesemonger. Samuel Foote's *The Commissary* (1765),
a play that Burney mentions in *Evelina* (188), contains a reference to "old Mite the
cheesemonger" (III.i).

2   *knocked up*: financially ruined.

3   *Whiskey*: a light, two-wheeled, one-horse carriage.

4   *Crocodile ... Lives upon air*. Katharine Rogers, citing Delery, notes that "Herodotus
reported that crocodiles eat nothing for four months in the year."

MRS. WHEEDLE. No, ma'am, the thing is she Laces so tight,[1] that she can't Eat half her natural victuals.

MRS. VOLUBLE. Ay, ay, that's the way with all the Young Ladies; they pinch for fine shapes. 30

BOB. Mother, I wish you'd help *me*,—I'm just starved.

MRS. VOLUBLE. Would you have me help you before I've helped the Company, you greedy fellow, you? Stay till we've done, can't you? and then if there's any left, I'll give you a bit.

MISS JENNY. I'll give Master Bobby a piece of mine, if you please, 35 ma'am.

MRS. VOLUBLE. No, no, he can't be very hungry, I'm sure, for he Eat a Dinner to frighten a Horse. And so, as I was telling you, she has agreed to stay here all night, and to be sure, poor Thing, she does nothing in the World but Cry, all as ever I 40 can say to her, and I believe I was talking to her for a matter of an Hour before you came, without her making so much as a word of answer. I declare it makes one as melancholy as a Cat[2] to see her. I think this is the nicest cold Beef I ever Tasted,— you *must* Eat a bit, or I shall take it quite ill. 45

MRS. WHEEDLE. Well, it must be *leetle* tiny morsel, then.

MRS. VOLUBLE. I shall cut you quite *a fox-hall* slice.[3]

BOB. Mother, if Mrs. Wheedle's had enough, you'd as good give it me.

MR. VOLUBLE. I declare I don't believe there's such another fel- 50 low in the World for gormondizing! — There,— take that, and be quiet. So, as I was saying —

BOB. Lord, Mother, you've given me nothing but fat!

MRS. VOLUBLE. Ay, and too good for you, too. I think, at your age, you've no right to know fat from lean. 55

MRS. WHEEDLE. Ah, Master Bobby, these are no Times to be dainty! one ought to be glad to get Bread to Eat. I'm sure, for my part, I find it as hard to get my Bills paid, as if the fine Ladies had no money but what they earned.

---

1 *Laces so tight*: the practice of tightly lacing corsets to create narrow waists was fashionable among women for much of the century.

2 *melancholy as a Cat*: proverbial.

3 *a fox-hall slice*: fox-hall was a common corruption of Vauxhall Gardens (visited by Evelina and Cecilia), at which the extreme thinness of the sliced ham was a popular jest.

60 MRS. VOLUBLE. If you'll take my advice, Mrs. Wheedle, you'll
send in your account directly, and then, if the young lady has
any money left, you'll get it at once.
MRS. WHEEDLE. Why that's just what I thought myself, so I
made out the Bill, and brought it in my Pocket.[1]
65 MRS. VOLUBLE. That's quite right. But, good lack, Mrs. Wheedle, who'd have thought of a young lady's being brought to
such a pass?—I shall begin soon to think there's no trusting
in any body.
MISS JENNY. For my part, if I was to chuse, I should like best to
70 be a Lady at once, and follow no Business at all.
BOB. And for my part, I should like best to be a Duke.
MRS. VOLUBLE. A Duke? you a Duke, indeed! you great num-
scull I wish you'd learn to hold your Tongue. I'll tell you
what, Mrs. Wheedle, you must know it's my notion this
75 young lady expects something in the money way out of the
City, for she gave me a Letter, just before you came, to send
by a Porter; so as I was coming down Stairs, I just peeped in
at the Sides —

*Enter* CECILIA.

O Law! — I hope she did not hear me!
80 CECILIA. I beg your pardon, Mrs. Voluble for this intrusion, but I
rang my Bell three Times, and I believe nobody heard it.
MRS. VOLUBLE. I'm sure, ma'am, I'm quite sorry you've had such
a trouble; but I dare say it was all my son Bobby's fault, for he
keeps such a continual Jabbering, that there's no hearing any
85 thing in the World for him.
BOB. Lord, Mother, I'll take my Oath I ha'n't spoke three words
the whole Time! I'm sure I've done nothing but knaw that
nasty fat this whole night.
MRS. VOLUBLE. What, you are beginning again, are you? —
90 CECILIA. I beg I may occasion no disturbance; I merely wished to
know if my messenger were returned.
MRS. VOLUBLE. Dear no, ma'am, not yet.

---

1 *Pocket*: until the end of the century, when handbags came into fashion, women wore
pear-shaped bags as pockets, tied round the waist under the dress.

CECILIA. Then he has certainly met with some accident. If you will be so good as to lend me your Pen and Ink once more, I will send another man after him.                                               95

MRS. VOLUBLE. Why, ma'am, he could not have got back so soon, let him go never so fast.

CECILIA (*walking apart*). So Soon! Oh how unequally are we affected by the progress of Time! Winged with the gay Plumage of Hope, how rapid seems its flight,—oppressed   100 with the Burden of Misery, how tedious its motion! — yet it varies not,—insensible to Smiles, and callous to Tears, its acceleration and its tardiness are mere phantasms of our disordered Imaginations. How strange that that which in its course is most steady and uniform, should, to our deluded Senses,   105 seem most mutable and irregular!

MISS JENNY. I believe she's talking to herself.

MRS. VOLUBLE. Yes, she has a mighty way of Musing. I have a good mind to ask her to Eat a bit, for, poor Soul, I dare say she's hungry enough. Bobby, get up, and let her have your   110 chair.

BOB. What, and then a'n't I to have any more?

MRS. VOLUBLE. Do as you're bid, will you, and be quiet. I declare I believe you think of nothing but Eating and Drinking all Day long. Ma'am, will it be agreeable to you to Eat a bit of   115 Supper with us?

MRS. WHEEDLE. The young lady does not hear you; I'll go to her myself. (*Rises and follows* CECILIA.) I hope, Miss Stanley, you're very well? I hope my lady's well? I believe, ma'am, you don't recollect me?                                             120

CECILIA. Mrs. Wheedle? — yes, I do.

MRS. WHEEDLE. I'm very sorry, I'm sure, ma'am, to hear of your misfortunes, but I hope things a'n't quite so bad as they're reported?

CECILIA. I thank you. Mrs. Voluble, is your Pen and Ink here?   125

MRS. VOLUBLE. You shall have it directly; but pray, ma'am, let me persuade you to Eat a morsel first.

CECILIA. I am obliged to you, but I cannot.

MRS. VOLUBLE. Why now here's the nicest little miniken bit you ever saw;—it's enough to tempt you to look at it.             130

BOB. Mother, if the lady don't like it, can't you give it me?

MRS. VOLUBLE. I was just this minute going to help you, but now you're so greedy, you sha'n't have a bit.

CECILIA. Mrs. Voluble, can I find the Pen and Ink myself?

135 MRS. VOLUBLE. I'll fetch it in two minutes. But, dear ma'am, don't fret, for bad things of one Sort or other are always coming to pass; and as to Breaking, and so forth, why I think it happens to every body. I'm sure there's Mr. Grease, the Tallow Chandler, one of my most particular acquaintance, that's

140 got as genteel a Shop as any in all London, is quite upon the very point of ruination: and Miss Moggy Grease, his Daughter—

CECICIA. I'll Step up Stairs, and when you are at leisure, you will be so good as to send me the Standish.[1] (*going.*)

145 MRS. WHEEDLE (*stopping her*). Ma'am, as I did not know when I might have the pleasure of seeing you again, I took the liberty just to make out my little account, and bring it in my Pocket; and I hope, ma'am, that when you make up your affairs, you'll be so good as to let me be the first Person that's considered,

150 for I'm a deal out of Pocket, and should be very glad to have some of the money as soon as possible.

CECILIA. Dunned already! good Heaven, what will become of me! (*bursts into Tears.*)

MRS. VOLUBLE. Dear ma'am, what signifies fretting?—better Eat

155 a bit of Supper, and get up your Spirits. Betty, go for a clean Plate.

*Exit* BETTY.

MRS. WHEEDLE. Won't you please, ma'am, to look at the Bill?

CECILIA. Why should I look at it?—I cannot pay it,—I am a destitute Creature,—without Friend or resource!

160 MRS. WHEEDLE. But, ma'am, I only mean—

CECILIA. No matter what you mean!—all application to *me* is fruitless,—I possess nothing—The Beggar who sues to you for a Penny is not more powerless and wretched,—a tortured and insulted Heart is all that I can call my own!

---

1  *Standish*: a stand containing ink, pens, writing materials, etc.

MRS. WHEEDLE. But sure, ma'am, when there comes to be a 165
Division among your Creditors, your Debts won't amount to
more than—

CECILIA. Forbear, forbear!—I am not yet inured to Disgrace, and
this manner of stating my affairs is insupportable. *Your* Debt,
assure yourself, is secure, for sooner will I famish with want, 170
or perish with Cold,—faint with the fatigue of labour, or
consume with unassisted Sickness, than appropriate to my
own use the smallest part of my shattered Fortune, till your—
and every other claim upon it is answered.

MRS. WHEEDLE. Well, ma'am, that's as much as one can expect. 175

*Re-enter* BETTY, *with a Plate and a Letter.*

BETTY. Ma'am is your name Miss Stanley?

CECILIA. Yes; is that Letter for me? (*takes it.*)

MRS. VOLUBLE. Betty, why did not you bring the Letter first to
me? Sure I'm the Mistress of my own House. Come, Mrs.
Wheedle, come and finish your supper. (MRS. WHEEDLE 180
*returns to the Table.*)

CECILIA. I dread to open it! Does any body wait?

BETTY. Yes, ma'am, a man in a fine lace livery.

CECILIA (*reading*). "Since you would not hear my message from
Mr. Censor, I must try if you will read it from myself. I do
most earnestly exhort you to go instantly and privately into 185
the Country, and you may then depend upon my Support
and protection. Beaufort now begins to listen to reason—"
Oh Heaven! "and, therefore, if you do not continue in Town
with a view to attract his notice, or, by acquainting him with
your retirement, seduce him to follow you—" Insolent, inju- 190
rious woman! "I have no doubt but he will be guided by one
whose experience and studies entitle her to direct him. I shall
call upon you very soon, to know your determination, and to
supply you with Cash for your Journey, being, with the
utmost sorrow for your misfortunes, Dear Miss Stanley, Yours 195
&c Judith Smatter." What a Letter!

BETTY. Ma'am, if you please, is there any answer?

CECILIA. No, none.

BETTY. Then, ma'am, what am I to say to the Footman?

200 CECILIA. Nothing. — Yes, — tell him I have read *this* Letter, but if he brings me another, it will be returned unopened.

BETTY. Yes, ma'am. Laws![1] what a comical answer.

*Exit.*

MRS. VOLUBLE. I wonder who that Letter was from!

MISS JENNY. I dare say I can guess. I'll venture something it's
205 from her Sweetheart.

MRS. VOLUBLE. That's just my Thought! (*they whisper.*)

CECILIA. Is then every Evil included in poverty? and is the deprivation of Wealth what it has least to regret? Are Contempt,
Insult, and Treachery its necessary attendants? — Is not the
210 loss of affluence sufficiently bitter, — the ruin of all Hope
sufficiently severe, but that Reproach, too, must add her
Stings, and Scorn her Daggers?

MRS. VOLUBLE. When I've Eat this, I'll ask her if we guessed
right.

215 CECILIA. "Beaufort begins to listen to reason," — mercenary
Beaufort! Interest has taken sole possession of thy Heart, —
weak and credulous that I was to believe I had ever any share
in it!

MRS. VOLUBLE. I'm of ten minds whether to speak to her, or
220 leave her to her own Devices.

CECILIA. "To listen to reason," — is, then, reason another word
for baseness, falsehood and Inconstancy?

MRS. WHEEDLE. I only wish my money was once safe in my
Pocket.

225 CECILIA. Attract his notice? seduce him to follow! — am I already
so Sunk? already regarded as a designing, interested Wretch? I
cannot bear the imputation, — my swelling Heart seems too
big for its mansion, — O that I could quit them all!

MRS. VOLUBLE (*rising and approaching* CECILIA). Ma'am, I'm
230 quite sorry to see you in such trouble; I'm afraid that Letter
did not bring you agreeable news; — I'm sure I wish I could
serve you with all my Heart, and if you're distressed about a

---

1 *Laws*: a corruption of "Lord."

Lodging, I've just thought of one in Queen Street, that, in a week's Time,—

CECILIA. In a week's Time I hope to be far away from Queen 235
Street,[1]—far away from this hated City,—far away, if possible, from all to whom I am known!

MRS. VOLUBLE. Dear ma'am, sure you don't think of going beyond Seas?

MRS. WHEEDLE. If you should like, ma'am, to go abroad, I 240
believe I can help you to a thing of that sort myself.

CECILIA. How?

MRS. WHEEDLE. Why, ma'am, I know a Lady who's upon the very point of going, and the young Lady who was to have been her Companion,[2] all of a sudden married a young Gen- 245
tleman of Fortune, and left her without any notice.

CECILIA. Who is the lady?

MRS. WHEEDLE. Mrs. Hollis, ma'am; she's a Lady of very good fortunes.

CECILIA. I have heard of her. 250

MRS. WHEEDLE. And she wants a young lady very much. She sets off the beginning of next week. If it's agreeable to you to go to her, I shall be proud to shew you the way.

CECILIA. I know not what to do!

MRS. VOLUBLE. Dear ma'am, I would not have you think of such 255
a Desperation scheme; things may be better soon, and who knows but Mr. Beaufort may prove himself a true Lover at the last? Lord, if you could but once get the Sight of him, I dare say, for all my lady, the Day would be your own.

CECILIA. What odious interpretations! to what insults am I 260
exposed! — yes, I had indeed better quit the kingdom,—Mrs. Wheedle, I am ready to attend you.

MRS. WHEEDLE. Then, Master Bobby, bid Betty call a Coach.[3]

CECILIA. No,—stay! —

MRS. WHEEDLE. What, ma'am, won't you go? 265

---

1 *Queen Street*: several London streets were so named.
2 *Companion*: i.e., "humble companion": a woman who is the paid companion of anoth-er woman, and is thus expected to be both humble and dutiful. In *The Wanderer*, the heroine becomes the companion of a highly disagreeable employer, Mrs. Ireton.
3 *a Coach*: i.e., a hackney-coach, holding four to six people and available for hire; there were 1,000 licensed to trade in London.

CECILIA (*walking apart*). Am I not too rash?—expose myself, like a common Servant, to be Hired?—submit to be examined, and hazard being rejected!—no, no, my Spirit is not yet so broken.

270 MRS. VOLUBLE. I hope, ma'am, you are thinking better of it. For my part, if I might be free to advise you, I should say send to the young Gentleman, and see first what is to be done with *him*.

CECILIA. What humiliating suggestions! yes, I see I must be
275 gone,—I see I must hide myself from the World, or submit to be suspected of Views and Designs I disdain to think of. Mrs. Wheedle, I cannot well accompany you to this Lady myself, but if you will go to her in my name,—tell her my unhappy situation, as far as your knowledge of it goes—and that, alas,
280 includes but half its misery!—you will much oblige me. When did you say she leaves England?

MRS. WHEEDLE. Next week, ma'am.

CECILIA. I shall have Time, then, to arrange my affairs. Tell her I know not, yet, in what capacity to offer myself, but that, at all
285 events, it is my first wish to quit this Country.

MRS. WHEEDLE. Yes, ma'am. I'll get my Hat and cloak, and go directly.

*Exit.*

CECILIA. Alas, to what abject dependance may I have exposed myself!

290 MRS. VOLUBLE. Come, ma'am, let me persuade you to Taste my Raison Wine,—I do believe it's the best that—

CECILIA. I thank you, but I can neither Eat or Drink. (*going.*)

*Re-enter* MRS. WHEEDLE.

MRS. WHEEDLE. I suppose, ma'am, I may tell Mrs. Hollis you will have no objection to doing a little Work[1] for the Chil-
295 dren, and things of that sort, as the last young lady did?

---

1   *Work*: needlework.

CECILIA. Oh heavy Hour!—down, down, proud Heart!—Tell her what you will!—I must submit to my fate, not chuse it; and should servility and dependance be my lot, I trust, at least, that I shall not only find them new,—not only find them Heart-Breaking and cruel—but short and expeditious. 300

MRS. VOLUBLE. But, ma'am, had not you best—

CECILIA. I have no more directions to give, and I can answer no more Questions. The sorrows of my situation seem every moment to be aggravated,—Oh Beaufort! faithless, unfeeling Beaufort! to have rescued you from distress and mortification 305 such as this would have been my Heart's first joy,—my life's only pride!

*Exit.*

MRS. VOLUBLE. She's quite in a sad taking, that's the truth of it.

MISS JENNY. Poor young lady! I'm so sorry for her you can't think. 310

MRS. VOLUBLE. Come, Mrs. Wheedle, you sha'nt' go till you've drunk a Glass of Wine, so let's sit down a little while and be comfortable. (*They seat themselves at the Table.*) You need not be afraid of the dark, for Bobby shall go with you.

BOB. Mother, I'd rather behalf[1] not. 315

MRS. VOLUBLE. Who wants to know whether you'd rather or not? I suppose there's no need to consult all your ratherness-es. Well, Ma'am, so, as I was going to tell you, poor Miss Moggy Grease—(*A violent knocking at the Door.*) Lord bless me, who's at the Door? why they'll knock the House down! 320 Somebody to Mr. Dabler, I suppose; but he won't be Home this two Hours.

BOB. Mother, may I help myself to a drop of Wine? (*Takes the Bottle.*)

MRS. VOLUBLE. Wine, indeed! no,—give me the Bottle this minute (*snatches and overturns it*). Look here, you nasty fellow, 325 see how you've made me spill it!

---

1  *behalf:* for my part.

*Enter* BETTY.

BETTY. Laws, ma'am, here's a fine lady all in her Coach, and she asks for nobody but you.

MRS. VOLUBLE. For me? well, was ever the like! only see, Betty, what a Slop Bobby's made! There's no such a thing as having it seen. Come, folks, get up all of you, and let's move away the Table. Bob, why don't you stir? one would think you were nailed to your Seat.

BOB. Why I'm making all the haste I can, a'n't I? (*They all rise, and* BOB *over-turns the Table.*)

MRS. VOLUBLE. Well, if this is not enough to drive one mad! I declare I could flee the Boy alive! Here's a Room to see Company! you great, nasty, stupid Dolt, you, get out of my sight this minute.

BOB. Why, mother, I did not do it for the purpose.

MRS. VOLUBLE. But you did, you great Loggerhead, I know you did! get out of my sight this minute, I say! (*drives him off the Stage.*) Well, what's to be done now?—Did ever any body see such a Room?—I declare I was never in such a pucker[1] in my life. Mrs. Wheedle, do help to put some of the things into the closet. Look here, if my china Bowl i'n't broke! I vow I've a great mind to make that looby[2] Eat it for his Supper.—Betty, why don't you get a mop?—you're as helpless as a Child.—No, a Broom,—get a Broom, and sweep them all away at once.—Why you a'n't going empty Handed, are you? I declare you have not half the Head you was Born with.

BETTY. I'm sure I don't know what to do no more than the Dog. (*gets a Broom.*)

MRS. VOLUBLE. What do you talk so for? have you a mind to have the Company hear you?—(*The knocking is repeated.*)—There, they're knocking like mad!—Miss Jenny, what signifies your staring? can't you make yourself a little useful? I'm sure if you won't at such a Time as this—why, Betty, why don't you make haste? Come, poke every thing into the

---

1  *pucker*: a state of agitation or excitement, a flutter.
2  *looby*: a silly, lazy fellow.

Closet,—I wonder why Bobby could not have took some of the things himself,—but as soon as ever he's done the mis- 360 chief he thinks of nothing but running away. (*They clear the stage, and* MISS JENNY *runs to a looking Glass.*)

MISS JENNY. Dear me, what a Figure I've made of myself!

MRS. VOLUBLE. There, now we shall do pretty well. Betty, go and ask the lady in.

*Exit* BETTY.

I declare I'm in such a flustration! 365

MISS JENNY. So am I, I'm sure, for I'm all of a tremble.

MRS. WHEEDLE. Well, if you can spare master Bobby, we'll go to Mrs. Hollis's directly.

MRS. VOLUBLE. Spare him? ay, I'm sure it would have been good luck for me if you had taken him an Hour ago. 370

MRS. WHEEDLE. Well, good by, then. I shall see who the lady is as I go along.

*Exit.*

MISS JENNY. It's very unlucky I did not put on my Irish Muslin.

MRS. VOLUBLE. It's prodigious odd what can bring any Compa-ny at this Time of night. 375

*Enter* MRS. SAPIENT.

Mrs. Sapient! dear ma'am, I can hardly believe my Eyes!

MRS. SAPIENT. I am afraid my visit is unseasonable, but I beg I may not incommode you.

MRS. VOLUBLE. Incommode me? dear ma'am no, not the least in the World; I was doing nothing but just sitting here talking 380 with Miss Jenny, about one thing or another.

MRS. SAPIENT. I have a question to ask you, Mrs. Voluble, which—

MRS. VOLUBLE. I'm sure, ma'am, I shall be very proud to answer it; but if I had but known of the pleasure of seeing you, I 385 should not have been in such a pickle; but it happened so that we've been a little busy to Day,—you know, ma'am, in all Families there will be some busy Days,[1]—and I've the misfortune of a Son, ma'am, who's a little unlucky, so that puts one a little out of sorts, but he's so unmanageable, ma'am, that really—

MRS. SAPIENT. Well, well, I only want to ask if you know any thing of Miss Stanley?

MRS. VOLUBLE. Miss Stanley? to be sure I do, ma'am; why she's now in my own House here.

MRS. SAPIENT. Indeed?—And pray—what, I suppose, she is chiefly with Mr. Dabler?—

MRS. VOLUBLE. No, ma'am, no, she keeps prodigiously snug; she bid me not tell any body she was here, so I make it a rule to keep it secret,—unless, indeed, ma'am, to such a lady as you.

MRS. SAPIENT. O, it's very safe with me. But, pray, don't you think Mr. Dabler rather admires her?

MRS. VOLUBLE. O, ma'am, not half so much as he admires another lady of your acquaintance. Ha! Ha!

MRS. SAPIENT. Fie, Mrs. Voluble!—but pray, does not he write a great deal?

MRS. VOLUBLE. Dear ma'am yes; he's in one continual scribling from morning to night.

MRS. SAPIENT.—Well, and—do you know if he writes about any particular Person?

MRS. VOLUBLE. O yes, ma'am, he writes about Celia, and Daphne, and Cleora, and—

MRS. SAPIENT. You never see his Poems, do you?

MRS. VOLUBLE. O dear yes, ma'am, I see them all. Why I have one now in my Pocket about Cleora, that I happened to pick up this morning. (*aside to* MISS JENNY) Miss Jenny, do pray put me in mind to put it up before he comes Home. Should you like to see it, ma'am?—

MRS. SAPIENT. Why—if you have it at Hand—

MRS. VOLUBLE. Dear ma'am, if I had not, I'm sure I'd fetch it, for I shall be quite proud to oblige you. As to any common acquaintance, I would not do such a thing upon any account,

---

1  *busy Days*: the phrase used (in the singular) by Burney for the title of her comedy of c. 1800-02.

because I should Scorn to do such a baseness to Mr. Dabler, but to such a lady as you it's quite another thing. For, whenever I meet with a lady of Quality, I make it a point to behave 425 in the genteelist manner I can. Perhaps, ma'am, you'd like to see Mr. Dabler's Study?

MRS. SAPIENT. O no, not upon any account.

MRS. VOLUBLE. Because, upon his Table, there's a matter of an hundred of his *miniscrips*. 430

MRS. SAPIENT. Indeed?—But when do you expect him Home?

MRS. VOLUBLE. O not this good while.

MRS. SAPIENT. Well then—if you are certain we shall not be surprised—

MRS. VOLUBLE. O, I'm quite certain of that. 435

MRS. SAPIENT. But, then, for fear of accidents, let your maid order my Coach to wait in the next street.

MRS. VOLUBLE. Yes, ma'am. Here, Betty!

*Exit.*

MRS. SAPIENT. This is not quite right, but this Woman would shew them to somebody else if not to me. And now perhaps 440 I may discover whether any of his private Papers contain my name. She will not, for her own sake, dare betray me.

*Re-enter* MRS. VOLUBLE.

MRS. VOLUBLE. Now, ma'am, I'll wait upon you. I assure you, ma'am, I would not do this for every body, only a Lady of your honour I'm sure would be above— 445

*Exit talking, with* MRS. SAPIENT.

MISS JENNY (*alone*).

MISS JENNY. She's said never a word to *me* all the Time, and I dare say she knew me as well as could be; but fine ladies Seem to think their Words are made of Gold, they are so afraid of bestowing them.

*Re-enter* MRS. VOLUBLE.

450 MRS. VOLUBLE. O Miss Jenny, only look here! my apron's all
stained with the Wine! I never see it till this minute, and
now—(*a knocking at the Door.*) Oh! (*Screams*) that's Mr.
Dabler's knock! what shall we all do?—run up Stairs and tell
the lady this minute,—

*Exit* MISS JENNY.

455 Betty! Betty! don't go to the Door yet,—I can't think what
brings him Home so soon!—here's nothing but ill luck upon
ill luck!

*Enter* MRS. SAPIENT *with* MISS JENNY.

Come, ma'am, come in! Betty!—you may go to the Door
now.
460 MRS. SAPIENT. But are you sure he will not come in here?
MRS. VOLUBLE. O quite, ma'am; he always goes to his own
Room. Hush!—ay, he's gone up,—I heard him pass.
MRS. SAPIENT. I am quite surprised, Mrs. Voluble, you should
have deceived me thus; did not you assure me he would not
465 return this Hour? I must tell you, Mrs. Voluble, that, whatever
you may think of it, *I* shall always regard a Person who is
capable of deceit, to be guilty of insincerity.
MRS. VOLUBLE. Indeed, ma'am, I knew no more of his return
than you did, for he makes it a sort of rule of a 'Sprit night—
470 MISS JENNY. Ma'am, ma'am, I hear him on the Stairs!
MRS. SAPIENT. O hide me,—hide me this Instant anywhere,—
And don't say I am here for the universe! (*She runs into the
Closet.*)
MRS. VOLUBLE. No, ma'am, that I won't if it costs me my life!—
you may always depend upon *me.* (*shuts her in.*)
475 MISS JENNY. Laws, what a pickle she'll be in! she's got all among
the broken things.

*Enter* DABLER.

DABLER. Mrs. Voluble, you'll please to make out my account, for I shall leave your House directly.

MRS. VOLUBLE. Leave my House? Lord, Sir, you quite frighten me! 480

DABLER. You have used me very ill, Mrs. Voluble, and curse me if I shall put up with it!

MRS. VOLUBLE. Me, Sir? I'm sure, Sir, I don't so much as know what you mean.

DABLER. You have been rummaging all my Papers. 485

MRS. VOLUBLE. I?—no, Sir,—I'm sorry, Sir, you suspect me of such a mean proceeding.

DABLER. 'Tis in vain to deny it; I have often had reason to think it, but now my doubts are confirmed, for my last new Song, which I called Cleora is no where to be found. 490

MRS. VOLUBLE. No where to be found?—you surprise me!— (aside) Good Lank,[1] I quite forgot to put it up!

DABLER. I'm certain I left it at the top of my Papers.

MRS. VOLUBLE. Did you indeed, sir? well, I'm sure it's the oddest thing in the World what can be come of it! 495

DABLER. There is something so gross, so scandalous in this usage, that I am determined not to be duped by it. I shall quit my Lodgings directly;—take your measures accordingly. (going.)

MRS. VOLUBLE. O pray, Sir, Stay,—and if you won't be so angry, I'll tell you the whole truth of the matter. 500

DABLER. Be quick, then.

MRS. VOLUBLE (in a low Voice). I'm sorry, Sir, to betray a lady, but when one's own reputation is at stake—

DABLER. What lady? I don't understand you.

MRS. VOLUBLE. Hush, hush, Sir!—she'll hear you. 505

DABLER. She?—Who?

MRS. VOLUBLE. Why Mrs. Sapient, Sir (whispering), she's in that closet.

DABLER. What do you mean?

MRS. VOLUBLE. I'll tell you all, Sir, by and by,—but you must 510 know She came to me, and—and—and begged just to look at your Study, Sir,—So, Sir, never supposing such a lady as

---

1  Lank: like "Laws" above (p. 146, note 1), a corruption of "Lord."

that would think of looking at your papers, I was persuaded to agree to it,—but, Sir, as soon as ever we got into the Room, she fell to Reading them without so much as Saying a Word!—while I, all the Time, stood in this manner!—staring with stupification. So, Sir, when you knocked at the Door, she ran down to the closet.

DABLER. And what has induced her to do all this?

MRS. VOLUBLE. Ah, Sir, you know well enough! Mrs. Sapient is a Lady of prodigious good Taste; every body knows how she admires Mr. Dabler.

DABLER. Why yes, I don't think she wants Taste.

MRS. VOLUBLE. Well but, Sir, pray don't stay, for she is quite close crammed in the closet.

DABLER. I think I'll speak to her.

MRS. VOLUBLE. Not for the World, Sir! If she knows I've betrayed her, she'll go beside herself. And, I'm sure, Sir, I would not have told any body but you upon no account. If you'll wait up stairs till she's gone, I'll come and tell you all about it,—but pray, dear Sir, make haste.

DABLER. Yes, She's a good agreeable Woman, and really has a pretty knowledge of Poetry. Poor Soul!—I begin to be half sorry for her.

*Exit.*

MRS. VOLUBLE. I thought he'd never have gone. How do do now, ma'am. (*opens the closet Door.*)

*Enter* MRS. SAPIENT.

MRS. SAPIENT. Crampt to Death! what a strange place have you put me in! Let me begone this Instant,—but are you sure, Mrs. Voluble, you have not betrayed me?

MRS. VOLUBLE. I'm surprised, ma'am, you should suspect me! I would not do such a false thing for never so much, for I always—(*a Knocking at the Door.*) Why now who can that be?

MRS. SAPIENT. How infinitely provoking!—let me go back to this frightful closet till the Coast is clear. (*returns to the Closet.*)

Mrs. Voluble. Well, I think I've managed matters like a *match-* 545
*well.*[1]

*Enter* Mrs. Wheedle.

Mrs. Wheedle. O, I'm quite out of Breath,—I never walked so
fast in my life.
Mrs. Voluble. Where have you left Bobby?
Mrs. Wheedle. He's gone into the Kitchen. I must see Miss 550
Stanley directly.
Mrs. Voluble. We've been in perilous danger since you went.
Do you know (*in a low Voice*), Mrs. Sapient is now in the
Closet? Be sure you don't tell any body.
Mrs. Wheedle. No, not for the World. Miss Jenny pray step and 555
tell Miss Stanley I'm come back.

*Exit* Miss Jenny.

Mrs. Voluble. Well, and while you speak to her, I'll go and talk
over Mr. Dabler, and contrive to poke this nasty Song under
the Table. But first I'll say something to the poor lady in the
closet. Ma'am! (*opens the Door*) if you've a mind to keep Still, 560
you'll hear all what Miss Stanley says presently, for she's coming down.
Mrs. Sapient. Are you mad, Mrs. Voluble?—what do you hold
the Door open for?—Would you have that Woman see me?
Mrs. Voluble. Ma'am, I beg your pardon! (*shuts the Door.*) I 565
won't help her out this half Hour for that crossness.

*Exit.*

Mrs. Wheedle. These fine Ladies go through any thing for the
sake of curiosity.

*Enter* Cecilia.

---

1 *matchwell*: probably, as Rogers suggests in her edition, Mrs. Voluble's rendition of
Machiavel; from the Florentine political theorist Machiavelli (1469-1527), notorious
for his plotting and scheming.

Cecilia. Well, Mrs. Wheedle, have you seen Mrs. Hollis?

570 Mrs. Wheedle. Yes, ma'am, and she's quite agreeable to your proposal: but as she's going very soon, and will be glad to be fixed, She says she shall take it as a particular favour if you will go to her House to night.

Cecilia. Impossible! I must consult some friend ere I go at all.

575 Mrs. Wheedle. But, ma'am, she begs you will, for she says she's heard of your misfortunes, and shall be glad to give you her advice what to do.

Cecilia. Then I *will* go to her!—for never yet did poor Creature more want advice and assistance!

580 Mrs. Wheedle. (*calls at the Door*) Betty! go and get a Coach. I'll just go speak to Mrs. Voluble ma'am, and come again.

*Exit.*

Cecilia *alone.*

Cecilia. Perhaps I may repent this Enterprize,—my Heart fails me already;—and yet, how few are those human actions that repentance may not pursue! Error precedes almost every step,

585 and sorrow follows every error. I who to happiness have bid a long, a last farewell, must content myself with seeking Peace in retirement and Solitude, and endeavour to contract all my wishes to preserving my own Innocence from the contagion of this bad and most deseased World's corruptions.

*Enter* Betty.

590 Betty. Ma'am the Coach is at the Door.

Cecilia. Alas!

Betty. Mrs. Wheedle, ma'am, is gone up stairs to my *Mississ,* but she says she'll be ready in a few minutes.

*Exit.*

Cecilia *alone.*

Cecilia. Oh cease, fond, suffering, feeble Heart! to struggle thus

with misery inevitable. Beaufort is no longer the Beaufort he 595
appeared, and since he has lost even the semblance of his
Worth, why should this sharp regret pursue his Image?
But, alas, that semblance which *he* has lost, *I* must ever retain!
fresh, fair and perfect it is still before me!—Oh why must
Woe weaken all faculties but the memory?—I will reason no 600
longer,—I will think of him no more,—I will offer myself to
servitude, for Labour itself must be less insupportable than
this gloomy indolence of sorrowing reflection—where is this
Woman?—(*going.*)

*Enter* BEAUFORT, *who stops her.*

BEAUFORT. My Cecilia! 605
CECILIA. Oh—good Heaven!
BEAUFORT. My lov'd, lost, injured,—my adored Cecilia!
CECILIA. Am I awake?
BEAUFORT. Whence this surprise?—my love, my Heart's sweet
Partner— 610
CECILIA. Oh forbear!—these terms are no longer—Mr. Beau-
fort, let me pass!
BEAUFORT. What do I hear?
CECILIA. Leave me, sir,—I cannot talk with you,—leave me, I
say! 615
BEAUFORT. Leave you?—(*offering to take her Hand.*)
CECILIA. Yes (*turning from him*),—for I cannot bear to look at
you!
BEAUFORT. Not look at me? what have I done? how have I
offended you? why are you thus dreadfully changed? 620
CECILIA. *I* changed? comes this well from *you?*—but I will not
recriminate, neither will I converse with you any longer. You
see me now perhaps for the last Time,—I am preparing to
quit the Kingdom.
BEAUFORT. To quit the Kingdom? 625
CECILIA. Yes; it is a Step which your own conduct has compelled
me to take.
BEAUFORT. My Conduct?—who has belied me to you?—what
villain—
CECILIA. No one, Sir; you have done your work yourself. 630

BEAUFORT. Cecilia, do you mean to distract me?—if not, explain, and instantly, your dark, your cruel meaning.

CECILIA. Can it want explanation to *you*? have you Shocked me in ignorance, and irritated me without knowing it?

635 BEAUFORT. I shocked?—I irritated you?—

CECILIA. Did you not, in the very first anguish of a calamity which you alone had power to alleviate neglect and avoid me? Send me a cold message by a Friend? Suffer me to endure indignities without support, and sorrows without par-

640 ticipation? Leave me, defenceless, to be crushed by impending ruin? and abandon my aching Heart to all the torture of new-born fears, unprotected, unassured, and uncomforted?

BEAUFORT. Can *I* have done all this?

CECILIA. I know not,—but I am sure it has seem'd so.

645 BEAUFORT. Oh wretched policy of cold, unfeeling Prudence, had I listened to no dictates but those of my Heart, I had never been wounded with suspicions and reproaches so cruel.

CECILIA. Rather say, had your Heart sooner known its own docility, you might have permitted Lady Smatter to dispose of

650 it ere the deluded Cecilia was known to you.

BEAUFORT. Barbarous Cecilia! take not such a Time as this to depreciate my Heart in your opinion, for now —'tis all I have to offer you.

CECILIA. You know too well —'tis all I ever valued.

655 BEAUFORT. Oh take it then,—receive it once more, and with that confidence in its Faith which it never deserved to forfeit! Painfully I submitted to advice I abhorred, but though my Judgment has been over-powered, my truth has been invio-late. Turn not from me, Cecilia!—if I have temporized, it has

660 been less for my own Sake than for yours; but I have seen the vanity of my expectations,—I have disobeyed Lady Smat-ter,—I have set all consequences at defiance, and flown in the very face of ruin,—and now, will *you*, Cecilia (*Kneeling*), reject, disdain and spurn me?

665 CECILIA. Oh Beaufort—is it possible I can have wronged you?

BEAUFORT. Never, my sweetest Cecilia, if now you pardon me.

CECILIA. Pardon you?—too generous Beaufort—ah! rise.

*Enter* LADY SMATTER *and* MR. CODGER.

BEAUFORT (*rising*). Lady Smatter!

LADY SMATTER. How, Beaufort here?—and kneeling, too!

CODGER. Son Beaufort, I cannot deny but I think it is rather an 670
extraordinary thing that you should chuse to be seen Kneeling to that young lady, knowing, I presume, that your Aunt
Smatter disaffects your so doing.

LADY SMATTER. Beaufort, I see you are resolved to keep no terms
with me. As to Miss Stanley, I renounce her with contempt; I 675
came hither with the most generous views of assisting her,
and prevailed with Mr. Codger to conduct her to her Friends
in the country; but since I find her capable of so much baseness, since I see that all her little arts are at Work—

CECILIA. Forbear, madam, these unmerited reproaches; believe 680
me, I will neither become a Burthen to you, nor a Scorn to
myself; the measures I have taken I doubt not will meet with
your Ladyship's approbation, though it is by no means incum-
bent upon me, thus contemptuously accused, to enter into
any defence or explanation. 685

*Exit.*

BEAUFORT. Stay, my Cecilia,—hear me—

*follows her.*

LADY SMATTER. How? persue her in defiance of my presence?
Had I a Pen and Ink I should disinherit him incontinently.[1]
Who are all these People?

*Enter* MISS JENNY, MRS. VOLUBLE, *and* MRS. WHEEDLE.

MISS JENNY (*as she Enters*). Law, only look! here's Lady Smatter 690
and an Old Gentleman!

---

1   *incontinently*: immediately.

MRS. VOLUBLE. What, in my Parlour? well, I declare, and so there is! why how could they get in?

MRS. WHEEDLE. I suppose the Door's open because of the Hackney Coach. But as to Miss Stanley, I believe she's hid herself.

CODGER. Madam, I can give your Ladyship no Satisfaction.

LADY SMATTER. About what?

CODGER. About these people, madam, that your Ladyship was enquiring after, for, to the best of my knowledge, madam, I apprehend I never saw any of them before.

LADY SMATTER. I see who they are myself, now.

MRS. VOLUBLE (*advancing to* LADY SMATTER). My Lady, I hope your Ladyship's well; I am very glad, my lady, to pay my humble duty to your Ladyship in my poor House, and I hope—

LADY SMATTER. Pray is Mr. Dabler at Home?

MRS. VOLUBLE. Yes, my lady, and indeed—

LADY SMATTER. Tell him, then, I shall be glad to see him.

MRS. VOLUBLE. Yes, my lady. (*aside to* MISS JENNY) I suppose, Miss Jenny, you little thought of my having such a genteel acquaintance among the Quality!

*Exit.*

MISS JENNY (*aside to* MRS. WHEEDLE). I'm afraid that poor lady in the Closet will spoil all her things.

LADY SMATTER. Yes, I'll consult with Mr. Dabler; for as to this old Soul, it takes him half an Hour to recollect whether two and three make five or six.

*Enter* CENSOR.

CENSOR. I have, with some difficulty, traced your Ladyship hither.

LADY SMATTER. Then, Sir, you have traced me to a most delightful spot; and you will find your Friend as self-willed, refractory and opinionated as your amplest instructions can have rendered him.

CENSOR. I would advise your Ladyship to think a little less for Him, and a little more for yourself, lest in your solicitude for his Fortune, you lose all care for your own Fame.

LADY SMATTER. My Fame? I don't understand you.

CENSOR. Nay, if you think such Lampoons may spread without 725
doing you Injury —

LADY SMATTER. Lampoons? What Lampoons? — sure nobody
has dared —

*Enter* DABLER *and* MRS. VOLUBLE.

MRS. VOLUBLE. Why here's Mr. Censor too! I believe there'll be
Company coming in all night. 730

LADY SMATTER. Mr. Censor, I say, if there is any Lampoon that
concerns *me*, I insist upon hearing it directly.

CENSOR. I picked it up just now at a Coffee House. *(reads)*
Yes, Smatter is the Muse's Friend,
She knows to censure or commend; 735
And has of Faith and Truth such store
She'll ne'er desert you — till you're poor.

LADY SMATTER. What insolent impertinence!

DABLER. Poor Stuff! poor Stuff indeed! your Ladyship should
regard these little Squibs as *I* do, mere impotent efforts of 740
Envy.

LADY SMATTER. O I do; I'd rather hear them than not.

DABLER. And ill done, too; most contemptibly ill done. I think
I'll answer it for your Ladyship.

CENSOR. Hark ye, Mr. Dabler *(takes him aside)*, do you know this 745
Paper?

DABLER. That Paper?

CENSOR. Yes, Sir; it contains the lines which you passed off at
Lady Smatter's as made at the moment.

DABLER. Why, Sir, that was merely — it happened — 750

CENSOR. It is too late for equivocation, Sir; your reputation is
now wholly in my power, and I can instantly blast it, alike
with respect to Poetry and to Veracity.

DABLER. Surely, Sir —

CENSOR. If, therefore, you do not, with your utmost skill, assist 755
me to reconcile Lady Smatter to her Nephew and his choice,
I will shew this original Copy of your extemporary abilities
to every body who will take the trouble to read it: otherwise,

I will sink the whole transaction, and return you this glaring
760   proof of it.
DABLER. To be sure, Sir,—as to Mr. Beaufort's choice—it's the
      thing in the World I most approve,—and so—
CENSOR. Well, Sir, you know the alternative, and must act as you
      please.
765 DABLER (aside). What cursed ill luck!
LADY SMATTER. Mr. Censor, I more than half suspect you are
      yourself the author of that pretty Lampoon.
CENSOR. Nay, madam, you see this is not my Writing.
LADY SMATTER. Give it me.
770 CENSOR. Hold, here's something on the other side which I did
      not see. (reads)
            Were madness stinted to Moorfields[1]
            The World elsewhere would be much thinner;
            To Time now Smatter's Beauty yields—
775 LADY SMATTER. How!
CENSOR (reading).
            She fain in Wit would be a Winner.
               At Thirty she began to read,—
LADY SMATTER. That's false!—entirely false!
CENSOR (reads).
            At Forty, it is said, could spell,—
780 LADY SMATTER. How's that? at Forty?—Sir this is your own
      putting in.
CENSOR (reads).
            At Fifty—
LADY SMATTER. At Fifty?—ha! ha! ha!—this is droll enough!
CENSOR (reads).
            At Fifty, 'twas by all agreed.
785         A common School Girl she'd excell.
LADY SMATTER. What impertinent nonsense!
CENSOR (reads).
            Such wonders did the World presage—
LADY SMATTER. Mr. Censor, I desire you'll read no more,—'tis
      such rubbish it makes me quite Sick.

---

1   Moorfields: the site of "Bedlam," the popular name for Bethlehem Royal Hospital, a
    hospital for the insane until 1815.

CENSOR (*reads*).

> Such wonders did the World presage                    790
> From Blossoms which such Fruit invited,—
> When Avarice,— the vice of Age,—
> Stept in,— and all expectance blighted.

LADY SMATTER. Of Age!— I protest this is the most impudent
thing I ever heard in my life! calculated for no purpose in the    795
World but to insinuate I am growing old.

CENSOR. You have certainly some secret Enemy, who avails himself of your disagreement with Miss Stanley to prejudice the
World against you.

LADY SMATTER. O, I'm certain I can tell who it is.                 800

CENSOR. Who?

LADY SMATTER. Mrs. Sapient—

MISS JENNY (*aside*). Law, I'm afraid she'll hear them.

LADY SMATTER. Not that I suspect her of the Writing, for miser-
able Stuff as it is, I know her capacity is yet below it; but she   805
was the first to leave my House when the affair was discovered, and I suppose She has been tatling it about the Town
ever since.

MRS. VOLUBLE (*aside*). Ah, poor lady, it's all to fall upon her!

CENSOR. Depend upon it, madam, this will never rest here; your   810
Ladyship is so well known, that one satire will but be the prelude to another.

LADY SMATTER. Alas, how dangerous is popularity! O Mr.
Dabler, that I could but despise these libels as you do!— but
this last is insufferable,— yet you, I suppose, would think it    815
nothing?

DABLER. No, really, ma'am, I can't say that,— no, not as *nothing,*—
that is, not absolutely as nothing,— for — for libels of this
sort — are rather —

LADY SMATTER. How? I thought you held them all in contempt?      820

DABLER. So I do, ma'am, only —

CENSOR. You do, Sir? —

DABLER. No, Sir, no; I don't mean to absolutely say that,— that is,
only in regard to *myself,*— for we men do not suffer in the
World by Lampoons as the poor Ladies do;— they, indeed,      825
may be quite — quite ruined by them —

LADY SMATTER. Nay, Mr. Dabler, now *you* begin to distress me.

*Enter* JACK, *Singing.*

JACK.

She has ta'en such a Dose of incongruous matter
That Bedlam must Soon hold the Carcase of Smatter
830 LADY SMATTER. How?—what?—the Carcase of Who?
JACK. Ha! Ha! Ha! faith, madam, I beg your pardon, but who'd
have thought of meeting your Ladyship here?—O Dabler, I
have such a thing to tell you! (*whispers him and Laughs.*)
LADY SMATTER. I shall go mad!—What were you Singing,
835 Jack,—what is it you Laugh at?—why won't you Speak?
JACK. I'm so much hurried I can't stay to answer your Ladyship
now. Dabler, Be sure Keep counsel. Ha! Ha! Ha,—I must go
and Sing it to Billy Skip and Will. Scamper, or I sha'n't Sleep
a Wink all night. (*going.*)
840 LADY SMATTER. This is intolerable! Stay, Jack, I charge you!
Mr. Codger, how unmoved you stand! Why don't you make
him stay?
CODGER. Madam I will. Son Jack, Stay.
JACK. Lord, Sir,—
845 LADY SMATTER. I am half Choaked!—Mr. Codger you would
provoke a Saint![1] why don't you make him tell you what he
was Singing?
CODGER. Madam he is so giddy Pated he never understands me.
Son Jack, you attend to nothing! Don't you perceive that her
850 Ladyship seems curious to know what Song you were hum-
ming?
JACK. Why, Sir, it was only a new Ballad.
LADY SMATTER. A Ballad with *my* name in it? Explain yourself,
instantly!
855 JACK. Here it is,—shall I Sing it or Say it?
LADY SMATTER. You shall do neither,—give it me!
CENSOR. No, no, Sing it first for the good of the Company.
JACK. Your Ladyship won't take it ill?

---

1  *provoke a Saint*: proverbial, but perhaps Lady Smatter is alluding to Pope's "Epistle to
Cobham" (*Moral Essays*, I): "Odious! in woollen! 'twould a Saint provoke" (1. 246).

LADY SMATTER. Ask me no Questions,—I don't know what I shall do.                                                                    860
JACK (*Sings*).

> I call not to Swains to attend to my Song;
> Nor call I to Damsels, so tender and young;
> To Critics, and Pedants, and Doctors I clatter,
> For who else will heed what becomes of poor Smatter.
> with a down, down, derry down.                                             865

LADY SMATTER. How? is my name at full length?
JACK (*sings*).

> This lady with Study has muddled her head;
> Sans meaning she talk'd, and sans knowledge she read,
> And gulp'd such a Dose of incongruous matter
> That Bedlam must soon hold the Carcase of Smatter.            870
> with a down, down, derry down.

LADY SMATTER. The Carcase of Smatter?—it can't be,—no one would dare—
JACK. Ma'am if you stop me so often, I shall be too late to go and sing it any where else to night. (*Sings.*)                                            875

> She thought Wealth esteem'd by the foolish alone,
> So, shunning offence, never offer'd her own;
> And when her Young Friend dire misfortune did batter,
> Too wise to relieve her was kind Lady Smatter.
> with a down, down, derry down.                                             880

LADY SMATTER. I'll hear no more! (*walks about in disorder.*)
CENSOR. Sing on, however, Jack; we'll hear it out.
JACK (*Sings*).

> Her Nephew she never corrupted with pelf,
> Holding Starving a Virtue—for all but herself
> Of Gold was her Goblet, of Silver, her platter                          885
> To shew how such Ore was degraded by Smatter.
> with a down, down, derry down.
> A Club she supported of Witlings and Fools,
> Who, but for her Dinners, had scoff'd at her rules;
> The reason, if any she had, these did shatter                          890
> Of poor empty-Headed, and little-Soul'd Smatter.
> with a down, down, derry down.

LADY SMATTER. Empty-Headed?—little Souled?—who has dared write this?—Where did you get it?

895 JACK. From a man who was carrying it to the Printers.

LADY SMATTER. To the Printers?—O insupportable!—are they going to Print it?—Mr. Dabler why don't you assist me?—how can I have it suppressed?—Speak quick, or I shall die.

DABLER. Really, ma'am, I—I—

900 CENSOR. There is but one way,—make a Friend of the Writer.

LADY SMATTER. I detest him from my Soul,—and I believe 'tis yourself!

CENSOR. Your Ladyship is not deceived;—I have the honour to be the identical Person. (*Bowing.*)

905 LADY SMATTER. Nay, then, I see your drift,—but depend upon it, I will not be Duped by you. (*going.*)

CENSOR. Hear me, madam!—

LADY SMATTER. No, not a Word!

CENSOR. You must! (*holds the Door.*) You have but one moment
910 for reflection, either to establish your Fame upon the firmest foundation, or to consign yourself for life to Irony and Contempt.

LADY SMATTER. I will have you prosecuted with the utmost severity of the Law.

915 CENSOR. You will have the thanks of my Printer for your reward.

LADY SMATTER. You will not dare—

CENSOR. I dare do any thing to repel the injuries of Innocence! I have already shewn you my *power*, and you will find my *Courage* undaunted, and my *perseverance* indefatigable. If you
920 any longer oppose the union of your Nephew with Miss Stanley, I will destroy the whole peace of your Life.

LADY SMATTER. You cannot!—I defy you! (*walks from him.*)

CENSOR (*following her*). I will drop Lampoons in every Coffee-House,—

925 LADY SMATTER. You are welcome, Sir.—

CENSOR. Compose Daily Epigrams for all the Papers,—

LADY SMATTER. With all my Heart,—

CENSOR. Send libels to every corner of the Town,—

LADY SMATTER. I care not!—

930 CENSOR. Make all the Ballad Singers resound your Deeds,—

LADY SMATTER. You cannot!—*shall* not!

CENSOR. And treat the Patagonian Theatre[1] with a Poppet to represent you.

LADY SMATTER (*bursting into Tears*). This is too much to be borne, Mr. Censor, you are a Daemon! 935

CENSOR. But, if you relent,—I will burn all I have written, and forget all I have planned; Lampoons shall give place to panegyric, and libels, to songs of Triumph; the liberality of your Soul, and the depth of your knowledge shall be recorded by the Muses, and echoed by the whole Nation! 940

LADY SMATTER. I am half distracted!—Mr. Dabler, why don't you counsel me?—how cruel is your Silence!

DABLER. Why, certainly, ma'am, what—what Mr. Censor says—

CENSOR. Speak out, man!—Tell Lady Smatter if she will not be a lost Woman to the Literary World, should she, in this trial of 945 her magnanimity, disgrace its expectations? Speak boldly!

DABLER. Hem!—you,—you have Said, Sir,—just what I think.

LADY SMATTER. How? are *you* against me?—nay then—

CENSOR. Every body must be against you; even Mr. Codger, as I can discern by his looks. Are you not, Sir? 950

CODGER. Sir, I can by no means decide upon so important a Question, without maturely pondering upon the several preliminaries.

CENSOR. Come, madam, consider what is expected from the celebrity of your character,—consider the applause that 955 awaits you in the World ;—you will be another Sacharissa, a Second Sapho,[2]—a tenth muse.

LADY SMATTER. I know not what to do!—allow me, at least, a few Days for meditation, and forbear these scandalous libels till— 960

CENSOR. No, madam, not an Hour!—there is no Time so ill spent as that which is passed in deliberating between meanness and Generosity! You may now not only gain the esteem

---

1 *the Patagonian Theatre*: a puppet theatre that came to London from Dublin in 1776 and performed there for five years. It was noted for its satirical treatment of contemporary individuals and institutions.

2 *Sacharissa, a Second Sapho,—a tenth muse*: Sacharissa was Edmund Waller's poetic name for Lady Dorothea Sidney. Sappho (born c. 600 BC), a Greek lyric poet, was much admired and regarded as the tenth Muse.

of the Living, but—if it is not Mr. Dabler's fault,—consign
965 your name with Honour to Posterity.
LADY SMATTER. To Posterity?—why where is this Girl gone?—
what has Beaufort done with himself?—
CENSOR. Now, madam, you have Bound me yours for-ever!—
here, Beaufort!—Miss Stanley!—

*goes out.*

970 JACK. Huzza!—
CODGER. Madam, to confess the verity, I must acknowledge that I
do not rightly comprehend what it is your Ladyship has
determined upon doing?
LADY SMATTER. No; nor would you, were I to take an Hour to
975 tell you.

*Re-enter* CENSOR, *with* BEAUFORT *and* CECILIA.

BEAUFORT. O madam, is it indeed true that—
LADY SMATTER. Beaufort, I am so much flurried, I hardly know
what is true;—save, indeed, that Pity, as a certain author says,
will ever, in noble minds, conquer Prudence. Miss Stanley—
980 CENSOR. Come, come, no speeches; this whole Company bears
Witness to your Consent to their marriage, and your Ladyship (*in a low voice*) may depend upon not losing sight of *me*
till the Ceremony is over.
CECILIA. Lady Smatter's returning favour will once more devote
985 me to her Service; but I am happy to find, by this Letter, that
my affairs are in a less desperate situation than I had appre-
hended. (*gives a Letter to* LADY SMATTER.) But here, Mr. Censor, is another Letter which I do not quite so well understand;
it contains an order for five thousand pounds, and is signed
990 with your name?
CENSOR. Pho, pho, we will talk of that another Time.
CECILIA. Impossible! Liberality so undeserved—
CENSOR. Not a word more, I entreat you!
CECILIA. Indeed I can never accept it.
995 CENSOR. Part with it as you can! *I* have got rid of it. I merit no

thanks, for I mean it not in Service to you, but in Spite to Lady Smatter, that she may not have the pleasure of boasting, to her wondering Witlings, that she received a Niece wholly unportioned. Beaufort, but for his own Stubbornness, had long since possessed it,—from a similar motive.  1000

CECILIA. Dwells Benevolence in so rugged a Garb?—Oh Mr. Censor—!

BEAUFORT. Noble, generous Censor! you penetrate my Heart,— yet I cannot consent —

CENSOR. Pho, pho, never praise a man for only gratifying his own  1005 humour.

*Enter* BOB, *running.*

BOB. Mother, mother, I believe there's a Cat in the closet!

MRS. VOLUBLE. Hold your Tongue, you great oaf!

BOB. Why, mother, as I was in the Back Parlour, you can't think what a rustling it made.  1010

MISS JENNY (*aside*). Dear me!—it's the poor lady!—

MRS. WHEEDLE. Well, what a thing is this!

MRS. VOLUBLE. Bob, I could beat your Brains out!

BOB. Why Lord, mother, where's the great harm of saying there's a Cat in the Closet?  1015

JACK. The best way is to look. (*goes toward the closet.*)

DABLER. Not for the World! I won't suffer it!

JACK. You won't suffer it?—Pray, Sir, does the Cat belong to you?

BOB. Mother, I dare say she's Eating up all the Victuals.

JACK. Come then, my Lad, you and I'll hunt her. (*brushes past*  1020 DABLER, *and opens the Door.*)

ALL. Mrs. Sapient!

MRS. SAPIENT (*coming forward*). Sir, this impertinent curiosity —

JACK. Lord, ma'am, I beg your pardon! I'm sure I would not have opened the Door for the World, only we took you for the Cat. If you please, ma'am, I'll shut you in again.  1025

LADY SMATTER. That's a pretty snug retreat you have chosen, Mrs. Sapient.

CENSOR. To which of the Muses, madam, may that Temple be Dedicated?

1030 JACK. I hope, ma'am, you made use of your Time to mend your furbelows?

CODGER. Madam, as I don't understand this quick way of Speaking, I should be much obliged if you would take the trouble to make plain to my comprehension the reason of your chusing to be shut up in that dark closet?

1035 CENSOR. Doubtless, Sir, for the Study of the Occult Sciences.

LADY SMATTER. Give me leave, madam, to recommend to your perusal this passage of Addison; Those who conceal themselves to hear the Counsels of others, commonly have little reason to be satisfied with what they hear of themselves.

1040 MRS. SAPIENT. And give *me* leave, ma'am, to observe,—though I pretend not to assert it positively,—that, in *my* opinion, those who speak ill of people in their absence, give no great proof of a sincere Friendship.

1045 CENSOR (*aside*). I begin to hope these Witlings will demolish their Club.

DABLER (*aside*). Faith, if they Quarrel, I'll not Speak till they part.

BEAUFORT. Allow me, Ladies, with all humility, to mediate, and to entreat that the calm of an Evening succeeding a Day so agitated with Storms, may be enjoyed without allay. Terror, my Cecilia, now ceases to alarm, and Sorrow, to oppress us; gratefully let us receive returning Happiness, and hope that our Example,—should any attend to it,—may inculcate this most useful of all practical precepts: That Self-dependance is the first of Earthly Blessings; since those who rely on others for support and protection are not only liable to the common vicissitudes of Human Life, but exposed to the partial caprices and infirmities of Human Nature.

# THE WOMAN-HATER

## A COMEDY

## IN FIVE ACTS

## PERSONS OF THE DRAMA

SIR RODERICK
WILMOT
OLD WAVERLEY
YOUNG WAVERLEY, his son
BOB SAPLING
STEWARD ⎫
BUTLER ⎬ SERVANTS OF SIR RODERICK
FOOTMAN ⎭
SERVANT TO LADY SMATTER
LADY SMATTER
ELEONORA
MISS WILMOT
SOPHIA
MISS HENNY SAPLING, sister to BOB
NURSE TO MISS WILMOT
PRIM, maid to LADY SMATTER
PHEBE, maid to ELEONORA

# ACT I

## Scene i

*An apartment at* SIR RODERICK'S, *with Chairs and Tables.*

OLD WAVERLEY *and* YOUNG WAVERLEY.

YOUNG WAVERLEY. O, curse it, Sir, 'won't do! 'twon't do, by any
means. —'Tis leading such a shabby, paltry, pitiful life—
OLD WAVERLEY. You're boisterous, Jack, you're boisterous. —
YOUNG WAVERLEY. I can't help it, Sir, I can't help it! 'tis so
abominable! What! after immuring me from my boyhood in    5
this old Cage—where no sweet singing Bird ever warbles the
smallest air to amuse my captivity, where but to name a
female—a lovely female! sets the whole house in a blaze, and
to parley with one would be looked upon as parleying with
the enemy—    10
OLD WAVERLEY. You're hot, Jack, you're hot.
YOUNG WAVERLEY. After all this, to disinherit me at last, if I will
not bind myself to be as unnatural as himself! consent to live
the life of a Monk—and enter into a covenant to die a fusty
old bachelor!    15
OLD WAVERLEY. You're peppery, Jack, very peppery. Sir Roderick is a little crabbed against the female sex, I own; but then,
he has been rather unkindly treated by them, you must allow.
Miss Wilmot's marrying Lord Smatter, just as his own wedding day was fixed with her, and all the knick-knacks were    20
prepared, was but a bad sort of joke to a man. It was rather
skittish of Miss Wilmot to do such a thing; especially as Sir
Roderick says it was only because Lord Smatter sent her his
proposals in verse. It was certainly skitty.
YOUNG WAVERLEY. But what's all that musty old story to me?    25
Has not Miss Wilmot been Lady Smatter, Wife or Widow,
these seventeen years? and am I to be pent up in a Monastary,
and denied the sight of half my species—the best half, the
fairest half, the most delightful half!—because a vain fool jilted him so long ago for a copy of verses?    30

OLD WAVERLEY. There's nothing pat[1] in your reasoning, Jack;
'ti'n't a bit pat. If it had not been for all that combustion, how
would you have been made heir to Sir Roderick? For he
don't care a fig for you! He only chose you in spite! We are
but his distant kinsmen, neither of us: and if Lady Smatter had
not jilted him, he might have had a family of his own; and if
his Sister, Eleonora—

YOUNG WAVERLEY. Oh, don't name his Sister, Sir, I beg! I never
think of her without confusion. To cast her off only because
she married Lady Smatter's Brother! Poor Wilmot! was not
Eleonora engaged to him before the quarrel? Was not the
double marriage projected first by Sir Roderick himself? And
if he liked jilting so little, why the plague should he make
such a point of recommending it to another? And why
should Wilmot, who was faithful to Eleonora, be deserted
because his Sister was false to Sir Roderick?

OLD WAVERLEY. Jack, Jack, it does not become you to find fault
with all that, for you owe to it that Sir Roderick settled all his
fortune upon you; and that I brought you to his house, and
have put up with all his whim whams ever since; for he's
whimy, I own; very whimy: but it's all for your sake that I
pocket being treated so like a dog by him, and that I am so
contented to see you treated like a puppy.

YOUNG WAVERLEY. Sir, you are extremely good! I am much
beholden to you, no doubt! but I've been ready to hang
myself these six years—though that does not lessen my
obligation, I know. Shut up with a choleric fellow, that won't
hear an opinion, or a word, that is not an eccho of his own—
but I am indebted to you all one—plague take it!

OLD WAVERLEY. Why, Jack, how do I bear it? I have not been
fairly answered to one argument since here I have been: it's
nothing but foaming and storming—for he's very stormy;
very foamy and stormy; yet I swallow it all, Jack! and never
take your part, if I see you used ever so ill. Never!

YOUNG WAVERLEY. You are a great deal too good, Sir! a great
deal, indeed!

OLD WAVERLEY. Ah, Jack, you young fellows think to turn the

---

1   *pat*: apposite, appropriate.

World round with your finger and thumb, like a tetotum![1] Poor Jack! I that am twice your age, and can't but have twice your wisdom—poor Jack!—never have been able to make it 70 wag an inch to my own fancy. However, as to Sir Roderick's Sister, don't be uneasy about her, Jack. She deserved no better. She played naught, and ran away from her husband, and forsook her Child—

YOUNG WAVERLEY. Yes, Sir; but Sir Roderick had renounced 75 her before her ill conduct and flight; so they make no excuse for him. And as to the Child—his Niece—I doubt not but Wilmot is now bringing her from the West Indies, to plead for a reconciliation.

OLD WAVERLEY. That's the very thing I am afraid of, Jack; I am 80 afraid of some wheedling. Girls are very apt to be wheedling, Jack. If any thing saves us, 'twill be Lady Smatter's Letter this morning to destroy us; for she has put Sir Roderick into such a passion, by taking the liberty to give him her advice about his niece that I don't think he'll be cool again these ten days. 85

YOUNG WAVERLEY. And if he is not? Why the plague can't he hate Lady Smatter, without hating all womankind, and bidding me turn Woman-Hater too?

OLD WAVERLEY. Why look at me, now, Jack. Do you think I don't like women as well as you do? yet see how I submit. Do 90 you ever catch me chattering to Mrs. This and Miss That? no, Jack; I never say a word to them; for, bless me! if once one begins, who can tell, before one knows where one is, how one shall end? Females, Jack, have very sly ways; I've often noticed that; very sly ways; one can't be over snappish with 95 them, when one looks at them: there's no being very snappy.

Scene ii

*Enter the* STEWARD.

STEWARD. Sir Roderick begs the favour of speaking with you, Sir.

---

1 *tetotum*: a child's top with four flat sides, each marked with a letter. When the top falls, the letter facing upwards tells the spinner's fortune.

OLD WAVERLEY. I'll come, I'll come. Now am I going to be baited like a Bull![1] contradicted before I so much as find out myself what I intend to say, and treated like an Ass, only because I was not born, the Lord knows how, without a woman for my Mother!

*Exit.*

## Scene iii

YOUNG WAVERLEY, *and the* STEWARD.

YOUNG WAVERLEY. 'Twon't do! no, no, 'twon't do any longer; and, one way or another, I'll put an end to it. Come hither, Steward. My dear Stephanus, thou hast been, from my boyish days, my chief comfort, in this musty old Cloister. Do you remember what I said to you, when Sir Roderick flung that pail of milk over me, only for asking the Dairy Maid how she did?

STEWARD. Yes, Sir, I remember it; but I no more mind what a young Gentleman says, than what an old Gentleman does, when he's out of temper.

YOUNG WAVERLEY. Did not I tell you 'twas the last gambol I should allow to his outrageous humours? and that, at the very next, I should declare off, though at the risk of becoming bankrupt for life? Well, what do you think has been his frolic this morning?

STEWARD. I know it all, Sir: but Sir Roderick means no harm. He is only a spoilt Child, grown into an old Man. His Father died early, and his Mother never gainsay'd him; so that, till Lady Smatter played him false, he never knew what it was to be crossed in his days; though since then, to be sure, he can't so much as see the shadow of a Woman, but it puts him in a passion.

YOUNG WAVERLEY. So it does me, too!—but 'tis the passion, my old boy, the sweet passion of Love! In short, Stephanus, I'll tell

---

1   *baited like a Bull*: bull baiting, in which dogs were set at a tethered bull, was popular throughout the century.

thee what: he has kept me at such an unnatural distance from 25
the Women, that I have hardly ever seen a laundress, but I
have become enamoured of her. And he has so irritated and
inflamed me, by this last monkish interdiction never to marry,
that it no sooner passed his lips, than I internally vowed—
what do you guess I vowed, Stephanus? 30
STEWARD. To beg him to change his mind.
YOUNG WAVERLEY. No! to be ruled by my own, like a man, and
take unto myself a Wife within a Week.
STEWARD. That's a bold word, indeed, Sir!
YOUNG WAVERLEY. I am sick, sick to death, Stephanus, of lead- 35
ing this life of a slavish, mercenary parasite; and if I had but
ten pound a year I could call my own, I'd gallop off to-morrow morning to Gretna Green,¹ with the beautiful daughter
of that charming Widow.
STEWARD. I am concerned you should think so much of that 40
young woman, Sir.
YOUNG WAVERLEY. How handsome she is, Stephanus!
STEWARD. But she mayn't be worth a Guinea because of that, Sir!
Nobody knows either her or her mother, nor whence they
come, nor what they want. They are never so much as even 45
seen, but just strolling about round our house, and in the
great avenue.
YOUNG WAVERLEY. And there, Stephanus, it is, that I watch for
them, that I meet them, and that I adore them!
STEWARD. Them? what, both? That's comical enough! 50
YOUNG WAVERLEY. Ay, Stephanus, both! for while the Daughter
is all softness and sweetness, the Mother has a grace, a manner,
so dignified, yet so winning—by my faith, Stephanus, I
should have fallen in love with her at once,—if her Daughter
had not been by her side! 55
STEWARD. My dear young Gentleman, if I may make bold to say
so, you are really a little crazy.
YOUNG WAVERLEY. So I am, Stephanus! but as I don't intend to
make them crazy too—I shall pursue them no more; for I
don't know how to work,—and I have no taste for starving. 60

---

1  *Gretna Green*: the Scottish village closest to the border with England, and hence popular as a destination for eloping couples; see *The Witlings*, p. 131, note 2.

But I am sure I may trust thee, Stephanus, so I'll tell thee my plan. I am bent upon marrying! in pure spite to Sir Roderick, I am bent upon marrying! I mean, therefore, to mount my Horse, make my escape, and gallop off for town directly.

65 STEWARD. To Town? And what will you do in town, Sir?

YOUNG WAVERLEY. Search out some pliant old Dowager, worth fifty thousand pounds—and invite Sir Roderick to my wedding.

STEWARD. Nay, Sir, for the matter of that, you need not go to
70 Town for an old Dowager—if it were not for fear of Sir Roderick.

YOUNG WAVERLEY. What do you mean?

STEWARD. Why Lady Smatter herself, Sir—only I would not for the World my Master should meet with such an affront,—but
75 Lady Smatter herself, with her noble mansion and jointure—

YOUNG WAVERLEY. What!

STEWARD. Lady Smatter herself has been heard to say, to twenty persons, and upwards, who have told it me again, that she did not think, in the whole country, there was a Gentleman to
80 compare with young Mr. Waverley.

YOUNG WAVERLEY. You dear old fellow!—why did not you tell me this before?

STEWARD. Because of my Master, Sir; for, else, I could tell you as much again; how she praised your air, and your look, and
85 your walk, and your Eyes—

YOUNG WAVERLEY. I'll marry her in three days!—But how must I go to work?

STEWARD. Why you would not think of such a thing in earnest? Sir Roderick would be *non compos*.[1]

90 YOUNG WAVERLEY. A small return of compliment! he has made me so an hundred times.

STEWARD. Lady Smatter is old enough to be your Mother.

YOUNG WAVERLEY. If she'll free me from this thraldom, I'd marry her, though she were old enough to be my Grand-
95 mother.

STEWARD. She gives her whole time to reading and scribbling, and thinks nothing worth talking of but Authors and Books.

---

1    *non compos*: i.e., *non compos mentis*; see *The Witlings*, p. 77, note 2.

YOUNG WAVERLEY. If she will but give me her money, her time and her talk shall be at her own disposal. But which way can I get at her to make my overtures? Must I break my shins just 100 before her door? or provoke her house dog to bite me? or risk a tumble from my Horse? — Has Sir Roderick sent any answer to her note?

STEWARD. Answer? He would not answer it to save her life! he looks upon her writing to him as such a piece of impudence, 105 as to authorize his reviling the whole Sex worse than ever. Besides, according to her usual fashion, she has told him so much of the sayings of Shakespeare, and Pope, and Swift, and the Lord knows who, upon what he ought to do, that he declares he wishes all the Books in the Kingdom collected 110 into a national bonfire; and all the Pens into Wing dusters;[1] and all the Ink cast into Reservoirs, in which the women should be made to bathe, that their outsides and their insides might be of one colour.

YOUNG WAVERLEY. He's a brute! a woman hater must be a 115 brute. But if you can hit upon nothing to help me, I'll e'en present myself at her Ladyship's door, and commit my pretence for entering it to the chapter of accidents.[2]

*going.*

STEWARD. But, my dear young Gentleman, think a moment what you are doing: they say she is so tiresome, and so self- 120 conceited —

YOUNG WAVERLEY. She may be what she will, so she has but the money! 'Tis all one to me. Sharp, snappish, shrewish — 'tis all one! sore-eyed, bandy-legged, hump-backed — 'tis all one! so she have but the rhino,[3] and free me from these trammels, 125 though she squint from Eye to Eye, and grin from Ear to Ear — I shall be sure to adore her.

*Exit.*

---

1  *Wing dusters*: feather dusters.
2  *chapter of accidents*: in philosophy, a miscellany of effects of which the causes are occult or unknown.
3  *rhino*: colloquial for money.

## Scene iv

### STEWARD.

STEWARD. Well, if this can be brought about, it may be the making of me. —

## Scene v

*Enter the* BUTLER, *with a Back Gammon board.*

BUTLER. Mr. Stephens! — are you alone?

STEWARD. Yes; what puts you in such a hurry, Mr. Smith?

5  BUTLER. I've been within an Ace of having my head broke! Just as I had slipt the Back Gammon board out of Sir Roderick's closet, who should I hear upon the stairs but himself? — if Thomas had not popt between us —

## Scene vi

*Enter* FOOTMAN.

O, Thomas, where is he now?

THOMAS. Up in his room, beating and banging the furniture about, for all the World as if there were not a Chair nor a Table but what had done him a mischief.

5  STEWARD. Hush! I hear him!

SIR RODERICK, (*within*). Smith! Thomas!

BUTLER. Oh Lud! he's coming! pop the Back Gammon board under the Table!

SIR RODERICK, (*within*). Stephens! Smith! Thomas!

*They get the Back Gammon board under the Table; the* BUTLER
*stands before it.*

## Scene vii

*Enter* SIR RODERICK.

SIR RODERICK. Why where are you all got to? What do you do

here? Which of you was it took in that cursed Letter this morning?

BUTLER . I did not, Sir, I am sure.

THOMAS. Nor I, indeed, Sir.

SIR RODERICK. You didn't, and you didn't,—Who did, then?

STEWARD. I happen'd to be in the Servant's Hall, Sir.

SIR RODERICK. And who brought it?

STEWARD. Lady Smatter's Butler, Sir.

SIR RODERICK. Then why did not you tell him to take it back unopened?

STEWARD. I did not know I might, Sir.

SIR RODERICK. Then why could not you come and ask?

STEWARD. You were not up, Sir.

SIR RODERICK. Not up? What the deuce! is that any reason I was not to be called? Was I to lie a bed all day? And how long was he here?

STEWARD. Not above a quarter of an hour, Sir.

SIR RODERICK. A quarter of an hour? A quarter of an hour in my house? And who the d—l did he make that long visit to? Which of you is it he came to see?

STEWARD. Not me, I'm sure, Sir.

THOMAS. Nor me, for I hardly ever spoke to him.

BUTLER. Nor me, for I scarcely know his face.

SIR RODERICK. Not you, and not you, and not you? Then who did he come to see? Ha? The Chairs and Tables? Do you take him for a Cabinet-Maker?—And why did not you bring me the Letter at once?

BUTLER. I never go up Stairs, Sir.

STEWARD. And I was wanted below, Sir.

THOMAS. And I never go to the Bed-rooms, Sir.

SIR RODERICK. Ay, that's the way with you! not I, and not I! that's always the case! Every thing's done by Nobody! You are a pretty set of fellows, indeed! a very pretty set of fellows! so not one among you could be found to bring the Letter to my Chamber? And I might have out-slept the Seven Sleepers,[1] if I would, and never have known it was come?

---

1   *Seven Sleepers*: the seven sleepers of Ephesus were seven young Christian men who fell asleep during the reign of the Roman emperor Decius c. 249 AD and awoke two hundred years later, thus escaping the persecutions of Christians during that time.

STEWARD. You are always so angry, Sir, if one wakes you —

SIR RODERICK. Angry? And who the devil may be angry if I
mayn't? Ha? Who has a better right? Can you tell? A'n't I
your Master? A'n't you all my hirelings? Who pays for the
house that shelters you? Who pays for the cloaths that cover
you? Who pays for the food that crams you till you are all
sick? Why I, I, to be sure. And what do you all do to make
me amends, Ha?

BUTLER. We all work as hard as we can, Sir.

SIR RODERICK. Work? What at? You don't earn twopence a day
among you.

THOMAS. I'm sure, Sir,—

SIR RODERICK. Why what do you do? Tell me that?—clean my
house,—for fear of hurting your own credit; dress my victuals—that it may be ready for your own dinners; and come
when I call you—that I mayn't break all your bones. And
now, for the same reason, you may go! Off, I say! get out of
my sight! what do you mean by standing there, Smith?

BUTLER. I'm going directly, Sir.

SIR RODERICK. What are you shuffling with your feet?

BUTLER. It's a — a — a — only a Box, Sir.

SIR RODERICK. A Box? What Box? Stand away — as I'm alive, it's
my own Back Gammon board!

BUTLER (*taking it up*). Indeed, Sir, I was only going to take it back
to your closet.

SIR RODERICK. And how came it out of my closet?

BUTLER. I'm sure, Sir, I was only just going to play one Game.

SIR RODERICK. To play one Game? What! with my own Back
Gammon Board? There's impudence! I'll teach you, however,
another sort of Game! I'll teach you to throw dice! There!
There! There!

*dashes the Back Gammon board from his hands, and, picking up the
men, pelts him off with them.*

*Exeunt* Servants.

## Scene viii

### SIR RODERICK.

SIR RODERICK. There's a set of Rapscallions, now! letting me feed them, and pamper them, and shew them the road to extravagance and ruin, and then, in return, purloining my favorite Back Gammon Board! They have no more sense of gratitude for all one can stuff and cram them with than so 5 many Hogs for what one flings into their swill tub. I wonder whether old Waverley saw the man that brought that Letter. Smith! Thomas!—call Mr. Waverley again!—Smith, I say!—Thomas!—Now they have all hid themselves!—call Mr. Waverley, I say! 10

## Scene ix

### *Enter* OLD WAVERLEY.

OLD WAVERLEY. Here I am, my good Friend, here I am. Don't be in such a hurry.

SIR RODERICK. Don't be in a hurry? And why not, Mr. Waverley? Do you think I am to spend all my time in creeping and crawling about, like a Snail, as you do? 5

OLD WAVERLEY. Nay, nay, I meant no harm. Don't be in a passion, my friend.

SIR RODERICK. Don't be in a passion? And who said I was in a passion? Why I am no more in a passion than you are.

OLD WAVERLEY. A'n't you? Why then you a'n't. It was my mis- 10 take; that's all.

SIR RODERICK. In a passion? And what for? What about? A woman, perhaps?—Lady Smatter, may be? A likely matter! Besides, what do you call being in a passion, Mr. Waverley? Where do you see any signs of it? What have I done? Have I 15 flung any thing at any body's head? A'n't all the Chairs in their places? I'n't my Wig on my Pate? Why you don't know what being in a passion means!

OLD WAVERLEY. Well, 'ti'n't your fault if I don't, I'm sure, my
20   good friend! However —
SIR RODERICK. I'll lay my life you thought I was in a passion
      about that note from Lady Smatter? But you're out, Mr.
      Waverley! You'll never find me in a passion about any thing
      done by a woman.
25   OLD WAVERLEY. Shan't I? — Well, no more I shall, then.
SIR RODERICK. I hate the whole Sex.
OLD WAVERLEY. Do you? Well, so you do, then.
SIR RODERICK. A poor sickly, mawkish set of Beings! What are
      they good for? What can they do? Ne'er a thing upon Earth
30    they had not better let alone.
OLD WAVERLEY. May be so, may be so.
SIR RODERICK. If you meet with e'er a one, by accident, that i'n't
      a wicked hussey, it's only because she's such a cursed fool,
      such a dawdle,[1] such a driveler, such a mince-mouthed, lisp-
35    ing Ideot, that she don't know how to set about it.
OLD WAVERLEY. Very likely, Sir Roderick, very likely.
SIR RODERICK. I never believe what they say, and I never care for
      what they think; and as for taking their word — I'd sooner
      trust myself with a Tiger, who had had nothing but a Mouse
40    for his breakfast.
OLD WAVERLEY. They are rather apt to be a little tricksey, to be
      sure; rather tricksey.
SIR RODERICK. Tricksey? What do you mean by tricksey? Ras-
      cally, you should say. Perhaps you call it tricksey in Lady
45    Smatter that she married that young Lord, because he wrote
      her his fine compliments in verse? Tricksey, forsooth?
OLD WAVERLEY. You are right, Sir Roderick, you are right.
SIR RODERICK. But I a'n't right, I a'n't right, Mr. Waverley! If I
      had been right, I should have found her out before hand —
50    with her Books and her Authors! One Day, when I wanted to
      see her, she sent me word she was finishing a new pamphlet![2]
      a woman reading a pamphlet! what could she understand of
      it?

---

1   *a dawdle*: a slow-witted girl or woman.
2   *pamphlet*: a small treatise normally concerned with political or other controversial mat-
    ters, and hence supposedly incomprehensible to women. In *Evelina*, the mannish Mrs.
    Selwyn "had business at a pamphlet-shop" (318-19).

OLD WAVERLEY. Why not much, to be sure; not over-much.

SIR RODERICK. Another time, she sent for excuse she was writ-   55
ing a Letter! Women writing Letters! What can they have to
say? And then, she'd stand me out by the hour together that I
was wrong, because Pope, forsooth, was of a different opinion!
or Shakespeare had said something quite to the contrary! As if
I cared a fig for Pope and Shakespeare! I hate all such pedan-   60
tic gibberish.

OLD WAVERLEY. Why that was a little pert, indeed; a little pert
of her ladyship. Yet—Pope and Shakespeare are very well in
their way.

SIR RODERICK. Women ought to be ashamed of talking such jar-   65
gon; what can their little heads make out of such matters?
What do they know? And what ought they to know? except
to sew a Gown, and make a Pudding?[1]

OLD WAVERLEY. Two very good things, Sir Roderick; very good
things indeed; serving outside and inside.   70

SIR RODERICK. And now, after all, to have the impudence to
write me her advice! There's brass! Ask me to adopt her
niece! And tell me her niece is mine! So much the worse!
That's the very reason I'll never own her. Did not I renounce
the Girl's Mother, though she's my only Sister, merely because   75
she married Wilmot? And has not she turned out to deserve
it, by running away with an officer, and leaving her husband
and brat behind?

OLD WAVERLEY. That was very unseemly; very unseemly,
indeed, Sir Roderick.   80

SIR RODERICK. And who the deuce could expect any better
from such a connexion? Marrying the Brother of a woman
that talks of nothing but Pope and Swift and Otway! trying to
make one believe she shakes hands with the Moon and the
Stars every night of her life,—when, all the time, I'd bet an   85
hundred to one, she does not know a Pig from a Rabbet.[2]

OLD WAVERLEY. Very true, very true; yet she could see what a
pretty man Lord Smatter was—

---

1   *make a Pudding*: a similar phrase is used by another of Burney's misogynists, Captain
    Mirvan in *Evelina*, who laments that modern women know nothing of "making pud-
    dings and pies" (109).
2   *a Pig from a Rabbet*: a variant of the proverbial "knows not a pig from a dog."

SIR RODERICK (*stamping*). How? Ha? What?

90 OLD WAVERLEY. Bless me!

SIR RODERICK. Lord Smatter a pretty man? Do you mean to insult me?

OLD WAVERLEY. I have not such a thought, my friend!

SIR RODERICK. He was the ugliest little wizen fright in the uni-
95 versal world!

OLD WAVERLEY. Was he? Well, so he might.

SIR RODERICK. I suppose you want to make it out she only jilted me because I was not handsome enough for her? If ever I hear such a word from you again, Mr. Waverley, I'll throw
100 every shilling I am worth into the sea—and there, you and your Son may go and dive for them.

OLD WAVERLEY. No, no, don't say that, my good friend—don't go too far. I can't put up with being talked to unlike a Gentleman.

105 SIR RODERICK. A pretty young Man, was he? So then I am ugly enough to frighten a Horse, I suppose?—For half a Crown,[1] I'd turn Jack out of doors for this!

OLD WAVERLEY. Turn Jack out of doors? No, Sir Roderick, no! I have borne a great deal; and very properly,—but as to turning
110 Jack out of doors—don't take it ill, my friend, but I must needs say, it's a phrase no Gentleman makes use of; especially in his own house. Don't storm, my friend; I'll walk out till you are a little cooler.

*Exit.*

Scene x

SIR RODERICK.

SIR RODERICK. There's a fellow! There's a pettish fellow, now! Off in a huff for a Straw! yet always trying to insinuate I am in a passion. And what is it to him if I am? I've a good right, I hope? I'll have him called back, however. Here, Stephens!

---

1 *For half a Crown*: a silver coin, with a value of two shillings and sixpence; i.e., for next to nothing.

Smith! Thomas!—There, now! they are all shamming deaf! 5
Always at some trick or other. Lord Smatter a pretty man?—
I would not affront old Waverley, however. Stephens, I say!—
Thomas!—Smith! Now though those fellows know I am
ready to blow all their brains out, not one of them will come
near me! As I'm alive, I've a mind to set fire to my house— 10
and if I do, by the lord Harry, I'll lock them all into it!

*Exit.*

### Scene xi

*A Dressing Room at* LADY SMATTER's.
LADY SMATTER *seated, a paper in her hand.*
PRIM *waiting.*

LADY SMATTER (*reading*).
  Fair Type of every liberal art,
  That shin'st resplendant to our Eyes,
  Perform'st thou not some heav'nly part?
  Mecenas[1] sure, in female guise!
How pretty! how amazingly pretty! Prim, did you hear it? 5
This is a dedication to me, in verse, of a new work upon
female power.
PRIM. I am afraid, my Lady, they'll dedicate your ladyship soon
into female poverty, if your ladyship goes on so, giving them
such sums for all they keep inventing. 10
LADY SMATTER. Why, Prim, what can one do? Fame, fame, as
Waller justly says, is not to be had for nothing. Yet I am the
only person, now, I am told, that rewards the Poets. Certainly,
if Sir Roderick had renewed his addresses, after I lost my dear
lord, his fine estate would have been very convenient for 15
these sort of things. Though I don't think I should have softened to him. —No!—as Butler says,—or Cowley,—I forget
which,—

---

1  *Mecenas*: Maecenas, a Roman statesman and patron of the arts, known for his patronage
   of poets such as Virgil and Horace.

In Constancy, and nuptial Love
20          I learn my duty of the Dove.[1]
PRIM. That's very pretty, I'm sure, my lady.
LADY SMATTER. I never remember any thing but what is pretty,
    Prim. My soul, as Parnel somewhere says, is the soul of poet-
    ry. But I wonder I should have no answer from Sir Roderick.
25  I expected him at my feet. But ever since I broke that poor
    wretch's heart, I am told he has been a perfect Brute. I am
    glad of it; for I should certainly have again rejected him.
    Though, really—it's surprising he should not come. Howev-
    er, I must positively make him adopt my niece, since my
30  Brother Wilmot is actually bringing her amongst us. For Jus-
    tice—as Prior, I think, says—or Wycherley,—
                 The quality of Justice must prevail.[2]
PRIM. Why I think, my lady, every body wants to keep their own
    money, except your ladyship.
35 LADY SMATTER. O, as to me, I really can do nothing for her. My
    own necessary expenses almost ruin me. Don't you remem-
    ber, Prim, 'twas but last week that sonnet cost me ten
    Guineas? But then, how pretty it was! And the beginning of
    this, the inscription of that tract was fifteen; but then, again,
40  what a precious morsel! And now, the dedicary ode this
    morning has cost me twenty—but who could offer less?
                 Fair type of every liberal art—
PRIM. It's very pretty, to be sure, my lady.
LADY SMATTER. Now, when one has such serious, indispensable
45  claims upon one's current income, how is it possible to pro-
    vide for all one's indigent Relations? No; Sir Roderick must
    take her. To prefer a distant kinsman, like young Waverley, to
    a niece, would be immoral, would be scandalous, since, as
    Shakespeare says, or Shenstone—no! Swift;—
50          An honest man's the noblest work of God.[3]

---

1  *In Constancy … Dove*: from John Gay's Introduction to the *Fables* (1727), ll. 45-46;
   "from the dove," not "of the Dove" in Gay.
2  *The quality of Justice must prevail*: apparently Lady Smatter's invention, echoing "The
   quality of Mercy is not strained" from Shakespeare's *The Merchant of Venice* (IV.i).
3  *An honest man's the noblest work of God*: Lady Smatter quotes the line correctly, but it is
   from Pope's *An Essay on Man* (1733-34), IV.248.

## Scene xii

*Enter a* SERVANT.

SERVANT. Young Mr. Waverley, my lady.
LADY SMATTER. Young Mr. Waverley? How extraordinary! Ask
him up stairs.

*Exit* SERVANT.

Perhaps he comes with some excuse from Sir Roderick. Go,
Prim.                                                                      5

*Exit* PRIM.

## Scene xiii

*Enter* YOUNG WAVERLEY.

YOUNG WAVERLEY (*bowing two or three times, hesitating and stam-
mering*). I have the honour, madam,—I have done myself the
honour—
LADY SMATTER (*aside*). What amiable diffidence! You are so
obliging, Sir, as to bring me an answer from Sir Roderick?
YOUNG WAVERLEY. Not—absolutely ... an answer, ma'am,—        5
that is, not positively ... an—an answer—but, I have taken
the liberty—I have presumed—I—I—that is, I—I—
LADY SMATTER (*aside*). He is quite confounded! modest youth! I
beg, Sir, you will not distress yourself, for distress—as a certain Writer remarks, distress is very painful, to a delicate   10
mind.[1]
YOUNG WAVERLEY. Were it possible for me, madam, to be
able—that is, to find means—I would say, to express—
but—but—the awe of your presence—

---

1   *distress is very painful, to a delicate mind*: in his *Dictionary of the English Language* (1755),
    Samuel Johnson illustrates the meaning of the word "distress" with a similar phrase
    from Samuel Richardson's novel *Clarissa*: "People in affliction or *distress* cannot be
    hated by generous minds."

LADY SMATTER (*aside*). He is absolutely struck! Recollect yourself, Sir. It has been finely said, by some of our poets — I forget which, but Gay, or Dryden, — that our memories, when
we are hurried, are very apt to be fugitive.

YOUNG WAVERLEY. Your ladyship is condescension itself. I
merely presumed to call in order to — to — to — I am sure
your ladyship can comprehend what I would say far — far —
far better than — than — I can express it myself.

LADY SMATTER. Your delicacy, Sir, is disturbed, I see, how to
come to so nice a point; but I understand you entirely; you
are so polite as to call for the purpose of shewing your concern at Sir Roderick's strange silence.

YOUNG WAVERLEY. Your ladyship has read into my bosom.

LADY SMATTER. I thought so; for there are minds, as my friend
Cowley has it, that understand one another with half a word.
I hope you are an admirer of Cowley?

YOUNG WAVERLEY. The warmest!

LADY SMATTER. If you are an admirer of Cowley, you and I
ought certainly to be no strangers to one another; for sympathy — as a very great writer expresses it, — sympathy — let's
see, — I forget how the phrase runs — you can help me, I dare
say. How is it?

YOUNG WAVERLEY. I don't — I can't say — I don't quite — that
is, not exactly — I really —

LADY SMATTER. You are fluttered. You don't do yourself justice.
Be composed.

YOUNG WAVERLEY. Your Ladyship's kind reception really gives
me a — a — a — takes away, I would say, — my memory.

LADY SMATTER. I see your sensibility. It is not thrown away upon
me. What the philosophers say upon that subject is always
uppermost in my mind: 'tis a feeling, says one of them, —
Seneca, or Newton, or one of the others — 'tis a feeling rather
than a study. You remember the passage I don't doubt?

YOUNG WAVERLEY. Yes, ma'am, — that is, no, ma'am, — that is —
I remember it perfectly — only — only — I can't recollect
it! —

LADY SMATTER. Have you read the new little ode upon the mag-
netism of the Eye?

YOUNG WAVERLEY. Let me see—have I? let's see—no! I am so unfortunate—I—I—I rather think—I believe—

LADY SMATTER. Do me the favour to let me recommend it to you; for, though dedicated to me, it is so ingenious, that my blushes must give way to candour; for true merit,—as the immortal Shenstone says,—I dare say you remember the line? 55

YOUNG WAVERLEY. Ma'am I—I—really—you permit me, then, to take away this poem?—And may I also,—may I presume—when I have read it—to—to— 60

LADY SMATTER. O yes, certainly! you may bring it me back.

YOUNG WAVERLEY. How quick will be my perusal!

LADY SMATTER. I shall be gratified myself by beginning a literary intercourse in a place where, hitherto, my knowledge has pined—in the phrase of Gray—or Beaumont and Fletcher—I forget which, but one of that set—my knowledge has pined in thought.[1] 65

YOUNG WAVERLEY (*bowing*). Madam!—(*aside*) The thing is done! 70

*Exit.*

Scene xiv

LADY SMATTER.

LADY SMATTER. How charming a youth! Sir Roderick cannot, must not disinherit him for a niece he has never seen! the offspring of a dishonoured Sister! No! to relinquish, for such an object, so accomplished a youth, would be unfeeling, preposterous—unjust! Otway says— 5

Scene xv

*Enter* SERVANT.

SERVANT. Bob Sapling brings this note from the Inn, my Lady.

---

1  *pined in thought*: from Viola's speech in Shakespeare's *Twelfth Night*: "she pined in thought, / And with a green and yellow melancholy / She sat like Patience on a monument" (II.iv.113-15).

LADY SMATTER. From my Brother! (*reads*) "Just arrived—short conference—my Daughter—extremely hurried—" Let me speak to the young man.

*Exit* SERVANT.

5      How unlucky they should come to day! If I receive them, they will just be here as this amiable and diffident youth will be returning—no, no; I must put them off till the Evening.

Scene xvi

*Enter* BOB SAPLING.

LADY SMATTER. Well, young man, my Brother and his Daughter are, I find, at your Mother's house?
BOB. Yes, mawm.
LADY SMATTER. And how are they?
5   BOB. Pure dull, mawm, both. The Gentleman looks gruff and dismal, and walks him up and down, like as he'd got a distemper; and the young Miss seems mainly moped. Vast sulky, like. Yet she's got a pair of Eyes of her own, I can tell you!
LADY SMATTER. Well, I'll write an answer. You'll wait.
10  BOB. Yes, mawm.

*Exit.*

LADY SMATTER. No, I must not embarrass this youth. I must spare his trembling sensibility, yet encourage his love of literature, and admit him—as Butler has it, or Congreve, to
The feast of Reason, and the flow of Soul.[1]

*Exit.*

---

1   *The feast of Reason, and the flow of Soul*: Lady Smatter quotes the line correctly, but it is from Pope, *Imitations of Horace*, "To Mr. Fortescue" (1733), l. 128.

# ACT II

## Scene i

*A room at an Inn. A table covered with Books.* WILMOT *is discovered reading, and* MISS WILMOT *with a Book in her hand.* WILMOT *puts down his Book, and leans his head upon his hand, sighs deeply; again looks at the Book; then, casting it upon a Table, rises, and walks about the room.*

WILMOT. I cannot read—the words swim before my Eyes, but paint no images, communicate no ideas. We must share, in some degree, an author's powers, to be capable of enjoying them: and My powers, My faculties, are they not annihilated? Gone, gone—with Thee, Eleonora, gone! *(returns to his seat)* 5
Are you reading, my dear?

MISS WILMOT *(starting)*. Sir!

WILMOT. Have you found any thing in that Book to amuse you?

MISS WILMOT *(half rising, and letting the Book drop)*. Book, Sir?

WILMOT. I hope you have not slept over it? 10

MISS WILMOT *(hastily picking it up)*. No, Sir.

WILMOT. What Book is it?

MISS WILMOT. What Book?—that you gave me, Sir.

WILMOT. But who is the Author? What is the title?

MISS WILMOT. I'll look, Sir. 15

WILMOT. I recollect,—Thompson's *Seasons*.[1] How have you been pleased with them?

MISS WILMOT. Very well, Sir.

WILMOT *(walking away)*. Unfortunate Child of the most unhappy of Parents! by one neglected, by the other deserted!—How 20
couldst thou abandon her, Eleonora? Did no voice plead within for so sacred a charge? Because offended thyself, didst thou deem thy own duties cancelled?—*(returns to his seat)* My poor Girl!—let me give thee a Book easier of comprehension, and of more immediate utility. Chapone's Letters.[2] My 25

---

1   *Thompson's Seasons*: see *The Witlings*, p. 135, note 1.
2   *Chapone's Letters*: Hester Mulso Chapone's *Letters on the Improvement of the Mind Addressed to a Young lady* (1773), a popular guide to female conduct.

Sister will soon come, or send for us, and, till then—(*walks from her*) An only Child—a daughter, too, thus to forsake!—(*returning*) Do you approve what I have now given you?

MISS WILMOT (*starting*). Sir?—Yes, Sir. (*reads*)

30 WILMOT. Poor fearful Girl! thy timidity subdues thy faculties! Why did I not grant thee to the prayers of thy Mother? How would she have modelled, polished thee! Yet, while I believed her guilty, could I repose in her such a trust? O Eleonora! even now, that I know thee innocent, that my Soul is racked

35 with the conscious horror of having wronged thee, even now, the cloud that hangs upon thy flight, its secresy, and thy concealment, darkens my views, confuses my intellects—Does my walking about disturb thee, my dear?

MISS WILMOT. No, Sir.

40 WILMOT. Yet—for Me is it to censure her? Me? Her oppressor, her bane, her destroyer?—

MISS WILMOT. Sir!

WILMOT. Do not mark me! read on, I conjure thee.—Ah, rather let me look within! Eleonora, yes! self-condemned I stand:

45 unconvicted, I blighted thy fair fame—untried, I chased thee from the honours of thy house, and doomed thy youth, thy sweetness, thy graces, to ignominious obscurity!—How! can I have done this?—to Eleonora? to my love? to the Wife of my bosom? O monstrous! monstrous!

50 MISS WILMOT. Did you speak, Sir?

WILMOT. My dear?—O, ay, true,—you have read that passage, have you? Look, then, for another.—That poor Thing will think me mad: and, at times, the acute remorse of my soul seems to touch on the verge of distraction. Nay, what else has

55 been my influence? Jealousy is madness of the worst species, seeking to wound what is most dear, to dishonour what is most sacred. O fie! fie! fie!—My Girl, your attention is, I hope, caught?

MISS WILMOT. Yes, Sir.

60 WILMOT. 'Tis amazing my Sister should be so late—Give me the book. I will read you a passage.

MISS WILMOT. Here, Sir.

WILMOT. I'll find some place directly. (*Takes the book with an absent air, and walks away.*) How could I crush the soft feelings of her sensitive soul, and change them into the bitter repin- 65 ings of unavailing resentment? 'Tis strange! incomprehensible to myself!—Did I say I would read to you?

MISS WILMOT. Yes, Sir.

WILMOT. Come, then, let me sit by you. Listen to this charming Letter—When will my Sister arrive, that I may begin my 70 tremendous search, and end—one way or other, my long, long misery?—Now, then, my dear Girl, are you ready?

MISS WILMOT. Yes, Sir.

WILMOT (*rising*). But how, Eleonora, wilt thou meet me? with hatred implacable?—or with deadly disdain? Intolerable 75 expectation!—O Eleonora!—

MISS WILMOT. Sir!

WILMOT. Read, read, my Girl!—What strange combinations entwine our complex, yet discordant feelings? Even in that fatal paroxysm of madness, when I believed her guilty, while 80 my heart recoiled from her iniquity, it clung to her idea! and while I renounced her sight, I doated on her remembrance! But this she will never know, and her indignation—her hatred—I cannot bear the thought!—I feel, I feel, if so she meet me—'twill soon be all over—soon, soon— 85

Scene ii

*Enter the* NURSE.

NURSE. Dear Sir, be any thing the matter?

WILMOT. The matter?—no.—I am tired; that's all. (*casting himself upon a chair*) Miserably tired!

Scene iii

*Enter* MISS HENNY SAPLING.

MISS HENNY. Ladies and Gentlemen, if you please, Brother Bob is come back from my lady's.

WILMOT. Has he brought me an Answer?

MISS HENNY. If you please, Sir, he won't tell me. He's in one of his humours. But he stands at the door.

WILMOT. Bid him come in.

## Scene iv

*Enter* BOB.

BOB. Why I told you so, did not I? only you will always be so dominationing.

MISS HENNY. Come, don't be saucy, Bob.

WILMOT. Have I no answer?

MISS HENNY. Give the Gentleman his answer, Bob, and don't be so stupid.

BOB. It's more like you're stupid yourself, Miss. Can't you let a body alone?

WILMOT. My Answer!

BOB. Sir, she puts me out, so,—but it's my notion it's this here (*taking a Letter from his waistcoat pocket*).

WILMOT (*snatching it*). Your notion? are you not certain? (*he reads it.*)

MISS HENNY. If you please, Sir, Brother Bob can't read writing hand.

BOB. And what do you lug that out for, pray, Miss?

MISS HENNY. Why you can't deny it, for you don't know printing hand neither.

BOB. And what business is that of yours, Mrs. Tell-Tale?

MISS HENNY. I'll fit[1] you for that, I'm resolved. If you please, Sir, Brother Bob can't write, nor can't read, neither.

WILMOT (*folding up his Letter*). Not till the afternoon? Severe delay! I must quiet my nerves in solitude. If you are not disposed to read, my dear, let Nurse stay with you. Nurse, you will take care of her. O!—

*Exit.*

---

1   *fit*: answer.

NURSE. Yes, Sir, that I will.

MISS HENNY (*going*). Poor young lady! She don't seem to dare 25
say her Soul's her own.

BOB (*going*). She's but mumpy,[1] indeed.

NURSE. Why a young lady, Miss Henny, can't be supposed to be
as free and easy as you are. Good by, Miss Henny, good by,
Mr. Bob. 30

MISS WILMOT (*peeping over the shoulders of the* NURSE). Is Papa
gone?

NURSE. Yes, Miss.

MISS WILMOT. Are you sure?

NURSE. Yes, Miss, up stairs to his own room. 35

MISS WILMOT ( *jumping up and singing*).

Then hoity, toity, whiskey, friskey,
These are the joys of our dancing days —

Come, now let's get rid of all this stupifying learning! so
march off, Mr. Thompson! decamp, Mrs. Chapone! away,
Watts' improvement of the mind,[2] and off! off! off! with a 40
hop, skip, and a jump, ye Ramblers, Spectators, and Adventurers![3] (*throwing about the Books, and dancing round them*)

So hoity, toity, whiskey, friskey,
These are the joys of our dancing days —

MISS HENNY. Good la me! (*holding up her hands*) 45

NURSE. Fie, Miss, fie!

BOB. He! He! He!

MISS WILMOT. Now, Nurse, don't you begin to be cross! Have
not I been curbed long enough? Jammed up there, with a
parcel of mopeish[4] old Books, that I don't understand a word 50
of—and that I won't understand a word of, Nurse! So Hoity,
toity, whiskey—Now, Nurse, suppose you dance, too?

NURSE. For shame, Miss, for shame!

---

1  *mumpy*: sullen, depressed, melancholy.

2  *Watts' improvement of the mind*: Isaac Watts's *The Improvement of the Mind* (1741), a popular didactic work.

3  *Ramblers, Spectators, and Adventurers*: periodicals containing moral essays. *The Rambler*
(1750-54) was edited by Samuel Johnson, who also contributed to *The Adventurer*
(1753-54). For *The Spectator* see *The Witlings*, p. 118, note 1.

4  *mopeish*: causing moping; foolish.

MISS HENNY (*to* NURSE). La, me, ma'am, I'm afeard Miss is not
quite right here! (*pointing to her Forehead*)
MISS WILMOT. Come, Nurse, let's allemande.[1] (*seizing her hands*)
NURSE. Don't, Miss!—don't, then!—don't pull me so!
MISS WILMOT. Why, Nurse, you want practice. You are as stiff as
a wooden Doll.
NURSE (*whispering*). Out upon it, Miss! before them low people!
You need not to stay, Miss Henny; Mr. Bob, you need not to
stay.
MISS WILMOT. And why not, Nurse? I won't have you put on
that long crabbed Face. That's the look that used to make me
cry so when I was a baby. Miss Henny may dance too. Can
you cut capers, Miss Henny?
MISS HENNY. I'm sure, Miss, I am very ready to be agreeable: but
Brother Bob can't dance at all.
MISS WILMOT. Can't he? Why then he shall sing.
MISS HENNY. No, Miss, Brother Bob can't sing.
MISS WILMOT. O, I'll give him a lesson.
NURSE. Miss! Miss! Is this behaving for a young lady?
MISS WILMOT. I'll teach him what the sailors sung all the way
we came along sea. (*sings*)
          O the roast Beef of old England,
          And O, the old English roast beef.[2]
D'ye hear? Can you sing roast beef, Bob?
MISS HENNY. No, Miss; Brother Bob don't know how. He's no
voice, Miss, and he's no Ear, Miss, and he's no—
BOB. Who told you that, Henny? (*grinning*) I know as good a tune
to roast beef as e'er a man in England—when I've got my
knife and fork to play it with!
MISS WILMOT. Well said, Bob! And what else do you know,
Bob?
BOB. Why I can skate, Miss; and I can swim, Miss; and I can cud-
gel, Miss; and I can Box,—

---

1  *allemande*: i.e., dance an allemande, a German dance.
2  *O the roast Beef ... roast beef*: a song from Fielding's *The Grub-Street Opera* (1731),
   III.iii.46-7, subsequently expanded by Richard Leveridge. Martin C. Battestin notes of
   "roast beef," "it became traditional for theatre audiences throughout the century to
   sing it heartily before and after *any* new play, and even between acts" (*Henry Fielding: A
   Life* [London: Routledge, 1989], 114).

MISS WILMOT. What! can you fight? O delightful! How I should like to see you! But I'm shut up from every thing—except a heap of musty old books. Do, Bob, let me see how you fight!

NURSE. Suppose, Miss, your Papa was to come down, and ask 90 what you are about? What would you say then?

MISS WILMOT. O, I should leave you to find excuses, Nursey. I never speak before Papa.

NURSE. No, Miss, you make your Papa believe you're as meek as a lamb; and the moment he goes away, you turn the house out 95 of windows.

MISS WILMOT. Why, Nurse, Papa's so dismal dull! always setting one to study! I wonder what's the use of Books, Nurse? If Papa had as many words of his own as I have, he would not be always wanting to be poring over other people's so. I can 100 find enough to say of myself. And I'm sure that's cleverer. Do you love reading, Miss Henny?

MISS HENNY. Yes, Miss, I like my book well enough; but Brother Bob's a great Dunce at it. Mother never could beat his learning into his head. 105

BOB. You might be ashamed of yourself Henny!

MISS WILMOT. Not at all, Bob. I like you the better. I hate reading, too. Come hither, Bob.

NURSE (*whispering*). Miss, you're enough to drive one crazy! Did not I tell you I had something to say to you of the most high- 110 est consequence?

MISS WILMOT. Come hither when I bid you, Bob. Can you play at questions and commands?

MISS HENNY. No, Miss, Brother Bob can't; but I can, Miss.

MISS WILMOT. Then I'll teach him. 115

NURSE. Miss, I declare I'll tell your Papa.

MISS WILMOT (*to* BOB). If you were placed at the tip top of a high precipice, with me, and Miss Henny, and Nurse—which would you throw down into the Sea? And which would you leave to have her Eyes pecked out by the crows? And which 120 would you carry down in your arms?

BOB. I know which I'd carry down in my arms!

MISS WILMOT (*laughing*). What, Miss Henny?

BOB. No; I'd leave her to be pecked by the crows, because she'd peck well again: but I know who! 125

MISS WILMOT (*smiling*). Nurse, then?

BOB. No; I'd throw her into the Sea.

NURSE. Well, Miss, if I don't go and call your Papa,—say I'm a rogue! (*going*)

130 MISS WILMOT (*running after her*). And if you do go and call him, Nurse—say I'm a fool!

NURSE. I won't be held, Miss! I won't!

MISS WILMOT (*throwing her arms round* NURSE'*s neck*). What! not in my Arms, Nursy?

135 NURSE. Nor I won't be coaxed, Miss, I won't! I'll go and tell your Papa all your tricks at once.

MISS WILMOT. What, Nurse, what! be unkind to your own Popsey? No, Nurse, no! dear sweet Nurse, no! You have not the heart. You look so pretty, Nurse!

140 NURSE. But I have! but I have!

MISS WILMOT. Ah, Nurse, do you forget how you used to love me? And to dandle me in your arms? And how you fondled me, and fed me, and patted me, and danced me? And how you called me your own sweet little popsey? Ah, Nurse! And

145 how you tossed me up and down so merrily, with (*sings*)

> O my Kitten, my Kitten,
>  And O my Kitten, my dearee!
> Such a sweet Child as This
>  There neither is far nor nearee;

150 Here we go up, up, up —[1]

Ah, Nursey, Nursey! (*kissing her*)

NURSE. Ah, Miss, Miss, you'd coax over a Lion! If you'd only be quiet a minute, now, and listen to what I've got to say to you—

155 BOB (*peeping out of the room*). Lud! there's the Gentleman's door opening!

MISS WILMOT. O help! help!—up with the Books!—quick!—quick!

---

1 *O my Kitten ... up*: from stanza one of "The Nurse's Song," published in volume four of Allan Ramsay's *Tea-Table Miscellany* (1740), and once attributed to Jonathan Swift. See Iona and Peter Opie, eds., *The Oxford Dictionary of Nursery Rhymes* (Oxford: Clarendon Press, 1951), 255.

*They scamper about, and pick up all the Books, and* MISS WILMOT
*seizes one of them, and seats herself demurely,*
*as at the beginning of the Scene.*

MISS HENNY. Why now, Bob, I've peeped, and the Gentleman's
door's as fast shut as can be! 160
MISS WILMOT. How! Is it a trick?—Come hither, Bob! I'll give
you such a command!—Here! stand on your Elbows, and
sing a song!
BOB. No, Miss, thankee; I'd rather run on my feet! (*runs off*)
MISS WILMOT. Stop him! (*running after him*) stop him! 165
NURSE. Stop her! (*following*) stop her!
MISS HENNY. La, me! that a young lady can behave so comical!

Scene v

*A Lawn before the house of* LADY SMATTER.

YOUNG WAVERLEY *and the* STEWARD, *meeting.*

STEWARD. I am glad to meet you so near this house, Sir. I hope
you have made a good beginning?
YOUNG WAVERLEY. O Stephens, I am a lost man—and a made
man at once! Here, all prospers;—but there!—O Stephens,
there!—in our old avenue, just by—the loveliest Girl in the 5
World is now wandering with the loveliest Mother!
STEWARD. What do you mean, Sir?
YOUNG WAVERLEY. Mean? That I am the unhappiest fellow
breathing! that I have been conversing with the Mother,
while looking at the Daughter, that my wits are gone to one, 10
and my heart is flown to the other, and that—
STEWARD. Ah, Sir, I see, plainly enough, how you are a lost man!
But I want to find out how you are a made one; what did you
mean by that, Sir?
YOUNG WAVERLEY. That I am the luckiest rogue upon Earth!— 15
That Lady Smatter's first reception authorized a second
attack; and her second, has invited a third; and that I have not
a doubt but the mansion and jointure will be mine upon the
first summons.

20 STEWARD. See, my dear young Gentleman—the door opens!—
YOUNG WAVERLEY. Why then—I must needs enter—and take
possession! There's no help!—'Tis, at least, the shortest way
to riches; and, as my brain has no relish for study, and my
hands have none for labour, the easiest. (*Goes to the* PORTER)
25 Is Lady Smatter at leisure, Sir?
PORTER. Yes, Sir.
YOUNG WAVERLEY. Well! it must be so!—(*aside, and entering the
house*) Adieu, then, sweet Girl of the avenue, adieu!
STEWARD. I would not desire a better business than this. I war-
30 rant Sir Roderick will be tired of looking out for another
heir! and then I, who have served him so long, must needs
stand next. This may turn out as pretty an affair as a man
could wish.

*Exit.*

Scene vi

LADY SMATTER's *Dressing Room.*

LADY SMATTER *seated*; PRIM *waiting.*

LADY SMATTER. Didst thou observe that youth as he went hence,
Prim?
PRIM. Yes, my lady. A sweet young man, indeed.
LADY SMATTER. Ah, Prim, youth is attractive—but how he
5 comes to find such attractions in me, who certainly am not—
quite—so young as himself—
PRIM. Ah, my lady, but your Ladyship is so wise!—I'm sure I
believe your ladyship knows all the books in the whole
world!
10 LADY SMATTER. Why no, Prim, not quite; but most of them, I
confess. My only misfortune is a bad memory. It puzzles my
quotations amazingly.
PRIM. That's pity, I'm sure, my lady. I suppose your ladyship was
not troubled with that misfortune before being in years?
15 LADY SMATTER. In years?

PRIM. I beg pardon, I am sure, my lady, for speaking so unthinking.

LADY SMATTER. In years? Why a bad memory is a sign of youth.
Don't you know what the Poet says?

PRIM. No, my lady.                                                    20

LADY SMATTER. A warm imagination, says Goldsmith—ay,
Goldsmith,—or else Otway,
    Where beams of warm imagination play,
    The memory's soft powers fade away.[1]
Now Imagination, Prim, as has been observed by the Philoso-     25
phers, is our earliest gift;—earliest, in the language of poetry,
means most youthful; now which do you think likely to be
wrong, Otway and the Philosophers, or you, Mrs. Prim?

PRIM. Why I don't know the Gentlemen, my lady, but I suppose
it most likely to be me; for I dare say the Book Writers know     30
best.

LADY SMATTER. 'Tis strange, however, Sir Roderick should not
have answered my note. Could I once force him to see me, he
would struggle in vain: my chains again would entangle him,
and, as Prior—                                                       35

Scene vii

*Enter* FOOTMAN.

FOOTMAN. Young Mr. Waverley, my lady.

*Prim goes out.*

*Enter* YOUNG WAVERLEY.

LADY SMATTER. Is it possible? Have you been so obliging as to
run over that thick quarto so expeditiously?

YOUNG WAVERLEY. Yes Ma'am, I have … run over it!

LADY SMATTER. Well, I envy the facility of a general lover of lit-    5

---

1   *Where beams … fade away*: from Pope's *An Essay on Criticism* (1711): "Where Beams of
warm *Imagination* play, / The *Memory's* soft Figures melt away" (ll. 58-9).

erature amazingly! But alas! the danger, as a very great writer
has said, of popularity! Painful pre-eminence![1] says Parnel. I,
now, am absolutely obliged, by my extended reputation, to be
difficult.

10 YOUNG WAVERLEY. How a poor Author must tremble, madam,
when he comes under your examination!

LADY SMATTER. Why yes, I am a little formidable, I am afraid.
But how can one help being celebrated?

YOUNG WAVERLEY. Talents, madam, such as your ladyship's—

15 LADY SMATTER. Why,—to be candid,—there is something
rather elegant, I own, in a taste for these kinds of pursuits.
The study of the fine arts certainly gives a sort of glow to the
polish of a complete education. I hope you think so, Mr.
Waverley?

20 YOUNG WAVERLEY. I?—O yes, Ma'am! perfectly!

LADY SMATTER. The learned, Mr. Waverley, are all of one opinion. And yet, study, study, as my friend Waller says, is but a
fatiguing thing. It requires such thought! I assure you, sometimes, I think till I am quite stupid.

*Enter* PRIM.

25 PRIM. A gentlewoman below, my lady, begs to see your ladyship.

LADY SMATTER. A Gentlewoman? O, some votary to the Muses,
with a new dedication, I suppose. Well, tell her to wait.

*Exit* PRIM.

'Tis astonishing how I am found out by these daughters of
Apollo.[2] The Sages of old were fond of asserting, as I doubt
30 not you have remarked, that we are all open to distinction. I
rather think the observation is Bacon's. Is it?—or the elder
Pliny's? one of those Fathers of the arts and languages.

---

1   *Painful pre-eminence*: from Addison's *Cato* (1713). In *The Witlings* (p. 90, note 3) Lady
Smatter misquotes the phrase as "fatal pre-eminence." Her favourite, Pope, also uses the
phrase in *An Essay on Man*: "Painful preheminence! yourself to view / Above life's
weakness, and its comforts too" (IV. 267-8).

2   *daughters of Apollo*: Apollo was traditionally depicted as the patron of poetry and music.

*Re-enter* PRIM.

PRIM. The Gentlewoman, madam, says she comes upon an affair of great importance, and begs your ladyship will be so good as to admit her. 35

LADY SMATTER. Observe, Mr. Waverley, how burthensome is Fame. In what sort of way does she come?

PRIM. Only on foot, my lady. 'Tis the Gentlewoman that nobody knows, that came t'other day to the village.

YOUNG WAVERLEY. Indeed!—Her?— 40

LADY SMATTER. Tell her, then, some other time—

YOUNG WAVERLEY. No!—admit her now!—dear madam, admit her now!—

LADY SMATTER. How? do you know her?

YOUNG WAVERLEY. N ... o,—but if she be distressed,—'twill be 45 so good, so amiable in your ladyship—

LADY SMATTER. Well, then, let's e'en see what sort of a Sappho we have got so near us. Bid her come in.

PRIM. She desires, my lady, to speak to your ladyship by yourself.

YOUNG WAVERLEY. I'll be off instantly. 50

LADY SMATTER. By no means. You must positively see how I Mecenas it with these fair Muses. Tell her I have only a friend with me.

*Exit* PRIM.

YOUNG WAVERLEY (*aside*). This must be my divine widow—O, should her daughter, too,— 55

LADY SMATTER. You look thoughtful, Mr. Waverley. I fear this intrusion disconcerts you: for sensibility, says a favorite author of mine, sensibility is soon embarrassed.

Scene viii

*Enter* PRIM, *followed by* ELEONORA.

PRIM. Here's the Gentlewoman, my lady.

*Exit.*

ELEONORA, *a handkerchief held to her Face, and her Eyes fixed on the ground, courtsies gravely to* LADY SMATTER, *and stands still.* LADY SMATTER *returns a little nod, and seats herself on an arm Chair.*

YOUNG WAVERLEY (*aside*). Yes! 'tis She! and her daughter must be left walking alone! How the deuce can I get to her?

LADY SMATTER. Won't you have a Chair, Mr. Waverley?

5 ELEONORA (*starting*). I had entreated the honor of seeing your ladyship alone.

YOUNG WAVERLEY. O, ay, true; I'll take a little turn.

*Exit abruptly.*

LADY SMATTER. Mr. Waverley!—I beg,—I insist—(*rising to follow him*).

ELEONORA (*advancing*). I beseech you, madam!—one little
10 instant—to privacy—and to pity!

LADY SMATTER. To pity I am always open, for, as Dryden, you doubtless know, says, Pity is the Muse's friend: but as to privacy—

ELEONORA. Ah, madam! think but how many are the interests
15 that here demand it!

LADY SMATTER. How many? Are you come to me, then, as one of the Nine,[1] to plead the cause of the other Eight?

ELEONORA. Lady Smatter!

LADY SMATTER (*returning to her seat*). Mrs. Sappho?

20 ELEONORA. Do you not know me?

LADY SMATTER. Know you? Have you ever brought me any of your works before?

ELEONORA. Alas, I ought not to wonder I am forgotten! Sorrow is a yet more fatal foe to remembrance than even Time,—
25 though Time has dragged on seventeen heavy years since last we met; but Sorrow—O Lady Smatter! in the scales of Sorrow they have weighed as so many centuries!

LADY SMATTER. How? What!—why surely—you are not—you cannot be—

---

1  *one of the Nine*: i.e., the nine muses.

ELEONORA. Yes, madam,—you see before you the unhappy Wife 30
of your misguided Brother!
LADY SMATTER. Eleonora!
ELEONORA. The hapless, persecuted, fugitive Eleonora!
LADY SMATTER. And is it possible you have the courage to present yourself at my door? 35
ELEONORA. O Lady Smatter! forbear this scorn, this cruelty!
LADY SMATTER. Cruelty? upon my word! the term is curious!
Your absconding, then, from your husband and family, and
selecting—as Shakespeare has it,—Your own Companion for
your chosen days—[1] 40
ELEONORA. Hold, madam, hold! I pretend not to ignorance of
these barbarous aspersions; I cannot be unconscious of the
calumny and contumely to which I am a victim; yet even
while my heart is sinking beneath their pressure, my Ear is
not familiar to their shock! 45
LADY SMATTER. Well, if this is not,—as Parnel says,—ineffably
amazing, I am no judge! Is it thus a person should speak, who
ought to be bowed down to the Earth, and begging for
mercy?
ELEONORA. I thought myself subdued! I came with the most 50
abject views of imploring your compassion and assistance; but
the spirit which silent affliction had sunk, indignant resentment now rouses! and since you venture, Lady Smatter, to vil-
ify me to myself, I no longer conjure—I demand a hearing!
LADY SMATTER. O Day and Night—as Pope has it—but this is 55
wond'rous strange![2] And what is it can thus embolden you in
my presence?
ELEONORA. Innocence, and Injury!
LADY SMATTER. Innocence? Well, indeed, may the confidence of
vice be a topic for Locke and Newton! After sixteen or sev- 60
enteen years concealment, with a person with whom one
elopes—
ELEONORA. Have a care, Lady Smatter! There is a certain point
beyond which endurance ceases! Change not the courage of

---

1  Your own Companion for your chosen days: misquoting Oliver Goldsmith's The Deserted
   Village (1770): "The fond companion of his helpless years" (l. 376).
2  O Day and Night ... strange: Horatio's words in Shakespeare's Hamlet (I.v.172).

65 innocence, for the defiance of Despair! Hear me!—Hear
me!—

LADY SMATTER. Nay, then, I must really ring for my people. (*rising*) A conference such as this is too great a degradation.
Bacon, the great Bacon himself—

70 ELEONORA. Nay, I must be heard! The time of mute forbearance
is over; I must be heard!—Ring—call your people, if you
please; your people, then, will hear me, too! will hear—that it
is—your Brother! ... not his unhappy Wife, who should
bow to the Earth, and supplicate for mercy!

75 LADY SMATTER (*returning to her seat*). I am in a torpor!—from
very amazement! as the Poets have it.

ELEONORA. Ah, yet deign a moment, to spare my irritated nerves
this dreadful asperity! As a Suppliant, not a defier, I meant to
present myself; and as such, again, permit me, candidly, kindly

80 permit me to entreat your patience, while I claim your justice!

LADY SMATTER. Well, if I must hear you—tell me, at least, what
is become of your Captain?

ELEONORA. Insupportable! yet is this no more than I ought to

85 have expected, from the representations that have been made.
Hear, however, the plain narrative. The fatal partiality of Captain Ludlow, which proved as unconquerable as it was unwarrantable, began during our voyage to the West Indies. Your
Brother perceived it, with an inquietude that broke his peace,

90 and destroyed my happiness. —

LADY SMATTER. That was unfortunate, to be sure!

ELEONORA. His uneasiness I thought injurious; my displeasure at
it he deemed indifference. Always in the same vessel, I could
not avoid the sight of Captain Ludlow, whose regard, though

95 constantly demonstrated, was never avowed;—in brief, a few
weeks after we landed, they fought, and Captain Ludlow was
dangerously wounded. —O fatal day! overpowered with its
horror, my husband surprised me in a deluge of tears—

LADY SMATTER. For Captain Ludlow, no doubt?

100 ELEONORA. Again must I hear the unfounded accusation? No,
madam! my husband's safety was precious to my heart, of
which he was undivided master: but his jealousy—his vio-

lence—let me avoid detail! My resentment, though not so vehement, was as deep as his own; and, in a cruel moment of rash recrimination, we agreed to separate. He allowed me my settlement, but refused me my Child—and—and—

LADY SMATTER. You were forced, therefore, to console yourself with your Captain?

ELEONORA. O Lady Smatter, if with so little faith you have heard me, how ill am I repaid for the dreadful effort with which I have quitted my retirement, and ventured upon making this intrusion! My Brother Roderick refuses to see or to hear from me; it was, therefore, my desperate, yet last recourse, to apply to you as a mediatrix;—for your Brother—accident has informed me—your Brother is shortly expected in England.

LADY SMATTER. Expected? Don't you know he is come?

ELEONORA. Come?

LADY SMATTER. Yes.

ELEONORA. To England?

LADY SMATTER. To England? ay, to this village.

ELEONORA. To this village?

LADY SMATTER. To this village? yes; to the very Inn just by.

ELEONORA. O Heaven! can it be? And may these Eyes—that once doated on his sight—Alas, no! he comes but with confirmed hate, and determined belief in my unworthiness!—or comes but to claim the last treasured tie—Name me not to him! forget my application—my apparition—forget even my defence—yet no!—O rather plead my cause! Awaken his Soul to Justice—and his heart will soon return to Love, to generosity, to its original attributes! O! I know him well!—he has not known himself!

LADY SMATTER (aside). I think I hear young Waverley return; I must get rid of her. I presume, as I expect my Brother every moment—

ELEONORA. Ah, let me, then, begone! not here, not thus must I risk a meeting upon which hangs life or death! Pardon, Lady Smatter, the importunity with which I have assailed you;—I must leave my story—and my petition incomplete: your Brother will probably—but I will wait his purpose. I must not, it seems, commend myself to your friendship, but suffer me, even yet, to plead against your enmity!

LADY SMATTER. How truly have the Poets said Nothing is surprising! But—let me see; what of my manuscript offerings
145     shall I look out for this pleasing youth, to give him some idea
how I stand with the Muses of the day;
Mecenas, sure, in female guise!
Were Sir Roderick less flinty, with such noble powers of
patronage, I might awake every morning to an Ode or a Son-
150     net, meet an Elegy at my breakfast, a Lampoon at my dinner,
and find the whole Day interwoven between Tragedy and
Comedy.

*Exit.*

# ACT III

## Scene i

*A Cottage.*

*Enter* ELEONORA, *hastily shutting her door.*

ELEONORA. So! I am safe! Safe?—From whom? My husband?—
And is it I who fly him? I, who scarcely knew the use of
sight, but to seek his Eyes—of hearing, but to listen to his
voice? O Wilmot!—in what temper of mind com'st thou at
last? Is it utterly to demolish me, by snatching away my 5
Child? or to call back my lost happiness, by restoring me thyself?—Where is Sophia—? (*calling up a small stair case*)
Sophia! She is not returned. Should she meet him—but he
would not know her. My Child!

## Scene ii

*Enter* SOPHIA.

SOPHIA. My dear Mother!
ELEONORA. Why hast thou been so late?—Thou art agitated?
SOPHIA. A—little!—I—I met again—that young man—
ELEONORA. And did he speak to thee?
SOPHIA. O yes! 5
ELEONORA. He did?—And … on what subject?
SOPHIA. He talked of nothing but … you—and me, my dear
Mother.
ELEONORA. And how?
SOPHIA. O, with every mark of the kindest interest! He spoke of 10
our retirement, our coming hither, our motives, our plans, and
most of all, our wishes. If he could learn them, he said, it
would be his whole delight to fulfil them. How kind!—in so
new an aquaintance, my dear Mother!
ELEONORA. My innocent Girl!—yet, as I have discovered him to 15

be thy own distant Relation, I am not uneasy at his assiduity to please thee.

SOPHIA. O, if you had but seen him, my dear Mother!—

ELEONORA. Hast thou totally, then, forgotten to enquire about thy aunt?

SOPHIA. O no, indeed! I was just going to ask how she did.

ELEONORA. How she did?

SOPHIA (*confused*). I mean—how she received you!—

ELEONORA. As I might have expected—but not as I knew how to bear! That, however, once past, is unimportant.—Sophia!

SOPHIA. My Mother?

ELEONORA. Thy Father, my Child—

SOPHIA. What, my dear Mother?

ELEONORA. Thy Father—wilt thou yet cling to me, Sophia?

SOPHIA. O, while I live!

ELEONORA. Thy Father is arrived—is here!—I am sick,—oh!—

SOPHIA. My dearest Mother!

ELEONORA. O Sophia! that my husband should be here—and I should not fly to meet him!—that thy Father should arrive—and I should dread his fondness for thee!

SOPHIA. Let us hope the best, let us hope he comes to be good and kind to us, to chear us, my dear Mother, to receive and to protect us.

ELEONORA. Thee, my Child, could he view and know, he must indeed love: but my cruel uncertainty of his state of mind and intentions, compels me, now, to communicate all I have hitherto forborn revealing.

SOPHIA. I will be very prudent; trust me without fear.

ELEONORA. On the fatal morning of our separation, when I begged thee of him, his refusal was so peremptory, so disgraceful, and so heart-breaking, I could not submit to it;— my dear Child, I must now confess—I owe thee not to his consent!

SOPHIA. But I hope you soon will, my dear Mother!

ELEONORA. I pretend not to vindicate the desperate step of taking thee without his knowledge—yet how could I bear to leave thee? Not alone to be torn from the joy of thy loved sight—the charm of thy look, the fascination of thy infantine caresses, but to know that thou wouldst be bred to blush for me, and tutored to abhor me—all danger, all wrath, all vengeance were sooner endured, and I thought myself authorized by maternal duty to prevail with thy Nurse clandestinely to relinquish thee.

SOPHIA. She was a dear good Nurse to let me go with you. I shall always love her for it, I am sure.

ELEONORA. Yet though unknown to him I took thee, I did not unknown to him detain thee; I left for him a Letter, with the Nurse, which rather courted than deprecated a pursuit—a recall. Neither ensued; and from thy childhood to this moment, thou hast known but one Parent.

SOPHIA. Ah, what a Parent! O my Mother! 'twould have been too much happiness to have had another quite as kind!

ELEONORA. And yet—till this fatal warp of jealousy, not more noble than gentle was his nature. Immediately on my arrival in England, I wrote to my Brother Roderick; he sent back my Letter unanswered: I wrote then to Lady Smatter; but with no better success. Thee I have named to neither, lest, while spurning the Mother, they might propose,—with yet greater severity, receiving the daughter.

SOPHIA. Ah! could any one be so cruel!

ELEONORA. Since then, without a struggle, because without a hope, I have resigned myself to silent obscurity; living only, my Sophia, for thy sake and through thy cares.

SOPHIA. Let me hope you will now begin to live again for yourself, also! and that we may bless for ever the happy chance which brought to your view the news-paper, that announced my father's leaving the West Indies, and induced you to quit your retreat, that here, should he come, he might find you.

ELEONORA. Wouldst thou, then, Sophia, allure me again to the regions of Hope? Awaken the sensitive feelings that tremble at every sound? call forth the illusions of fond expectation? and bid my sad heart beat once more to a prospect of joy?

SOPHIA. And why not, my dear Mother?

ELEONORA. Ah, who can tell thy Father's purposes? I would fain have procured the support of Lady Smatter, or Sir Roderick; but with Lady Smatter I have wholly failed, and my plan of surprising Sir Roderick into an interview, I have no longer courage to execute. No! I have done. All must now take its course.

95 SOPHIA. Nay, lose not your spirits, my dearest Mother. This is just about the hour they told us Sir Roderick usually walks in the great avenue: one more effort!

ELEONORA. It cannot be, my Child! mental strength, as well as bodily, has its term. Mine is exhausted! (*seats herself*)

100 SOPHIA. You affright me! Shall I go to my Uncle Roderick myself?

ELEONORA. Could he see thee without reference to thy unhappy Mother, thy artless persuasions might perhaps engage his regard—Ill-fated Sophia! to belong to a Mother thus univer-
105 sally abandoned! Wilt thou not renounce me, too, that Fortune may be more propitious to thee?

SOPHIA. You affright me more and more! Let me go to my Uncle—let me bring him to comfort you!

ELEONORA. Thy Uncle, Sophia, will not hear my name;—nor
110 will thy Aunt; nor will thy Father!—Is it not time it should be obliterated from thy memory, too, my poor Girl?

SOPHIA. O do not talk so!—I will force myself into his presence—I will bring him without saying who you are—I can watch his leaving his house, that I may know him; and I will
115 plead to him, kneel to him, to accompany me hither, without naming you: and once here, once in your sight,—O my Mother, how soon will he love you again! May I go?

ELEONORA (*sighing*). Do what thou wilt!

SOPHIA. Come, then, my dear Mother, come to your room, and
120 repose till I return.

ELEONORA. Do what thou wilt! I have no life left but thine!

*Exeunt by the little stairs.*

# Scene iii

*An Avenue to* SIR RODERICK'S *house.*

*Enter* YOUNG WAVERLEY, *followed by the* STEWARD.

YOUNG WAVERLEY. O Stephens! Stephens! don't torment me! —
She's the loveliest Creature! —
STEWARD. But has she the fifty thousand pounds, Sir?
YOUNG WAVERLEY. She has youth, Stephens! Youth, beauty,
loveliness! —                                                  5
STEWARD. But the fifty thousand pounds, Sir?
YOUNG WAVERLEY. She has gentleness, Stephens! gentleness,
innocence, sweetness! Five hundred fifty thousands cannot
purchase such gifts. I have met her, at last, alone, I have con-
versed with her, Stephens, and—                                10
STEWARD. But have you forgotten the fifty thousand?
YOUNG WAVERLEY. What can they do for me, Stephens? What
can all the pelf [1] in the world do for me, without a Partner in
its enjoyment? Will a House give Happiness?—inhabit it
alone, 'tis a mere shelter from storms: a Carriage, delight?     15
enter it without a companion,—'tis a mere Machine to doze
in: a Table, pleasure? Eat at it singly —'tis a mere coaxer—to
Apoplexy!
STEWARD. Why, I understood, Sir, you thought all these things
quite necessary?                                                20
YOUNG WAVERLEY. So I did, Stephens, till I saw so divine a
Creature without any of them.
STEWARD. Can you really, then, Sir, give up such riches, just as
they are falling into your hands?
YOUNG WAVERLEY. No, I shan't give them up, neither; I am not  25
so mad as that: but drudgery, Stephens,—Man was not made
to live by drudgery alone. A little recreation mixt with it has
a very pretty effect. Off, therefore, I glide, to recruit my spirits
at the cottage of my dainty widow, and afterwards —
STEWARD. Ah, my dear young Gentleman, if you don't make all  30
sure at my lady's first, you may get yourself into such a scrape

---

1   *pelf:* property acquired by fraud or theft.

at your dainty widow's as you'll never get out of! And then—what becomes of the independance you were in such a hurry about?

35 YOUNG WAVERLEY. O, ay, true, Stephens! I must have my independence. You are right, there!

STEWARD. Better, then, declare yourself at once to her ladyship, after which—

YOUNG WAVERLEY. Declare myself, Stephens? Declare what?
40 You don't think I have the face to declare I am in love with her?

STEWARD. Why no, that may not be necessary, Sir, provided you can ask if she be in love with you.

YOUNG WAVERLEY. Why ay, Stephens, if that will do—But how
45 the devil can I enter upon such a subject with her? I am a horrid hand at keeping my countenance. I shall make some shocking grimace, and spoil all.

STEWARD. Suppose you write, then, Sir? She's prodigious fond of Letters.

50 YOUNG WAVERLEY. Write? So I will, Stephens.—You have just made me hit upon a short cut to her heart: I'll write in verse! Lord Smatter won her from Sir Roderick by one couplet; and I will win her from Books and Authors—of which she knows nothing but scraps and the names,—by another.

55 STEWARD. That will be the very thing, Sir. And, to avoid any accident, I will carry your Letter myself.

YOUNG WAVERLEY. Well, then, I'll e'en go scribble. 'Tis but a pitiful imitation of her first lord, to be sure; but it's better than telling a hundred lies at her feet. So now—favour me, ye
60 Muses!

*Exit.*

STEWARD. Well, this is managed as cleverly as a man need wish, and Sir Roderick's fortune will fall as naturally into my hands—Zooks! if the very Girl is not coming this way!—how lucky they did not meet! I'll go keep him tight to his job
65 till it's done.

*Exit.*

Scene iv

*Enter* SOPHIA, *frequently looking behind her.*

SOPHIA. I hope I have not mistaken his walk! It must certainly be
my Uncle who came out of the house: I distinctly heard him
say he should soon be home again. — O, here he is! —

Scene v

*Enter* OLD WAVERLEY, *thoughtfully, holding
a thick-headed stick to his mouth.*

SOPHIA (*aside*). Yes, 'tis the same! Now what can I say? — I don't
know how to begin!
OLD WAVERLEY (*to himself*). I was but a fool for being affronted,
neither.
SOPHIA (*aside*). If he should happen to fall into one of those terri-   5
ble passions to which they say he is subject! —
OLD WAVERLEY (*to himself*). But 'twas very provoking, very pro-
voking, certainly. I could have swallowed any thing else; I'm a
pretty good swallower.
SOPHIA. I had no notion how difficult—He is going! — I must   10
say any thing to stop him—Sir! (*running after him*)—Sir! —
OLD WAVERLEY (*looking round*). Does any body call?
SOPHIA. Sir—
OLD WAVERLEY. Ma'am?
SOPHIA (*aside, and retreating*). I am frightened to death!   15
OLD WAVERLEY. Did you speak to me, ma'm?
SOPHIA. Sir, I—I—I only —(*aside*) I am ready to sink! —
OLD WAVERLEY. I beg your pardon, ma'am; I thought you
spoke. (*walking on*)
SOPHIA (*aside*). What can I say? What can I do? He is going   20
again! —(*following him*) Sir! —
OLD WAVERLEY (*turning short round*). Ma'am?
SOPHIA. Sir, I—I—I beg—I—(*aside*) if he should fall into one of
his rages!
OLD WAVERLEY. Pray, ma'am, did you want any thing?   25
SOPHIA. No, Sir, I—I—

OLD WAVERLEY. No? And pray, ma'am, did not you call me?
SOPHIA. Yes, Sir,—that is, I—I—
OLD WAVERLEY. And what for, then, ma'am?
30 SOPHIA. I beseech you, Sir, not to be angry! I only —
OLD WAVERLEY. Angry? Bless me! what should I be angry for?
SOPHIA. O, if I dared hope you would not—
OLD WAVERLEY. Why I have not such a thought!—(*aside*) She's a prodigious pretty Creature!
35 SOPHIA. I should take courage, and conjure you—
OLD WAVERLEY. Why do so, then. Why should not you?— (*aside*) Quite a young Girl, I declare!
SOPHIA. May I? do you give me leave? How unexpected is this kindness! O Sir! you gladden my heart!
40 OLD WAVERLEY. Gladden your heart? Why that's a good thing; but I can't think how I have done it.
SOPHIA. You have filled me with hope and joy!
OLD WAVERLEY. Have I indeed? Well, that's odd enough! But pray, ma'am, what do you mean?
45 SOPHIA. I cannot, just now, explain—unless you command me!
OLD WAVERLEY. I command you?—Bless me!—how should I think of commanding you?
SOPHIA. If I might venture—might request—might entreat—
OLD WAVERLEY (*aside*). How timid she is! how modest and
50 timid!
SOPHIA. You would condescend to accompany me for a few minutes—
OLD WAVERLEY (*staring*). Ha?
SOPHIA. To that cottage—
55 OLD WAVERLEY. What!—
SOPHIA. Not twenty yards off—only down there—
OLD WAVERLEY (*after a pause*). O ho, that's the case, is it?— who'd have thought it? with such a squeamish air?—
SOPHIA. You are not offended, I hope? Indeed you must not be
60 offended.
OLD WAVERLEY (*looking another way*). Must not I?
SOPHIA. O no, dear Sir!—
OLD WAVERLEY (*to himself*). Dear Sir! ay, ay, I see how it is!
SOPHIA. Awaken not again the fears with which I first addressed
65 you!

OLD WAVERLEY (*aside*). O, she feared me, did she? I suppose she took me for the Justice!

SOPHIA. But which your gentleness has removed; for your goodness now opens to me such a support—

OLD WAVERLEY (*aside*). A support? Bless my heart!—She thinks to take me in to maintain her! I'd best be off. Good by to you, ma'am. 70

SOPHIA. Will you not grant my petition? Will you not go with me?

OLD WAVERLEY. No, ma'am; I never go to ... Cottages!— 75

SOPHIA. O, you must not refuse me! you must not say me nay! Dear Sir! say me not nay!

OLD WAVERLEY (*aside*). What a coaxing little vixen it is! Bless me! that a bad Girl can have such winning ways! (*going*) Good by, I say, ma'am. I can't go with you. 80

SOPHIA. Cruel disappointment!—Alas, my Mother!

OLD WAVERLEY (*returning*). Mother? Have you a Mother?

SOPHIA. Yes, and in the deepest distress!

OLD WAVERLEY. I'n't that a—tell the truth! tell the truth, now!—i'n't that a great story? 85

SOPHIA. O Heavens, no!

OLD WAVERLEY. Do you live, then, with a real Relation?

SOPHIA. I do, indeed! with the most deserving—and the most unhappy in the world!

OLD WAVERLEY. Do you? Why then I am very glad of it! for 90 here have I been ill-natured enough to think—well, I won't tell you what I thought: but I see you are a very modest young Girl. And how long has your poor Mother been in this sad way?

SOPHIA. Do not ask me just now, Sir; in a very short time, I will 95 explain every thing.

OLD WAVERLEY. In a very short time? why do you suppose you and I shall ever see one another again?

SOPHIA. O, I hope so! again, and again, and again!

OLD WAVERLEY. Do you indeed? odd enough! And pray what 100 do you hope it for?

SOPHIA. Ah, Sir, I must not let you know, at present, half I hope from you!

OLD WAVERLEY. Yes, you may; what is it?

105 SOPHIA. Protection, countenance, and benevolence!

OLD WAVERLEY (*aside*). She's as innocent as a Dove! (*feeling for his purse*) Well, I must send something, then, for your poor Mother.

SOPHIA. Send? O no! carry it yourself! honour our Cottage with
110     your presence. It is You, only, I wish for!

OLD WAVERLEY. Me? (*aside*)—Odder and odder! I can't tell what to make of her! So you'd really like to see me again?

SOPHIA. See you? O Sir, I should like to live with you!

OLD WAVERLEY. To live with me? (*aside*)—Well, this is particu-
115     lar, or nothing is! Who could have believed, at my time of life, such a modest young Girl could have taken such a fancy to me?

SOPHIA. May I hope you will put my truth to the test?

OLD WAVERLEY. Why, as to that,—as to our living together—
120     (*aside*) I can't say any thing cross to her, now!—as to that, I say, my dear,—it might set the World a prating, you know.

SOPHIA. The World?

OLD WAVERLEY. Yes; the World's duced[1] ill-natured, when it sets about it! very duced!

125 SOPHIA. O, let not that be an obstacle to your generosity! The World would only approve it!

OLD WAVERLEY. Approve it? Poor little Thing! she's as ignorant as a Lamb when it goes to the Butcher!—No, my dear, no! you don't know what you talk of. The World would say vile
130     things of us.

SOPHIA. O, but I know a way to prevent that!

OLD WAVERLEY. Do you?

SOPHIA. A way to make all right and clear to the whole World, and every body in it applaud the measure, and esteem you for
135     your kindness in befriending me.

OLD WAVERLEY (*aside*). If I don't believe she means I might marry her! bless my heart! But you spoke just now of your Mother; what would she say if you were to come and live with me?

140 SOPHIA. My Mother? O, she would be delighted! enchanted!

---

1   *duced*: variant of deuced, confounded; unlucky.

OLD WAVERLEY. (*aside*) Would she indeed?—why then her Mother, at least, must be stark naught! what a vile old Hag!— I must put an end to this: if Sir Roderick should come, and see me with a young Girl!—Well, good by, my dear.

SOPHIA. Will you not accompany me, then?—Can you, at last, be so cruel? 145

OLD WAVERLEY (*aside*). There, now, there! She's very touching! something very touching in her manner! Why no, no;—I can't be cruel to you, my dear;—I can't be that; so don't fret; I tell you what; suppose I follow you? We can't quite so well walk together, you know; but don't take on, my dear;—I'll follow you. 150

SOPHIA. O how kind! A thousand thanks! Down there, then, Sir,—that is the house.

OLD WAVERLEY. I see it, I see it! Good by. 155

SOPHIA. You'll surely not fail?

OLD WAVERLEY. I won't, I won't: only go first, my dear.

SOPHIA. I obey. Pray, pray come quickly!

*Exit.*

OLD WAVERLEY. Here's a thing, now! here's a sorceress, to entangle a man before he's aware. O she's a little witch!—And quite modest! But it's odd to take such a liking to a man at my time of day! And all at first sight, too!—She certainly wants me to marry her! She knows a way to make all the World approve our living together? Yes, yes, that was as broad a hint as a Girl could well give; and rather over-broad: only I suppose she's poor, and so wants me to marry her, to get a little richer. Well, that's natural, too. What do other Girls marry for? But that Mother must be a sad Jade! I'll go to her cottage directly, on purpose to take her out of the hands of such a vile baggage. And I'll place her somewhere honestly; to save her from bad ways. But I'll take a round, that none of Sir Roderick's people may see me going after her—a young Girl!— bless me!—they'd think—bless me!— 160 165 170

*Exit.*

## Scene vi

LADY SMATTER's *Dressing Room.*

LADY SMATTER. Pope,—or Swift,—no, Prior, I believe it was
Prior—'Tis amazingly provoking I can never retain an
Author's name! I remember them perfectly, but can't recollect
one from another. If I did not talk them over with Prim, I
5   should really be at a loss for a single quotation. Reading so
amazingly as I do, puzzles the understanding prodigiously.
Yes, yes, Shakespeare knew what he said!
True Wit to Madness sure is near allied —[1]

## Scene vii

*Enter* PRIM.

PRIM. Mr. Wilmot, my lady.
LADY SMATTER. My Brother? What, already?
PRIM. Yes, my Lady; and Miss Wilmot, and a sort of a Governess,
like. Mr. Wilmot has desired them both to be shewn into a
5   Parlour below, because he wants to see your ladyship alone.
O, here he is.

*Exit.*

## Scene viii

*Enter* WILMOT.

LADY SMATTER. My dear Brother, I rejoice to welcome you again
to our Island. Absence, as the Moralists say —[2]
WILMOT. I am glad you are so well, Sister, and glad to see you so
little changed.

---

1   *True Wit to Madness sure is near allied*: misquoting Dryden's *Absalom and Achitophel*
(1680): "Great Wits are sure to Madness near ally'd" (l. 163).
2   *Absence, as the Moralists say*: alluding to Propertius' famous line, "Absence makes the
heart grow fonder" (*Elegies*, II.xxxiii.43).

LADY SMATTER. Changed? Heavens! 5

WILMOT. After what I have written, of my resolution to finish my gloomy career in the West Indies, you are surprised, doubtless, at my return?

LADY SMATTER. Not at all. Waller is of opinion—

WILMOT. Pardon my interrupting you. An event has happened to 10 alter all my purposes: a ray of light has opened upon the long darkness of my despair; it has brought me once more to England, and may, perhaps, conduct me—I dare not yet trust myself to say to what happiness it may yet conduct me!

LADY SMATTER. You give me great pleasure; but the observation 15 I was going to quote is, I believe, not of Waller, but of Swift; he says—

WILMOT. Permit me to be brief. The business which brings me over, calls for my undivided attention: may I, then, for a few Days—perhaps a little longer—commit to you my daugh- 20 ter?

LADY SMATTER. Undoubtedly, for, as I have somewhere read—

WILMOT. Excuse my haste—my agitation. You will find her simple and unpolished, fearful as the Hare, who in every shadow sees a pursuer, invincibly shy, pensive, and nearly 25 mute.

LADY SMATTER. Precisely such a character as Shenstone has drawn in one of his pieces![1]

WILMOT. Unfortunate Girl! I sought not her early confidence, and now, 'tis too late to obtain it. 30

LADY SMATTER. That can be no very heavy loss, if she bear any resemblance to her frail Mother.

WILMOT. Sister! touch not that string with irreverence! Her Mother is spotless!

LADY SMATTER. Spotless? Why you wrote me word— 35

WILMOT. Forget what I wrote—I was mad! Hear me, however, speak, for my senses are restored. All I told you of the passion of Captain Ludlow has been verified, but most unjust, most untrue was my judgement of Eleonora, in whose prudent concealment of his love, I mistook the anxious fear of my 40

---

1 *Shenstone … in one of his pieces*: Wilmot is alluding not to Shenstone but to Gay's poem "The Hare and many Friends," no. fifty in his *Fables* (1727).

impetuous jealousy, for secret participation. All, to my "jaun-
diced Eye," seemed conviction of a mutual attachment—

LADY SMATTER. Yes, I well remember Gay upon that subject;—
no,—Hammond;—

45      All seems Yellow to the jaundic'd Eye.[1]

WILMOT. Yet deep as is now my horror in reflecting on the foul
suspicions which impelled our separation, every other circumstance seemed, at that period, to give them confirmation:
Eleonora, in quitting my house, demanded our Child; I
50     thought her unworthy the trust, yet concluded—perhaps
hoped—she would remain in its vicinity; but, in a few days, I
heard she had set sail for England,—and that Captain Ludlow, at the same Time, was sent out upon a secret expedition
to the Continent: I imagined this collusion—

55 LADY SMATTER. O, the collusion is as clear—in the words of
Churchill,

       As clear as the Brook which the Pebbles display.[2]

WILMOT. Distraction then seized me—I no longer lamented, but
raved, no longer accused, but condemned; nor, since that fatal
60     time, for sixteen years did Captain Ludlow again appear:
imagine then,—for I never can paint—the indignant aston-
ishment with which I was seized when, a few months ago, I
was suddenly accosted by him!—Imagine, too, if possible, the
emotions which succeeded, when I discovered that—far
65     from having secluded himself with Eleonora, he knew not
that she had left me! He had been surprised, with his whole
party, by a large body of Indians, carried up the Country a
Prisoner, and detained, a Slave, not a Captive, till nearly the
moment of our interview!

70 LADY SMATTER. Well, Armstrong—

WILMOT. Another enquiry led to a full explanation; he candidly
acknowledged his ill-fated passion, but proof opening upon
proof, cleared his Honour of all stain.

LADY SMATTER. Amazing! Eleonora, then—

75 WILMOT. Is the most injured of women! Execrably I have

---

1   *Hammond … jaundic'd Eye*: from Pope's *An Essay on Criticism*: "As all looks yellow to
    the Jaundic'd Eye" (l. 559).
2   *As clear as the Brook which the Pebbles display*: not identified.

wronged her; but if her heart be not steeled against me, I come over to seek her abode, and—

LADY SMATTER. You have not far to wander: she is only somewhere in this neighborhood.

WILMOT. She?—Who?—Eleonora? 80

LADY SMATTER. Yes; she came to me this very morning, with a long story of her innocence; but I did not believe a word of it, for, as Rowe observes—

WILMOT. You did not believe Her? Eleonora?—Has she lost then, that commanding mein? that dignified port? that look 85 so noble, which announced a Soul incapable, rather than unwilling to do wrong? You did not believe Her? Eleonora?—Yet alas!—am I—to censure others?—

LADY SMATTER. Wycherley, you know, Brother, asserts—

WILMOT. She is here, you say?—In this neighborhood?— 90

LADY SMATTER. It is not an hour since she was in this very room.

WILMOT. So soon, then, Eleonora, may I meet thee? Sister, Adieu. Believe every syllable she uttered! I, alone, am criminal, and groveling in the dust I will acknowledge it! Yes, Eleonora! Thy innocence shall be loudly proclaimed, and 95 justly will I take upon myself the shame from which I shall whiten thee!

*Exit.*

LADY SMATTER. Well, this may certainly be called a curious incident, and Pope—or Beaumont and Fletcher—I'll look among my Classics for the passage (*opens an elegant little Book* 100 *case*).

### Scene ix

*Enter* PRIM.

PRIM. Pray, my lady, what's to be done with that young lady?

LADY SMATTER. O, ay, true; what can I find to entertain her with? A Volume of my Classics, I think. Have you seen her, Prim?

PRIM. Only as she went into the Parlour, my lady.

LADY SMATTER. She never speaks, my Brother says; a poor little dumb shy thing. I must admit her, however: so let her come up.

PRIM. And the Governess, my lady?

LADY SMATTER. By all means.

*Exit* PRIM.

What shall I say to the poor frightened thing? I have really confined myself so exclusively to literary pursuits, that I am become almost quite unfit for common conversation.

Scene x

*Enter* MISS WILMOT, *and the* NURSE.

LADY SMATTER. How are you, Miss Wilmot? I am glad to see you in England.

MISS WILMOT *courtsies bashfully.*

I hope, too, you have some pleasure in coming amongst us?

*She courtsies again.*

The part of the World you have left is, I fancy, rather … uncivilized?

*She courtsies.*

You have been forced to live pretty much, I imagine, among savages?

*She courtsies.*

However, your Papa will have given you, I doubt not, some taste for reading; I shall look you out, therefore, one of my Classics (*going to her Book case*).

NURSE (*whispering* MISS WILMOT). Why don't you speak to your

Aunt, Miss? If your Papa was here, he'd be quite ashamed of you.

MISS WILMOT (*looking up*). My Papa? why … i'n't my Papa here?

LADY SMATTER. Don't be alarmed, my dear. He will soon be 15
here. Pray don't be frightened. Nobody will molest you. Take
courage.

MISS WILMOT. O, Papa's gone out, is he? I thought he was here
now. Dear! what a pretty room this is! And what a nice
delightful sofa! (*throwing herself upon a sofa*) How I should like 20
to take a nap upon it!

LADY SMATTER. Heavens!

NURSE. Why, Miss, what are you thinking of? lollopping in such
a way as that? Who'd believe the pains I've been at to teach
you how to behave! See how you make my lady stare! 25

MISS WILMOT. Do I, Nurse? O but she should not stare. Do you
know, Nurse, in one of those old Books that Papa made me
read, it is said that staring is very — guess what, Nurse?

NURSE. Not I, indeed, Miss!

MISS WILMOT. Why then, do you guess, Aunt. 30

LADY SMATTER. I am thunderstruck!

MISS WILMOT. Pray, Aunt, have not I got some Cousins?

LADY SMATTER. No, ma'am!

MISS WILMOT. What, have you no children, Aunt?

LADY SMATTER. No, Miss Wilmot—! 35

MISS WILMOT. Why then, I dare say that's what makes the house
so dull! Now I'll tell you what I'd do, if I had no Children,
and was as old as you are.

LADY SMATTER. As old as I am, Miss Wilmot?

MISS WILMOT. I'd look out for some poor Beggar, that had got a 40
dirty, ragged, squalling, hungry brat at its back, and if it were
ruddy, and chubby, and plump — I'd dip it in a pail of Water,
to clean it, and bring it up for my own.

LADY SMATTER. I am extremely obliged to you for favouring me
with your advice, ma'am! 45

MISS WILMOT. You can't think how I hate a house without
Children.

LADY SMATTER. This may be shyness in the West Indies! but —

MISS WILMOT. I like Children twenty times better than grown
up people. 50

LADY SMATTER. I am happy to be informed of your taste!

MISS WILMOT. They are so merry, and so good-humoured, and so playful, and so frisky!—Grown up people are so cross! always finding fault! always hating a noise! always bidding one take care!—I hate old people!

LADY SMATTER. Is This the timid Hare, trembling at its own shadow?—Waller, Miss Wilmot—

MISS WILMOT. What's Waller, Aunt?

LADY SMATTER. What's Waller? Are you ignorant of the name of one of our first Poets?

MISS WILMOT. O, he's one of the Poets? I like none of them! I hate Books.

LADY SMATTER. You do? What, then, may be the study you prefer? Painting? Music? Botany? Languages?—Geography?—

MISS WILMOT. O, I hate all those! Whenever I am forced to set about any thing of that sort, do you know, Aunt, it always makes me sleepy? See, now, if you have not made me yawn, only by mentioning them! Whenever any of those fusty old masters used to come to me, I always made Nurse say I was ill.—Don't tell Papa, now!—I hate study.

LADY SMATTER. You seem well practiced in hating. Perhaps you hate every thing?

MISS WILMOT. O no, I don't. I like a great many things; but my first best favourite of all is dancing. It makes one so light, and so blyth, and so gaysome, and so skipping! Do you ever dance, Aunt?

LADY SMATTER. I dance, Miss Wilmot?

MISS WILMOT. Nay, Nurse does; and I think she's much about your age.

LADY SMATTER. My Age, Ma'am! Nurse?

MISS WILMOT. Well, and the second next best thing that I like is singing. Can you sing, Aunt?

LADY SMATTER. Can I? What I can do, ma'am,—

MISS WILMOT. I sing, sometimes, do you know, Aunt, from morning to night? O, it makes the house all alive! But that's only when Papa's out.

LADY SMATTER. I am glad, at least, you are so considerate to his nerves.

MISS WILMOT. Well, and the third next best thing that I like—

NURSE. Miss, Miss, how you run on! 90

MISS WILMOT. Why, Nurse, you scold if I speak, and you scold if I hold my tongue![1] so I'll tell you what I intend.

NURSE. What, Miss?

MISS WILMOT. Why to talk or be dumb, as much as I will for my own amusement, and to let you scold, or look bluff, as much 95 as you will for your's. Now that I think fair play. I'n't it, Aunt?

LADY SMATTER. Really, it is a point of casuistry I cannot determine. Cowley—

MISS WILMOT. O, but, Aunt, I was going to tell you the third 100 best thing I like! You forget that! Now only guess?

LADY SMATTER. Such a transformation from silence to garrulity—no, Ovid, nor Otway, have nothing like it!

MISS WILMOT. Why, don't you see, Aunt? Can't you find out?— Swing, swang, swing, swang—Why, it's swinging! That's what 105 I like third best. Now my fourth best—

LADY SMATTER. Pray trouble yourself no more! I mean to enquire no farther! Parnel—

MISS WILMOT. Perhaps you think I've told you all? Why there's an hundred things besides! There's walking—and there's run- 110 ning—and there's jumping—

LADY SMATTER. Enough, enough! Swift—

MISS WILMOT. And then, when one's famished, and empty,— how delightful are minced veal, and Pancakes!

LADY SMATTER. Minced veal and Pancakes! (*aside*) Her vulgarity 115 is mundane to a degree! Pope—

MISS WILMOT. And O! when one's parched, and faint—how delightful is a Glass of lemonade!—or Punch! Punch, Aunt!—

LADY SMATTER. I must make my escape! Shakespeare himself 120 would plead to be heard in vain!

*Exit.*

---

1 *Why, Nurse … my tongue*: perhaps alluding to the words of the fool in Shakespeare's *King Lear*, who says: "They'll have me whipped for speaking true; thou'lt have me whipped for lying; and sometimes I am whipped for holding my peace" (I. iv.173-5).

NURSE. How rude you've been, Miss! How could you think of rattling on to your Aunt so?

MISS WILMOT. O, I did it without thinking, Nurse. I hate think-
125 ing.

NURSE. Ah, Miss, you would not be so giddy, if you knew all I've got to say to you! But why don't you coax your Papa to go back to the West Indies? If you knew but what a bad place this may turn out for you!

130 MISS WILMOT. Nurse, Nurse, hush!—Do you know I think I hear Bob Sapling below?

NURSE. Fie, Miss, to talk of Bob Sapling so! O Miss! I've something to tell you, that may make you serious for the rest of your days!

135 MISS WILMOT. Then I won't hear it! I hate to be serious.

Begone! old Care!

And let us be merry awhile![1]

*Exit, singing.*

NURSE. I shall never get it out! O that I was safe back in the Indies!

*Exit.*

### Scene xi

*The Cottage of* ELEONORA.

*Enter* SOPHIA.

SOPHIA. My dear Mother—She is still up stairs.—O, what joy I shall awaken in her breast! what consolation! (*a tap at the door*) Ah, this dear Uncle! so soon to follow! (*in opening the door*) O Sir, how kind, how good!

---

1  *Begone! old Care! ... awhile*: from a traditional song, no.13 in John Playford's *Musical Companion* (1687).

## Scene xii

### *Enter* Young Waverley

Heavens!

Young Waverley. How kind? enchanting Girl!—how kind didst thou say?

Sophia. No, I did not, indeed!—believe me! I said it quite—in a mistake! (*going towards the stairs*)—but I had better call my   5
Mother—

Young Waverley (*following*). No, no, no!

## Scene xiii

*Enter* Old Waverley, *cautiously coming by in the door* Young Waverley *had left open.*

Old Waverley. Yes, yes, this must be the house.—What do I see?—Jack here!

Young Waverley. I entreat—(*turning around*) How!—my Father!

Sophia (*looking back, aside*). Ah! 'tis my Uncle himself! (*advancing*)   5
Sir!

Young Waverley (*aside*). What the devil can bring the old Gentleman hither?

Old Waverley (*aside*). If I a'n't quite confounded to think what Jack can come for!   10

Sophia. I was almost afraid, Sir, you had repented your kind promise.

Old Waverley. No, my dear, no—What will Jack think of this?

Young Waverley (*aside*). Hey day! was it for my Father, then,   15
all that so good and so kind were intended?

Sophia. You will permit me, Sir, now, to call down my Mother?

Old Waverley. No, my dear, no; not at present.—(*aside*) I had better not stay, I believe. It may put odd thoughts into a young man's head. Young men are very apt to have odd   20
thoughts.—very apt to think something oddish!

SOPHIA. May I not, at least, tell my Mother you are here?

OLD WAVERLEY. No, no,—another time,—

YOUNG WAVERLEY (*aside*). Another time?—What the plague!—

25 OLD WAVERLEY (*aside*). How scowly Jack looks at me!—very scowly, indeed!—I must set him right. (*whispering* SOPHIA) Leave us a minute my dear,—I want to speak to that young man.

YOUNG WAVERLEY (*aside*). Insufferable! whispering her!—I 30 could pull his wig off for madness!

SOPHIA. Promise, then, I shall find you when I come back?

OLD WAVERLEY. I don't know—may be so! Go, you little Plague!

SOPHIA *walks slowly to the little stairs.*

YOUNG WAVERLEY (*aside*). This is too bad! I burn with rage! 35 What an old rogue! (*following her*) And can you, then, quit me without one word?

OLD WAVERLEY (*aside*). How's this! Jack following her? What a young knave!

SOPHIA. I must, I must!—but … don't take it ill!—

40 YOUNG WAVERLEY (*taking her hand*). So soft—and so cruel at once?

OLD WAVERLEY. Bless me! does he take her hand? The sweat drops down my face!

SOPHIA. Let me go!—pray!—I beg!—

45 YOUNG WAVERLEY (*detaining her*). A moment!

OLD WAVERLEY (*aside*). He holds her, I protest! Well, young men are the most impudent young fellows!—I quite quake!— (*angrily*) Jack!

YOUNG WAVERLEY (*letting her go*). Ah, cruel!

50 SOPHIA (*running to the Stair case, and then looking back*). Adieu!

*Exit, up the stairs.*

OLD WAVERLEY *and* YOUNG WAVERLEY *stand some time looking silently at each other.*

Young Waverley (*aside*). How the deuce can he have made acquaintance here? I'll see him out, however.

Old Waverley (*aside*). I must put an end to this at once. I won't leave him behind, I'm resolved. Pray, Jack, what brought you to this house? 55

Young Waverley. I am always glad, Sir, to come where I may have the pleasure of meeting you.

Old Waverley. But you did not know I should be here; so who did you come to meet?

Young Waverley. I was just going to take the liberty, Sir, of 60 asking you that very question.

Old Waverley. As to me, Jack, it's quite—another affair.—I am not a boy,—and I don't like to be catechised.

Young Waverley. I have the honour—the duty, at least,—to inherit precisely the same sentiment, Sir. 65

Old Waverley. Jack! Jack! I don't admire coming after young Girls! it don't look well.

Young Waverley. In me, Sir?

Old Waverley (*aside*). Very sly, that! Jack's duced sly! I tell you what, Jack; I am your Father, and must take care of your 70 morals; and you are my Son, and must follow—

Young Waverley. Your example, Sir!

Old Waverley. Lookee, Jack, if ever I find you in this house again—

Young Waverley. Nay, Sir, if you find me here yourself, Sir,— 75 you must at least compliment me on the similarity of our ways!

Old Waverley. Jack, Jack, I'll encourage no such doings.

Young Waverley. In others, Sir?

Old Waverley. Go, Jack, go! I won't leave you behind! Follow- 80 ing young women to their ruin is a very bad thing.

Young Waverley. So I think, Sir!

Old Waverley. Very unpardonable.

Young Waverley. Very unpardonable indeed, Sir!

Old Waverley. Then why do you do it? 85

Young Waverley. Did not I hear—an eccho, Sir? (*looking about*)

Old Waverley. An eccho?

YOUNG WAVERLEY. Yes,—that repeated Why do *you* do it?

OLD WAVERLEY (*aside*). Ay, ay, now he's got at some bad
90     thoughts, now! I must see you out, Jack.

YOUNG WAVERLEY. I wait your time, Sir (*bowing and holding open
the door*). You often tell me to be respectful.

OLD WAVERLEY (*aside*). There, now! he forces me to decamp
first!—However, as soon as I've seen him safe-housed, I'll be
95     back. Come, Jack, come!

YOUNG WAVERLEY. I am close at your side, Sir. (*aside*) The very
instant I have got rid of him, I'll be here again.

*Exeunt.*

# ACT IV

## Scene i

*The Apartment at* SIR RODERICK'S.

*The* STEWARD *alone, holding a Letter in his hand.*

STEWARD. Well, now I must look for my best pocket Book, to carry her ladyship the Letter all in order.

## Scene ii

*Enter* SIR RODERICK.

Zooks!

*Hastening to put away the Letter, it falls:*
*he picks it up, and stuffs it into his pocket.*

SIR RODERICK. I'n't Mr. Waverley come back yet?—why what have you got there?

STEWARD. Only a—a—a bit of paper, Sir.

SIR RODERICK. A bit of paper? Why it's a Letter! Who is it for?  5

STEWARD. For, Sir?—it's for—for me, Sir.

SIR RODERICK. For you? then why don't you read it?

STEWARD. I—I have read it, Sir.

SIR RODERICK. Read it? Why I saw the Seal unbroke? Who is it from?  10

STEWARD. From, Sir?—O,—it's from—from my Brother, Sir.

SIR RODERICK. Your Brother? With that fine broad seal? There's some roguery, Stephens! I see that plainly! Shew me the Letter.

STEWARD. Sir I—I—  15

SIR RODERICK. This moment!—(*stamping*) or else I shall lose my temper!

*The* STEWARD *takes out the Letter.*
SIR RODERICK *snatches it from him.*

How! What!—To Lady Smatter?—How came you by a Let-
ter for Lady Smatter?
20  STEWARD. Sir I—I only—
SIR RODERICK. Why it's Jack's hand!—How came Jack to write
to Lady Smatter?—
STEWARD. Sir, it's just ... it's only—
SIR RODERICK. By the lord Harry[1] I'll see what he says to her!
25    This fine seal sha'n't—How? Verses? (*reads*)
Fairest Daughter of the Nine,
Thy smiles have rivetted my heart
O that Hymen might entwine—
Why what's this? What the Devil's all this? Jack Waverley
30    writing Love Verses to Lady Smatter?—Lady Smatter smiles
upon him?—Hymen, too?—And all in verse?—What the
devil!—Am I in my senses?—Stephens! answer! If you don't
tell me all this moment, I'll blow your brains out!
STEWARD. Indeed, Sir, all I know is—is—
35  SIR RODERICK. Would you have me fetch my blunderbuss?
STEWARD. The young Gentleman, Sir, happened just to call on
Lady Smatter—
SIR RODERICK. Call on Lady Smatter?—Jack?
STEWARD. And so—her ladyship being a little civil to him—
40  SIR RODERICK. Civil?—Lady Smatter civil to Jack?—If you say
such another word—Go on!—be quick!—
STEWARD. So the young Gentleman thought, Sir, as she was so
agreeable, he might make her the offer.
SIR RODERICK. I have no breath! no breath left in my body!—
45    Make her the offer? what, Jack Waverley?—Jack Waverley
make the offer to Lady Smatter? I never heard any thing so
diabolic since I was born!—Jack Waverely make the offer to
Lady Smatter!
STEWARD (*aside*). How unlucky this is!
50  SIR RODERICK. So here I have kept him from the whole sex all
this time, for such an end as this? I can't believe my senses! A

---

1  Harry: a familiar name for the Devil.

Boy like that talking of Hymen! I'll disinherit him within an hour! Get me an attorney.

STEWARD. Yes, Sir.

SIR RODERICK. Did not I warn him from the beginning he must 55 never think of marrying? Did not I caution him never to like a woman as long as he lived? Have not you heard me tell him, an hundred times, the whole sex was good for nothing? A poor feeble, puling, useless Race! changing their minds every half hour; with more freaks in their composition than blood, 60 or bones; fit for nothing but making faces at bad dinners, and squalling at bad roads: and so helpless, if they fall into a ditch, they are drowned,—and if you don't put the meat into their mouths, they are starved!

STEWARD. They are but poor Helpmates, indeed, Sir. 65

SIR RODERICK. And now, after all, he must marry one of them, must he?—I'll never see his face again!—And he must make his offer to Lady Smatter, must he?—I'll cut him off without a Shilling!—And he must write verses to her, also?—Just as Lord Smatter did before him!—Write verses!—a Copy of 70 Verses!—By the lord Harry, I'll fit him for that! I'll look out for an heir that does not know his alphabet. He'll see, then, what he's got by writing verses! I'll do it directly. I'll do it to shame them both. If there's one thing I think more diabolic than another, it's writing verses. But I'll give him enough of 75 them!—Harkee, Stephens,—if you know e'er a looby[1] that can't either write or read,—send him to me directly. I'll make his fortune.—A copy of verses!—

*Exit.*

STEWARD. Ah ha! A looby that can neither write nor read! why this will just suit my poor Nephew Bob. I'll go tutor the lad 80 this minute, that he may catch Sir Roderick while he's in the humour.

*Exit.*

---

1   *looby*: variant of booby, an awkward ignorant fellow.

## Scene iii

*The Dressing Room at* LADY SMATTER'S.

*Enter* MISS WILMOT, *on tiptoe, looking carefully around.*

MISS WILMOT. I have a prodigious curiosity to peep at these
Classics my Aunt is so fond of. (*opening the little Book Case*)
La! Books! always Books!—nothing but Books!—I wonder
what's in this pretty little Box?—(*opening a small Box*) O my
5  Classics! my Classics!—what delightful Classics are these!
(*eating Bon Bons*) And O what sweet smells! (*taking out little
bottles, vials, and Boxes*) Jessamine—Rose—Lavander—

## Scene iv

*Enter* NURSE, *crying.*

NURSE (*wringing her hands*). O Miss, Miss!
MISS WILMOT. O Nurse, look but what delicious sweetmeats,
and smelling Bottles, and creams, and pomatums, I have found
in Aunt's Classics!
5  NURSE. Don't be so wild, Miss! don't be so wild! If you won't be
quiet a moment, and hear me, it will all come upon you in a
blow, like a clap of thunder!
MISS WILMOT. Smell, smell, Nurse!—Give me your Handkerchief—if you won't you shall take it upon your Gown, and
10  upon your Cap, and upon your Neck, and upon your
Arms—(*throwing Lavander over her*)

## Scene v

*Enter* PRIM.

PRIM. Miss Wilmot—Goodness, Ma'am, I hope you have not
meddled with my lady's Classics?
MISS WILMOT. O yes, but I have! And I like them of all things.
Will you have some? Here, eat!—smell!—
5  PRIM. It's the Books, ma'am, that are my lady's Classics. Those

things are only put there not to be touched.

MISS WILMOT. O, I won't touch the Books. I'll take a bon bon a piece for every one of them. So here's for Thomson—and here's for Chapone—and here's for Waller—and here's for Pope—and here's for Swift—and here's—O what a big 10 one!—for Shakespeare—

PRIM. This is a little parcel, Miss Wilmot, scissars, and I know not what, that you left at the Inn; and the young woman and her Brother have brought them.

NURSE. That's very civil, I am sure; I'll go thank Miss Henny 15 myself, as soon as I've put my things a little to rights; for you've made me such a figure—

*Exit.*

MISS WILMOT. And I'll thank her Brother, myself. Mrs. Prim, pray call up Bob.

PRIM. Ma'am!                                                              20

MISS WILMOT. Call up Bob. I want to speak to him.

PRIM. Call up Bob?—Into my lady's Dressing room?

MISS WILMOT. Well, then, I'll call him myself! I won't be kept in a prison, so! never doing any thing I have a mind. I am quite tired of it, I am so. (*calling*) Bob! Bob!                                 25

PRIM. Well, I believe this is such a young lady as never was seen in the World before!

Scene vi

*Enter* MISS HENNY.

MISS HENNY. May I come in, Miss?

MISS WILMOT. O, yes, Miss Henny: but where's Bob?

Scene vii

*Enter* BOB.

BOB. Why there, now, Henny! I said it was I Miss called. I heard her as plain as could be.

MISS HENNY. Well, if you did, Bobby, there's no reason I should not come in first.

5 PRIM. If my lady were to step up, and see such company as this in her dressing room, Miss Wilmot —

MISS WILMOT. O, I should scamper them off, then. You can't think, Mrs. Prim, what short work I make of getting rid of people, when I'm in a hurry. Come hither, Bob. I want to 10 speak to you. Come nearer. Nay, Miss Henny, I did not call you.

MISS HENNY. No, Miss; but I always come to answer for Brother Bob, because of his being so stupid.

BOB. Why now, Henny —

15 MISS WILMOT. O, but I only want Bob. Come hither, I say, Bob; and don't stare so. And shut your mouth. And don't hold your hands so stiff and strait down. Now mind me. Do you know, Bob,—let me speak in your Ear; it's a secret. Do you know Bob, I'm tired to death of living with Papa?

20 BOB. Be you, Miss?

MISS WILMOT. Yes. How do you like Papa?

BOB. Not a bit, Miss.

MISS WILMOT. No more do I, Bob; for I'm kept in such subjection, I've no comfort of my life.

25 BOB. Lauk, Miss, and so am I!

MISS WILMOT. There's nothing but ordering, and tutoring, and scolding, and managing … and reading!

BOB. And they do just the same by me!

MISS WILMOT. And I don't chuse to put up with it any longer, 30 Bob. I'm all for Liberty!—Liberty, Liberty, Bob!

## Scene viii

*Enter* NURSE.

NURSE. Good la! Master Bob up here! (*in a menacing tone*) Miss, Miss!

MISS WILMOT. I am all for Liberty, Nurse! (*Dances round her*) Liberty —Liberty!—

5 NURSE. You'll come to ruin, Miss! You'll come to ruin!—Don't

stay, Miss Henny;— you've no business here, Master Bob.

MISS HENNY. I'm sure I only —

BOB. Why Miss called me!

NURSE *hustles them out.*

PRIM. I hear my lady's Bell, I declare!

*Exit* PRIM.

MISS WILMOT (*singing*).

        Fie, nay, prithee, Nurse,          10

        Do not quarrel, Nurse,

NURSE. Have done with your singing, Miss!

MISS WILMOT (*skipping*). But be merry, and Dance about.

NURSE. And have done with your dancing, Miss! for I won't bear
it no longer; so I won't!          15

MISS WILMOT. Hey day, Nurse!

NURSE. It's no time for singing and dancing—unless you've a
mind to sing ballads in the street; or dance with the milk
maids on May Day.

MISS WILMOT. How dare you talk to me so, Nurse? Beg my par-  20
don this instant!

NURSE. I beg your pardon? You'd better come hither, and fall on
your marrow bones to beg mine!

MISS WILMOT. If I don't go this minute and call my Aunt Smatter—          25

NURSE. I desire you'd give yourself no such airs, madam! Stop, I
say!

MISS WILMOT. I won't!

NURSE. You must! … nay, you Shall!

MISS WILMOT. Shall?—I'll go fetch Papa, too!          30

NURSE. Stir a step at your peril! Do you know whom you speak
to?

MISS WILMOT. Do I? Yes, to be sure! to a frightful, wrinkled,
bold, old Nurse!

NURSE. No, you don't, Miss! you don't! I a'n't no such thing! and  35
I order you never to speak to me in that manner no more.

MISS WILMOT. You order me? And who are you to order me?

NURSE. Who? your Mamma!—your own Mamma!—There! now you have it!

40 MISS WILMOT. You my Mamma?

NURSE. Yes; your own natural mamma. That's who I am!

MISS WILMOT. How dare you tell me such a wicked, monstrous, horrible, vile fib, Nurse? I don't believe it; and I won't believe it. My mamma ran away.

45 NURSE. Yes; but she took her own Poppet[1] with her.

MISS WILMOT. What do you mean? What do you mean, Nurse? If you don't tell me the real truth directly—

NURSE. I will, I will! only don't hurry me so, Miss,—my dear, I should say,—for I'm all of a trimble, already, for it's all coming

50 out to every body.—But, when Mistress was gone, old Nick put it into my head to burn the Letter she left me for Master, and pop you into young Missy's place, making believe you yourself died up the Country. But I hope I shall be forgiven, for I should not have done it, if old Nick had not put it in my

55 head; which your Daddy did besides.

MISS WILMOT. My Daddy?

NURSE. Yes; and Master could not bear to see you, after Mistress was gone, for such a while, that he never found it out; though he used often to say he thought you vast altered. However, I

60 always kept you as much as I could out of his sight.

MISS WILMOT. What, then, i'n't Papa Papa?

NURSE. No, Miss. Your own Dad was a journeyman shoe-maker.

MISS WILMOT. A journeyman shoe-maker!

NURSE. Yes, my dear. And your own real christian name i'n't

65 Sophia; it's Joyce.

MISS WILMOT. Joyce?

NURSE. Yes; and it's all coming out, for I've just heard, from the servants, that my Mistress is in this very village! ay, and called on Lady Smatter this very morning! And that's what's put me

70 in this pother! O la! o la! we shall be turned back upon one another, and I may come to the work house,[2] and you may go for a kitchen maid!

---

1  *Poppet*: baby.

2  *work house*: throughout the century workhouses, where the indigent were supposed to earn their keep, were notorious for their inmates' ill-treatment.

MISS WILMOT. I? No, that I won't!—You nasty, old, vile impostor!—You ugly, wizen, wicked cheat!—you mean—

NURSE. O, Miss, that you can put yourself in such a passion with    75
your own right mamsey! that did it all for your sake, that hoped you'd have got a rich husband before it was found out, that let you have your own way in every thing, that hid all your faults from your Papa—

MISS WILMOT. So you did, Nurse! that's true, Nurse!—And I    80
always loved you, and I could never abide Papa, but what is it all come to now? What did you tell me I should be a kitchen maid for? And a ballad singer?

NURSE. O, Miss—my dear!—that was nothing but my little pet because you would not hear me. But I'll never say nothing    85
disrespectful to you again, if you'll only stand by me now. I'll be your dutiful servant all my days.

MISS WILMOT. O Nurse! Nurse! (*bursting into Tears*) how could you serve me so? setting me up for a lady, only to be made Game of! What must I do?—what will become of me?—I    90
can't scrub rooms—and I won't scrub rooms!—(*sobbing*) And I can't turn ballad singer, and—(*suddenly brightening*) yes, I can, though! that I can, Nurse! and if I must be something— I had rather be a ballad singer than any thing else.

NURSE. Yes, my dear; but there's no need, I hope, for what I think    95
is—

MISS WILMOT. How droll it would look, Nurse, to see me a real ballad singer! I saw two or three, at the great Inn we stopt at, in our way through London. Such comical, dumpty, mumpty[1] figures! and such squalling and bawling voices!    100

NURSE. What I think, is, we should go to your Uncle, as they call him, Sir Roderick—

MISS WILMOT. I bought one of the songs; and now only hear if I won't sing it just like them.

NURSE. O, don't play tricks, now, Miss! but let's see what we can    105
get from Sir Roderick before we're discovered.

MISS WILMOT. Lend me your handkerchief, Nurse. There!— that's to be tied under my Chin. Now lend me your apron;— nay, I will have it! There! that's to be tied so, and then swung

---

1   *mumpty*: a variant of "mumpy"; see above, p. 201, note 1.

110     up round me, so. There! Now I must stuff up my nose as if I
        were snuffy.
    NURSE. O come! and make him believe you're his real niece!
    MISS WILMOT. Now for my ballad. (*Takes a ballad from her pocket*)
        *Sings. Tune, Of all the Girls that are so smart.*[1]
115         Of all the Lovyers in the Town,
            The Masters and the Misses,
            There's none like little Bet and John,
            For they live on Love and Kisses.
            And though this fare's so wond'rous fine,
120         They never grow the thinner;
            Because they mix it well with Wine,
            And bread and cheese at Dinner.
    NURSE. Come, come, do come!

                                                    *Exeunt.*


                            Scene ix

                        *The Avenue.*

                        *Enter* WILMOT.


    WILMOT. She cannot forgive me!—perhaps she ought not!—
        Her fair Fame blighted—O heinous precipitance of iniqui-
        tous jealousy!—no! she cannot forgive me! There are injuries
        which we can only cease to resent, by ceasing to remember;
5       and what to My memory is cemented by remorse, to her's
        must be glued by indignation. Art thou, then, sovereign over
        evils, O Time! only because sovereign over life?—No!—I
        will not seek her pardon!—The pardon of the Lips! to which
        the heart cannot beat responsive!—The pardon ... of
10      Pity!—not the pity of tender feelings, but of feelings which
        have worn out their own energy,—of ... Contempt!—Hor-
        rible!—I revolt from such pardon. The fiercest resentment

---

    1   *Of all the Girls that are so smart:* the first line of Henry Carey's ballad *Sally in our Alley*
        (1729). Carey also wrote the music for this and others of his poems, published as *The
        Musical Century* (1737).

were preferable. I will see her, however. Lowly to the earth will I bend the proud spirit that wronged her, reinstate her in all her violated rights, make over to her the sole dominion of her unfortunate Daughter, and then, in a last farewell—I will not seek her habitation till midnight. Our interview must have no witnesses, no interruption.—Whither—whither—when it is over, shall I guide my desperate steps? 15

## Scene x

BOB SAPLING *crosses the stage above.*

Holla! young man!—I would view her abode by daylight, though by daylight I dare not enter it.—Can you direct me, Sir, to the house of a lady who arrived in this village a few days since?

BOB. What, she as nobody knows? 5

WILMOT (*walking away*). O fell barbarian!—Is it thus thou hast left her, a mark for scorn?—Where did you say is her house, Sir?

BOB. Why there,—down yonder.

WILMOT. There?—so near! … Is all I covet—all I dread—all I have wronged—and all I adore, so near? What if at once—my heart beats high!—Eleonora! my own Eleonora! wouldst thou receive me?—Young man, if I go to that house, am I likely to meet any company?—or to find the lady alone? 10

BOB. Company? lauk, no! She never sees nobody, and nobody never sees her. 15

WILMOT. I am strongly tempted—O Eleonora! were it possible to surprise thy compassion—a restoration to thy bosom—to thy Love—I should meet her, you think, by herself?

BOB. Yes, as sure as can be; except just for Miss. 20

WILMOT. For Miss? whom do you mean?

BOB. Why the young one.

WILMOT. What young one?

BOB. Why her Daughter.

WILMOT. Her Daughter? 25

BOB. What, don't you know she's got a Daughter as lives with her?

WILMOT. Some Companion, probably—some one who travels with her?—assists—associates—

30 BOB. No, no; it's her own born Child, I tell you! Sister Henny put the question to Phebe, their little maid; and she said that Miss asked her mamma's blessing every night of her life; and that madam was so fond of her, she often said she could not live without her.

35 WILMOT. 'Tis false!

BOB. Lauk! it's as true as ever you heard in your life! Besides, if you were only to set Eyes on 'em! Why they are as like one to t'other as ever you see a Chicken to a Hen.

WILMOT. Begone!—Another word may demolish you!

(*drives him away*)

40 Heaven and Earth!—Her Daughter?—Is This the mystery of her flight, her silence, her secresy?—Her Daughter?—Is Ludlow then clear, only because some other paramour is guilty? And has my poor Girl been abandoned, only that the pledge of lawless love might be cherished?—O barbarous

45 delusion of Hope! vain, fleeting phantoms of Innocence! Have ye given me this short luxury of Joy, only to lacerate my soul more terribly by the abrupt transition?—shall I bear it?— Am I base, abject enough to say There lives my Wife—but with what associate I know not?—There she rears the Child

50 of her shame, while the offspring of wedded Honour never learnt to lisp her name?—This shall I bear—and breath? No!—the catastrophe is at hand—Eleonora! thou art lost!

*Exit.*

Scene xi

*The Cottage of* ELEONORA.

ELEONORA *seated;* SOPHIA *leaning over her.*

ELEONORA. Since thou hast the courage to wish it, go, then, my Sophia, to my Brother. Ill, indeed, could I bear a blight on thy integrity! ah, rather—were such the alternative—rather would I find that on my own indelible!

SOPHIA. Indeed, my dear Mother, I do not fear applying to him. 5 He has none of the roughness I expected. I have found him all gentleness and kindness.

ELEONORA. There is a powerful influence in female youth; but my Sophia will simply use it as the instrument of filial piety. If, while we are yet unknown, thou canst again sooth him hither, 10 we will here try to soften him; if not, acknowledge at once who thou art, and openly seek his support and protection.

SOPHIA. I will, my dearest Mother. And you—will you keep up your spirits till I come back?

ELEONORA. Yes, yes!    15

*Exit* SOPHIA.

ELEONORA. Dear, innocent, ingenuous Girl! O Wilmot! when I reflect on the years thou hast missed of paternal joy and delight—of exultation in her improvements, of tenderness in her caresses—I forgive thee all!—I condemn only myself; Thee I think most injured, myself the most to be envied!—    20 some one taps at the door—Phebe!—see who is there.

Scene xii

*Enter* PHEBE, *who opens the door.*

PHEBE (*after speaking to someone at the door*). Please, ma'am, it's an old Gentleman, as asks for Miss.

ELEONORA. My Brother! How unfortunate! She must just have missed him!

PHEBE. Please, ma'am, shall I tell him Miss is gone out?    5

ELEONORA. Yes—no!—what had I best resolve? Shall I seize this moment?—or wait her return and assistance?—Alas, I have no courage! Tell him, Phebe,—

PHEBE. Please, ma'am, the Gentleman's coming in.

ELEONORA. Ah!—Leave the room, then, immediately.—    10

PHEBE *goes in.*

## Scene xiii

*Enter* OLD WAVERLEY.

OLD WAVERLEY. I must not wait at the door, for fear Jack should come by, and catch me. Where's the little Girl, now?—Bless me! I suppose that's the Mother!

ELEONORA (*aside*). I dare not look at him!

5 OLD WAVERLEY (*aside*). This is lucky enough. I'll ransom the poor Girl out of her hands without loss of time;—a vile Hag!

ELEONORA (*aside*). O, could I soften him!

OLD WAVERLEY (*aside*). I don't know how I shall command myself to speak to her without saying something affronting—

10 a naughty Jade!

ELEONORA (*aside*). How I dread the first instant!

OLD WAVERLEY (*aside*). I'll put the poor Thing out to some honest trade, two hundred miles off from her!

ELEONORA (*aside*). I must conquer my terror!

15 OLD WAVERLEY (*aside*). She's ashamed, now, to show her face to an honest man, with all her impudence!

ELEONORA *turns slowly round, clasps her hands*
*with an air of distress, and bows, but without raising her Eyes.*

OLD WAVERLEY (*starting back, aside*). Bless my heart! Who'd have thought to have seen such a fine looking woman as that?

ELEONORA (*aside*). He does not recollect me!—By every one—

20 and every way forgotten!

OLD WAVERLEY (*aside*). She has no more the look of a woman of that sort—

ELEONORA (*raising her Eyes, aside*). How? a stranger!—who can he be? and why has he asked for Sophia?

25 OLD WAVERLEY (*aside*). I could sooner have taken her for a Nun! one must never trust to appearances!

ELEONORA (*aside*). Is it some one sent by Wilmot to demand his daughter?—alas!—What, sir, are your commands with me?

OLD WAVERLEY. Why, ma'am—why—why, I say, ma'am—

30 (*aside*) There's something so particular in her Eye, it puts me quite out!

ELEONORA. Sir!

OLD WAVERLEY. I just called, ma'am, upon you, about—a little business, I say, ma'am—it's about—

ELEONORA. Won't you be seated, Sir? 35

OLD WAVERLEY. Thankee, ma'am, thankee (*sits*); (*aside*) Now I shall be a little more at my ease.

ELEONORA (*returning to her Chair, aside*). I dread an explanation!

OLD WAVERLEY. I come to you, I say, ma'am—(*aside*) I can talk to her better when I don't look at her! to speak about— 40 about—you've a daughter, I think?—

ELEONORA (*aside*). 'Tis so!—cruel Wilmot!—

OLD WAVERLEY. A Daughter, I say, ma'am?—Have not you, ma'am?

ELEONORA (*rising, with emotion*). I have, Sir!—my last, sole 45 resource upon Earth! all that softens—or sustains my existence!

OLD WAVERLEY (*aside*). There, now! She owns she sustains her! She's just the bad Jade I took her for! I'll speak to the point without ceremony. Well, ma'am, I come about that daughter. 50 I should be glad to know upon what terms you'd give her up.

ELEONORA. Give her up? Inhuman!—Can you come to me with so barbarous a proposition?

OLD WAVERLEY (*aside*). There, now, there! that's to make me bid 55 high! yes, yes, I must come down pretty handsomely, I see that. I don't mean, ma'am, to be shabby; but as to any thing out of the common road—

ELEONORA. Sir!

OLD WAVERLEY (*aside*). There, now! there's a look of an Eye! 60 one would think she had never so much as heard a naughty word in her life! I say, ma'am, as to any thing extravagant, I can't think of it; but if you will make her quietly and reasonably over to me—

ELEONORA. Never, Sir, never! no deputy, no substitute shall tear 65 her from me! If that last fatal wound must be inflicted, the Principal, himself, must at least come to witness its effect!

OLD WAVERLEY (*aside*). What does she mean now? The Principal?—Who is he, I wonder? Is she in treaty with somebody else, to set two or three of us together at loggerheads?—As to 70 the Principal, ma'am,—or the Underling, which I suppose you mean me for,—

ELEONORA. I mean not any offence, Sir; but concluding you the agent—

75 OLD WAVERLEY. Agent?

ELEONORA. Do you not come to me on a commission?

OLD WAVERLEY. Commission? no, ma'am, not I! I am no second-hand broker. I come on my own affairs.

ELEONORA. To what, then, Sir, do I owe so singular a visit? and
80 intcrrogatories so extraordinary?

OLD WAVERLEY (*aside*). There now she's at her Eye again! I wish I had not looked at it! How the plague a woman of that sort can have the impudence to have such a modest Eye! Why, ma'am, your daughter—

85 ELEONORA. What know you, Sir, of my daughter?

OLD WAVERLEY. O, I know her very well; and a pretty Girl she is; and as soft as a Dove. I don't mean to dispute that; very pretty and dovey.—

ELEONORA (*with agitation*). And where, Sir—when—how—
90 which way have you seen her?

OLD WAVERLEY. Here,—hard by,—in the avenue.

ELEONORA (*aside*). Good Heavens!—My poor Child!—She has mistaken this old man for her Uncle! (*calling*) Phebe! my cloak! I must run every risk to follow and protect her. I find,
95 Sir, I have addressed you under an error: I beg you, therefore, now, concisely and at once, to let me know your business.

OLD WAVERLEY. Why, ma'am, my business is this. You have got a young Girl here, that I have conceived a sort of fancy to; and therefore, out of regard to her, I am willing to take her
100 into my own hands: and so, any thing you may expect, that's reasonable, for letting her off, I shan't object to; and I'll make her as comfortable as I can; but as to any exorbitant sum, don't pretend to it, because I can't afford it.

ELEONORA. Do I live!

105 OLD WAVERLEY. O! now she's to be surprised!

ELEONORA. O my poor helpless Sophia! My abandoned—my fatherless Child!—are we sunk to this?—Is innocence no guard? Virtue, no bulwark?—And can Man alone from Man protect us?

OLD WAVERLEY. Protect you, ma'am?—why— 110
ELEONORA. I have heard you, Sir, in silence; in silence, now, hear
    Me!
OLD WAVERLEY. Ma'am!
ELEONORA. I shall not detain you. A single word will comprise
    my answer. I perceive, Sir— 115
OLD WAVERLEY. What, ma'am?
ELEONORA. You are a villain!
OLD WAVERLEY. What!—Bless my heart!—
ELEONORA. I deign no explanation. Conscience will be as able an
    Interpreter to your understanding, as Honour has been to 120
    mine! Phebe!—you will open the door for this Gentleman.

*Exit up the little Stair Case.*

Scene xiv

*Enter* PHEBE, *who crosses over the stage, and opens the house door.*

OLD WAVERLEY. Well, I've seen many odd turns in my life; but
    this is the oddest!
PHEBE. Please, Sir, I've opened the door, Sir.—La, who's here?
YOUNG WAVERLEY (*at the door*). Don't let me interrupt you from
    your business, my dear. I'll wait in this room till one of the 5
    ladies come. Pray go back to the kitchen, and don't mind me
    (*giving her money*).
PHEBE. Yes, sir. La! I wonder who all these visitors be!

*Exit.*

Scene xv

*Enter* YOUNG WAVERLEY, *disguised.*

YOUNG WAVERLEY (*to himself*). This old suit of the steward's
    squeezes me so horribly, I can hardly move. I fancy it was
    made before he had done growing. However, it answers my
    purpose, for I might pass my Father twenty times a day in it,
    without being guessed at. 5

OLD WAVERLEY. I've half a mind to sit me down stock still, till the little Girl comes in to give me an answer herself (*sits down on Eleonora's arm Chair*).

YOUNG WAVERLEY. I'll wait here till—How! my Father again!—what plaguy ill luck!—(*aside, and returning to the door*) I'll make off before he finds me out.

OLD WAVERLEY (*looking round, aside*). Who's that, now, that's come in without rapping at the door? Mighty familiar, methinks. It's the Principal, I suppose, that she told me of. Quite a young man, too, for all his queer dress, if I may judge by his motions.

YOUNG WAVERLEY (*aside*). No, hang it, no! I can't bear to leave him master of the field, neither. I must find out the reason of his haunts here. He'll never know me if I don't speak. He'll take me for just such another old Codger as himself.

OLD WAVERLEY (*aside*). He must be a young fellow of great particularity, now, to be dressed more old fashioned than I am!

YOUNG WAVERLEY (*aside, and looking about*). I think I'll go and ask the maid what he's waiting for. I wonder which is the way to the kitchen.

OLD WAVERLEY (*aside*). I should take him for an old man, too,— if I were not one myself: but I know the odds on't too well! bless my heart! if I were to whisk about in that jerking way, I should tumble me plump down at once!

YOUNG WAVERLEY (*aside*). What the deuce is it can bring him to the house again so soon?

OLD WAVERLEY (*aside*). There's something in his motions prodigiously like to Jack's!

YOUNG WAVERLEY (*aside*). No, I won't go to the kitchen; if I speak to the maid, he may know me by my voice.

OLD WAVERLEY (*aside*). His hat's slouched so, one can hardly see a bit of his face; but, upon my word, it's his exact size!

YOUNG WAVERLEY (*aside*). I had never the least suspicion of the old Gentleman's having such tricks!

OLD WAVERLEY (*aside*). Only Jack would no more be seen in such a dress as that—yet,—I protest, it's Jack's chin!

YOUNG WAVERLEY (*aside*). So soon to return to the charge!

OLD WAVERLEY (*aside*). It's his mouth, too—as near as ever I saw.

YOUNG WAVERLEY (*aside*). How he examines me! I must get out of his way! 45

OLD WAVERLEY. That's as like his skip — why it's Jack! — it's Jack himself! — Jack! —

YOUNG WAVERLEY (*aside*). Detected, by Jingo! — but I won't own myself!

OLD WAVERLEY. Jack, I say! 50

YOUNG WAVERLEY (*singing carelessly*). Tol de rol de rol —

OLD WAVERLEY. Surely I can't be mistaken! — Sir! — young man! —

YOUNG WAVERLEY (*singing*). La, la, la, la, la, —

OLD WAVERLEY. He don't much care to speak, be he who he 55 will. Pray, Sir, I say, (*rising*) a'n't you — yes, you are! — a'n't you — I say, — my son Jack?

YOUNG WAVERLEY (*clapping his hat lower over his face, and holding a handkerchief to his mouth*). Did you speak, sir?

OLD WAVERLEY. Speak, Sir? yes, Sir!

YOUNG WAVERLEY. Your pleasure, Sir? 60

OLD WAVERLEY. My pleasure, Sir? no, it's my displeasure, Sir! What do you do in this place again?

YOUNG WAVERLEY. This place, Sir? (*looking around*) Is any thing the matter with this place?

OLD WAVERLEY. The matter? why have you forgotten — 65

YOUNG WAVERLEY. Name your objection to it, Sir!

OLD WAVERLEY. My objection? bless my heart! —

YOUNG WAVERLEY. I see no harm in it, I protest. The place seems to me a very good place.

OLD WAVERLEY. Why if ever — 70

YOUNG WAVERLEY. But you are very kind to take so much interest in me, Sir. I'm very much obliged to you, Sir, I'm sure.

OLD WAVERLEY. Very kind? ay; so I think! I wonder what would become of you if I were not! 75

YOUNG WAVERLEY. I have the honour to wish you a good day, Sir.

OLD WAVERLEY. Why how now, Jack?

YOUNG WAVERLEY (*walking off*). Tol de rol de rol —

OLD WAVERLEY. Stop, Jack! Stop, I say! — Jack! — Jack! — 80

YOUNG WAVERLEY. Jack! — Jack! — why where the deuce can

this Jack be? Let me help you to call him, Sir. Jack! Jack! —

OLD WAVERLEY. Call him? Why, what's in the boy's head?

YOUNG WAVERLEY. I beg your pardon, I am sure, Sir. I only meant to assist you. Good day, Sir.

OLD WAVERLEY. Why what's all this, Jack? don't you know me?

YOUNG WAVERLEY. Not in the least, Sir.

OLD WAVERLEY. Well, this is a thing for the first time! A Boy not knowing his own Father!

YOUNG WAVERLEY. Not exactly the first time,[1] I believe, Sir! But I don't mean to criticize.

OLD WAVERLEY. You don't? You are prodigiously kind. So I don't know you, neither, I suppose?

YOUNG WAVERLEY. O, I apprehend you, now, Sir! You mistake me for somebody else? — some acquaintance? Yes, yes, I conceive how it is, now.

OLD WAVERLEY. Why what are you at?

YOUNG WAVERLEY. I dare say I can guess the person; for there's a young fellow — a pretty sort of a young fellow, I understand, — who lives somewhere here-abouts, that I am often taken for. Pray, Sir, with your patience, what was the name you mentioned just now? — the name you were calling?

OLD WAVERLEY. The name? Why Jack, to be sure; Jack Waverley.

YOUNG WAVERLEY. The very same! the identical same name! It's the oddest thing in the world how often I have heard I am like him!

OLD WAVERLEY. Like him? Like who?

YOUNG WAVERLEY. This Jack, Sir; this Jack Waverley.

OLD WAVERLEY. Why who would you be like? What do you mean?

YOUNG WAVERLEY. It's surprising what strong resemblances there sometimes are! I am frequently told nobody would know us asunder — except by our dress! And they say he has quite another taste in dress to what I have! But it's so familiar to me to be taken for him, that I am as much accustom-

---

1 *Not exactly the first time*: alluding to the proverbial "wise child that knows its own father."

med to be called Jack Waverley, as to be called by my own name.

OLD WAVERLEY. Why now can this really not be my son? It's very surprising if he i'n't. Yet to be sure it's no more like his style of dress—pray, Sir, if Jack Waverley i'n't your name—what is? 120

YOUNG WAVERLEY. I never tell my name, Sir. Good morning to you, Sir.

OLD WAVERLEY. You never tell your name? why then how is any body to know it? 125

YOUNG WAVERLEY. I never trouble myself about that, Sir. Good morning to you.

*Exit abruptly.*

OLD WAVERLEY. Well, this is as odd a visit as ever I made! very odd, indeed! Here's a paupau woman[1] makes it out I am worse than herself;—and either I don't know my own Son, or my own Son don't know me! I begin to think we are all either cracked, or addle-headed: very addle-headed and cracky, I am afraid! 130

*Exit.*

Scene xvi

*The Avenue.*

*Enter the* STEWARD, *and* BOB SAPLING.

STEWARD. Pho, pho, Bob, never talk to me of your strange Gentleman, but mind what I've told you about Sir Roderick. He is now coming this way. If you should be made his Heir, what a thing it will be for us all!

BOB. But you must begin, Nuncle. 5

STEWARD. He's coming! hush!

---

1 *a paupau woman*: a procuress.

## Scene xvii

*Enter* SIR RODERICK.

SIR RODERICK. What! not here, neither! That old man's grown
so touchy, one can't say a syllable to him, but he's off in a pet!
He must be talked to like a Gentleman, forsooth!—Stephens!
Why what do you do here? Have you met with Mr. Waver-
5    ley?
STEWARD. No, Sir.
SIR RODERICK. Why then I make no doubt but he's rode off to
York![1] well, a good journey to him. I must not so much as
speak to him now, but just to his own liking! And why?
10    because, truly, I am in my own house! A pretty reason in
faith!—Did you hear me, Stephens?
STEWARD. Yes, Sir.
SIR RODERICK. Then why can't you answer? Where is it a man
may speak his mind, if it i'n't in his own house?
15 STEWARD. I don't know, I am sure, Sir.
SIR RODERICK. What, if he be only a vagabond, a raggamuffin,
spunging upon who-ever he can get at, and living nobody
knows how,—then, I suppose, he may say what he likes—
may he?
20 STEWARD. I can't tell, indeed, Sir.
SIR RODERICK. But if he be a man of property, with a house over
his head, and a coat to his back, he must not utter a word but
in ceremony—ha?
STEWARD. I never knew how it was, I'm sure, Sir.
25 SIR RODERICK. So then, I may take a house, and pay the taxes,
and maintain the servants, and keep the Table;—and let
whosoever please come into my rooms, and consume my
time, and eat my meat, and drink my Wine—and I must not
let out a syllable but what's just to their own taste?
30 STEWARD. Very hard, indeed, Sir.
SIR RODERICK. I have never seen that young rascal, Jack, since
that impudence of his—writing Love verses to Lady Smatter!
And now here's his Father just as bad; for though I'll answer

---

1   *rode off to York*: i.e., ridden off at great speed; see *The Witlings*, p. 138, note 1.

for it he has heard, by this time, my resolution to cut his son off with a Halfpenny, he never comes near me! If there were any thing in the world I could hate like a woman, 'twould be those two fools. —But as to a woman—she's my complete abomination.

STEWARD. No wonder, Sir.

SIR RODERICK. Why what does a woman spend her life in? D'ye know? Doing nothing but mischief; talking nothing but nonsense, and listening to nothing but flattery! Sitting, with her two hands before her, all day long, to be waited on; and sighing and moping, because her noodle pate can't hit upon things to give trouble fast enough!

BOB (in a low voice to the STEWARD). Nuncle! I shall forget all I was to say.

STEWARD. Patience!—With your leave, Sir, here's one begs to speak with you.

SIR RODERICK. What does he want?

STEWARD. Sir, it's a young man that—

SIR RODERICK. Who the plague cares whether he be young or old? Can't you let me know his business, without telling me his age?

STEWARD. It's … Bob Sapling, if you please, Sir,—my Nephew.

SIR RODERICK. And who is he if I don't please? Ha?—Can you tell me that?

STEWARD. He is come, Sir, upon the notice of your wanting an Heir.

SIR RODERICK. What!

STEWARD. He's a very ignorant young man, I can assure you, Sir.

SIR RODERICK. What are you at now? Have you lost your wits?

STEWARD. Did not you say, Sir, you should disinherit poor Mr. Jack?

SIR RODERICK. And what if I did?

STEWARD. And that you'd leave your estate to somebody that could neither write nor read?

SIR RODERICK. Well, and what then?

STEWARD. No offence, I hope, Sir,—only the young man's friends thought it was such an opportunity as might not happen again.

SIR RODERICK. This is such an assurance as I never met with

yet!—Drive him away this minute!—Tell him it's all false!—
a mere lying report, of your own fabrication!—D'ye hear?

75 STEWARD. I am very sorry to have made such a mistake, I am
sure, Sir; but I thought, from your being so angry about Lady
Smatter—

SIR RODERICK. Why there, now, there! the next thing will be to
say I sha'n't disinherit Jack!—Stop, Stephens! what makes
80 you always in such a cursed hurry? I'll speak to the young
man, if it's only to frighten him.

STEWARD. Yes, Sir. Here, Bob!

SIR RODERICK. Your servant, friend.

BOB. Servant, Sir. Here I be, Sir.

85 SIR RODERICK. Yes, I see that. And pray, Sir, what brings you
here?

BOB. Uncle told me, Sir, you was a looking for a body to leave
your fortune to, upon your dying.

STEWARD (apart to Bob). You should not have mentioned that!

90 SIR RODERICK. What!

BOB. So I thought, if you'd no objections, I should like it very
well.

SIR RODERICK. You should?

BOB. Yes; for I know of one I should like hugely should go shares
95 with me.

SIR RODERICK. Very lucky, indeed! So you have made your
arrangements, have you? And pray, Sir, do you know mine?
Do you know what I require of you?

BOB. Yes, partly, Sir.

100 SIR RODERICK. And are you such a Booby that you have come
to these years, without learning how to write or read?

BOB (nodding). That you may depend upon!

SIR RODERICK. So you have been a dunce from your youth
upwards, have you?

105 BOB. A Dunce, Sir?

SIR RODERICK. Ay, Sir, a Dunce! If you don't know what that
means, it's a Noodle, Sir! And if you want to hear that
explained, it's a blockhead! And if that i'n't clear, it's an Ideot!
Now do you understand me?

110 BOB. Yes, fast enough. Sister Henny runs me on so by the hour
together.

SIR RODERICK. Sister Henny?

BOB. Yes she's mortal cross. 'Ti'n't She I shall go shares with
when you die.

SIR RODERICK. O, it i'n't? You are very good to let me into your 115
secrets!

BOB. No; it's one worth a hundred of She. And one as always
takes my part, for she knows what it is to be snubbed so; for
she's as bad off as I.

SIR RODERICK. She? and she? why what the D—l's this? do you 120
come hither to talk to me of your Shes?

BOB. No; I did not come 'cause of that; I come 'cause Uncle said
it might be the making of my fortune; for, he said, 'twas
unknown what a body might get from you, when you was in
one of your tantarums. 125

SIR RODERICK. One of my tantarums?—(*holding up his stick*) As
I'm alive, Stephens—

STEWARD. O Sir! Mercy!

*runs away.*

SIR RODERICK. Ay, off with you! And if ever you enter my Walls
again, I'll have you Horse-ponded. (*turning, with his raised stick* 130
*to* BOB) As to you, you young dolt—

BOB. O, if you come to that—I can out-run your old gouty feet,
I warrant me!

*runs off.*

SIR RODERICK. My old gouty feet!—By the lord Harry, if I
ha'n't a mind to knock down the first man I meet! 135

# ACT V

## Scene i

*An Apartment at* SIR RODERICK's.

SIR RODERICK. I detest and abominate the whole sex worse and worse every moment! A second time to be caught by a copy of Verses! —

## Scene ii

*Enter* OLD WAVERLEY.

O ho, Mr. Waverley! you've found your way back again, have you? I thought you were set off for New Zealand. So I suppose you have heard of the pretty tricks of your son? Writing Love Verses to Lady Smatter?

5 OLD WAVERLEY. Bless my heart! to Lady Smatter? Why he's following up a young person in the village at this very time!

SIR RODERICK. What, Jack?

OLD WAVERLEY. I detected him in the Girl's own house twice this very day.

10 SIR RODERICK. There's a young dog, now! After all I have said to him never to think of a woman as long as he breathed, to be after two at a time! And where's this that you detected him?

OLD WAVERLEY. Why at no very good house, I'm afraid! —

SIR RODERICK. Very pretty, truly! So you've been twice to day
15 yourself at a bad house, have you?

OLD WAVERLEY. I? O, but that was — that, my good friend — was only a matter of charity!

SIR RODERICK. By the lord Harry, I am come to a fine pass! surrounded by a pretty clan!

## Scene iii

*Enter the* STEWARD.

STEWARD. Sir, here's a young person who —

SIR RODERICK. What! you're at your youngs, again, are you? And pray what am I to keep a Register Office[1] of people's ages for? Ha?

STEWARD. It's a person, Sir, who begs to see you alone.

SIR RODERICK. Why then, tell him I beg to see him in company! what the plague! Are these young persons to come to my house to domineer over me? telling me to turn my company out of doors, because they want to have my rooms to themselves? Bid him come in directly.

STEWARD (*apart to* OLD WAVERLEY). What can I do, Sir?—It's a young lady! And I dare not for my life tell Sir Roderick so. But she persuades me she has something so particular to say, that she is sure Sir Roderick will forgive me, when he sees her.

OLD WAVERLEY. A young lady?

STEWARD. Yes; with an elderly one by her side, who seems to have the tutoring her.

OLD WAVERLEY. For a wager, it's my own little Girl, and her Mother! and it's me, all the time, she wants! (*turns to* SIR RODERICK) Sir Roderick, I have a notion this is a person who wishes to speak with Me; that's my notion; so, if you please, I'll step out and see.

SIR RODERICK. No, if you please, you may stay in, and let Me see! What the deuce! am I to be ordered by you, too? Bid him come in, I say!

STEWARD. Yes, Sir. (*aside*) We shall have rare work, now!

OLD WAVERLEY (*apart to the* STEWARD). Harkee, Mr. Stephens! don't let the elderly one come in! She dashes me prodigiously.

*Exit* STEWARD.

(*to himself*) It's very unlucky if it's that young Girl! very unlucky!—A young Girl coming after me!—There's no knowing what Sir Roderick may think of it!

---

1 *a Register Office*: the Universal Register Office was founded by Henry Fielding and his half-brother John in 1750; several other such offices opened later in the century. They assisted in the finding of employment, sales of goods, etc.

## Scene iv

*Enter* JOYCE.

No! it's another, I protest!

SIR RODERICK. How now? What's this? I can't believe my Eyes! A woman in my house? By the lord Harry, I'll make every man in it come and help turn her out! Here, Stephens! Smith!
5 Thomas! Jack Waverley! What are you all about? Here's a woman got into the house! Mr. Waverley, what do you mean by standing there, and doing nothing? Why don't you bid her go?

OLD WAVERLEY. Upon my word, my friend—

10 JOYCE. Pray, Gentlemen, will you tell me which of you two is Sir Roderick?—(*pointing to him*) I hope it i'n't That!—

SIR RODERICK. Why what is it to you?

OLD WAVERLEY. Yes, ma'am, it is That! That is Sir Roderick!

JOYCE. Is it? (*running up to him*) Why then, Uncle, do you know
15 you're my Uncle?

SIR RODERICK. I your Uncle?

JOYCE. They told me so in the West Indies, I am sure.

SIR RODERICK. How? do you come from the West Indies?

JOYCE. Yes, I do; and that's as true here as there! And if you'll call
20 in Nurse, she'll tell you so, too.

SIR RODERICK. What! are you my Sister Eleonora's Daughter?

JOYCE. That's what I heard in the West Indies. And they told me, too, I was your niece, as sure as I was Squire Wilmot's Daughter. And that's real truth! for I am just as much one as t'other!

25 SIR RODERICK. I am confounded!—And what do you come hither for?

JOYCE. I come hither—to see you, Uncle.

SIR RODERICK. Me? Why has no one ever told you I never let a woman come into my house? never see one? never hear of
30 one? and wish Bedlam¹ were large enough to hold every one of them?

JOYCE. Lord, Uncle, and what for?

---

1 *Bedlam*: the popular name for Bethlehem Royal Hospital, a hospital for the insane in Moorfields; see *The Witlings*, p. 164, note 1.

SIR RODERICK. What for? What right have you to ask me what for? Ha? Do you think I have not very good reasons? Do you come from the West Indies, to enquire into my private affairs? 35 Don't you know I've made a vow never to let a woman cross my threshold?

JOYCE. Lord Uncle, don't you like women?

SIR RODERICK. Like them? By the Lord Harry—

JOYCE. And why not? They are a great deal prettier than men;— 40 though I like the men best, too, because they are the good naturedest—except just my own Relations.

SIR RODERICK. There's a Tartar, now! there's a Tartar! come to my own house for nothing but to affront me!

JOYCE. No, I did not, Uncle; I did not come for that! 45

SIR RODERICK. Why what did you come for, then?

JOYCE. I came to see what you'd do for me, Uncle.

SIR RODERICK. There's impudence, now! never saw me in her born days before, and pops upon me all at once, to pick my pocket, and make me a beggar! This is the effect of marrying 50 into such a family! She's no more like her Mother—

JOYCE. Yes, but I be, though!

SIR RODERICK. You can't remember your Mother?

JOYCE. Yes, I do.

SIR RODERICK. Do you? why then you remember as modest, as 55 graceful, as elegant a woman—

JOYCE. No, I don't.

SIR RODERICK. Hey day! why what do you remember, then?

JOYCE. Nothing but a vulgar, jabbering old woman.

SIR RODERICK. If my head don't turn round!—Is this your 60 respect for your Mother?

JOYCE. O, that don't hinder my liking her. I like her better than any body; but she's a poor little mean old Soul, for all that.

SIR RODERICK. I protest I am choaked—suffocated—I don't know what step to take!— 65

JOYCE. I wish you'd let me tell you, Uncle!

SIR RODERICK (groaning). Oh!

JOYCE. Now will you, Uncle? Will you?

SIR RODERICK. Oh!—

JOYCE. Now do, Uncle, do! Only just hear me, Uncle. Now if 70

you'd be so kind, and so good-natured, as to give me a few of
your thousand pounds—

SIR RODERICK. This is past every thing! (*sitting down and panting*)

JOYCE. Why Nurse says it's no more than your duty!

75 SIR RODERICK (*groaning*). Oh!—

JOYCE. Why now, Uncle, what can you want with them all yourself? Such an old man as you are?

SIR RODERICK (*starting up, enraged*). As I'm alive—

JOYCE. It can't be to dress finer, because that would make you

80 look a good deal uglier; it can't be for your family, because
you've neither Child nor Chick;[1] it can't be for eating and
drinking, because you are past running about to get an
appetite; and it can't be to go to Balls, because you'd get
nobody to dance with you.—So—

85 SIR RODERICK. Where are all my people?

JOYCE. So what good can all that money do you, Uncle? Nurse
says a little snug annuity would get you all you want.

SIR RODERICK. Stephens!—

JOYCE. For it's only, she says, an oak stick to stump about with in a

90 morning; and an arm chair to doze in after dinner; and plenty
of Water Gruel for supper.—

SIR RODERICK. I am parched!—Smith!—Thomas!—

JOYCE. Now if you'd give the money to me, you'd see the difference! Now do try, Uncle, do! 'Twill make you quite giddy to

95 see how I shall whisk it about! I'll go to plays,—I'll go to
Balls,—I'll go to Operas,—I'll go to puppet-shews,—I'll see
all the wild beasts,[2] I'll eat all the tarts at the Pastry Cooks;—
and my Coach shall have such lovely brisk Horses—they'll
gallop over you before you can get out of the way!—Now

100 will you give me the money, Uncle? will you?

SIR RODERICK (*throwing himself stretched on an arm-Chair*).
Breath!—Breath!—Breath!—

JOYCE. If you will, Uncle—I'll love you, and kiss you, as if you
were as pretty as a little kitten!

SIR RODERICK (*groaning*). Oh!

---

1    *Child nor Chick*: a proverbial phrase meaning "no one to care for."
2    *wild beasts*: London's best-known menagerie, with a collection of lions, tigers, wolves,
     bears, etc., was kept at the Tower of London.

JOYCE. And I'll make a large, huge, gigantic bonfire of all Aunt 105
Smatter's Books and Authors for joy!
SIR RODERICK (*starting up*). Will you, faith?
JOYCE (*jumping and frisking about*). O, he smiles at last!—I've
gained the day! I've gained the day!

Scene v

*Enter the* STEWARD.

STEWARD (*to* JOYCE). The elderly person, who came with you,
ma'am, has something to say to you in very great haste.
JOYCE. Let her wait, let her wait!

*Exit* STEWARD.

Scene vi

*Enter* NURSE, *crying.*

NURSE. Miss! Miss! come directly!—I must speak to you this
minute! O my dear! my dear! (*dragging her away*)
JOYCE. The day's my own! the day's my own!
Rule, ye fair ones,—Ye fair ones, rule—the Men![1]

*Exit singing, pulled by* NURSE, *crying.*

OLD WAVERLEY. This young Girl is but giddy, my friend. How- 5
ever, one must not be over-strict.
SIR RODERICK. I have not a guess, yet, whether I am asleep or
awake!

---

1   *Rule, ye fair ones … Men!*: a parody of James Thomson's popular ode "Rule Britannia"
(1740), of which the refrain is "Rule, Britannia, rule the waves; / Britons never will be
slaves."

## Scene vii

*Enter* STEWARD.

STEWARD. Another young lady, Sir,—

SIR RODERICK. What!—

STEWARD. Another young lady, Sir, begs very hard to speak to you.

5 SIR RODERICK (*rubbing his Eyes*). Why this must be all passing in a dream!—Another young lady come to Me?—what the devil and all!—I hope you have not let her in?

STEWARD. Yes, I have, Sir.—

SIR RODERICK. Why then you may let her out!—go!—

10 STEWARD. She's here, Sir.

*Exit.*

## Scene viii

*Enter* SOPHIA.
*She stands fearfully at the door.*

OLD WAVERLEY (*aside*). Bless my heart!—This is she herself!

SIR RODERICK. Yes, as I live, it's another!—another young Girl!—Why here must be some juggling—some trick afloat—and, by the lord Harry,—if I find out who's making

5 their Game of me—

SOPHIA. I dare not advance—

OLD WAVERLEY (*aside*). I wish I were safe out of the room! She has such pretty little coaxing ways with her, that if once she begin to speak to me, Sir Roderick will think something, as

10 sure as can be!

SIR RODERICK. They shall pay for their hocus pocus work, I can tell them!

SOPHIA (*aside*). He will not speak first! I must take courage! (*to* SIR RODERICK, *but looking down*) Pardon, Sir, this intrusion,

15 and suffer me to hope, from your kindness, your indulgence—

SIR RODERICK. There, now, there!—just as I thought!—She's come on purpose to make a joke of me! I tell you what, young woman, if you don't let me know immediately who it is has set you on to this impudent frolic— 20

SOPHIA (*looking up*). Good Heaven! what a mistake have I made!—To whom am I come!—

OLD WAVERLEY (*aside, and retreating*). I wish she mayn't see me!

SOPHIA. I beg you, Sir, to pardon me: my commission was with another Gentleman— 25

SIR RODERICK. And it may be with another lady, for aught I care! What the deuce!—

SOPHIA. Indeed, Sir, I am utterly ashamed. I will be gone—

OLD WAVERLEY (*aside, and sideling off*). So will I, too!

SOPHIA (*turning round to go to the door, encounters* WAVERLEY). Ah! I am right at last! O Sir! what a relief is it to me to see 30 you!

SIR RODERICK. So, so, so! This is his own Girl, then!—Very pretty doings, Sir! So you let your Girl come after you to my very house, do you?

OLD WAVERLEY. Indeed, my friend—you may believe me, my 35 friend—this is a thing I am quite innocent in!—Fie, my dear! how could you do such a thing?—following me in this manner?—It's putting thoughts into people's heads!

SIR RODERICK. Why then it's putting what people's heads have great need of! What the devil! do you suppose this is to satis- 40 fy me?

OLD WAVERLEY. Go, my dear, go!—

SOPHIA. Hear me, I beseech you, Sir! Remember how kind, how encouraging you have been, and cast me not off, I entreat!

SIR RODERICK. There! there, now! This is your innocence, is it? 45 You have been kind and encouraging to her, have you? And so you only make a wry face, because I am by?

OLD WAVERLEY. I was never in such jeopardy in my life!—do go!—pray do!—I shall take it very ill if you don't!—I shall, indeed!— 50

SOPHIA. Suffer me but to speak to you a few minutes alone—

SIR RODERICK. As I'm alive, if I a'n't ashamed to hear them!

OLD WAVERLEY. Lack a day! if I a'n't ashamed too! I protest,

young Woman, I could not have thought you would have
55 been so bold!

SOPHIA. Two instants private discourse will clear all!

SIR RODERICK. Private? Ha? Private discourse? If ever the like of
this—

SOPHIA. What can thus have changed you, Sir? what is it can so
60 suddenly have robbed me of your promised protection?

OLD WAVERLEY. I'm in such a heat at her confidence—

SIR RODERICK. So am I, too, at yours!—A man at your Time of
life!— However, you may find some other place for your
gambols, I can tell you that!

65 OLD WAVERLEY. See, now, you little plague, see what you've
done!

SOPHIA. One word, one syllable, only, in another room—

SIR RODERICK. She's the impudentest baggage that ever entered
a house! So I am in your way, am I, ma'am? I am in your way,
70 am I, Sir? And you want me to walk off the premises to leave
you to yourselves, do you?

OLD WAVERLEY. I have been sadly taken in, I see! I could never
have believed it, but she's certainly a bad Girl, coming after
me with a design to take away my character!

75 SIR RODERICK. And I beg, then, she may take away your person,
too! for, by the lord Harry, I'll call up all the house to expose
you! Here, Stephens!—Smith!—Thomas!—

SOPHIA. O, no! no! no!—Let me speak to you first!—

OLD WAVERLEY. I can't, indeed; they may come and take you
80 away if they will!

## Scene ix

*Enter the* STEWARD, BUTLER, *and* FOOTMAN.

You may take her, I say! you may carry her off!

SOPHIA. Hold! hold! and hear me, Sir! Hear, and protect me! I
have a claim to your protection! I am ... your Niece!

SIR RODERICK (*bursts into a loud laugh*). Ha! Ha! Ha! Well, this is
5 the first good laugh I have had these seventeen years!—So
you've got a Niece, too, have you?

OLD WAVERLEY. Not that I know of, I am sure! I don't know

that I have ever a one in the World!

SOPHIA. I can give you proof immediately!—Indeed, my dear Uncle,— 10

SIR RODERICK. Ha! Ha! Ha! So you're an Uncle, as well as I! And we've both got nieces sprung up all in a moment, nobody knows how! Ha! Ha! Ha!

OLD WAVERLEY. Upon my word, Sir Roderick—

SOPHIA. What do I hear? Are not you Sir Roderick yourself, Sir? 15

OLD WAVERLEY. I? No!

SOPHIA. Not Sir Roderick?

OLD WAVERLEY. Bless me, no! I'm only John Waverley Esquire, Senior. That's Sir Roderick.

SOPHIA. I am confounded! in what a series of mistakes and errors 20 have I been involved!—Alas, Sir!—pardon an offense which has been so unintentional! It is Sir Roderick I have always meant,—it is Sir Roderick whose kindness and protection I come to implore—it is Sir Roderick who is my Uncle!

SIR RODERICK. Very clever, truly! And pray how many more of 25 you may there be, who intend to pop in upon me in this manner? As I'm alive, if I don't put an end to this, I shall have a niece of every Girl in the Parish! Harkee, Mrs. Minx—

Scene x

*Enter* YOUNG WAVERLEY.

YOUNG WAVERLEY. What do I see!

SIR RODERICK. Hey day! what has brought you back, Sir? How dare you shew your Face here again?

YOUNG WAVERLEY. Indeed, Sir, I am a true penitent—

SIR RODERICK. You are, are you, so?—Well, well, one of you at a 5 time. So first for you, Mrs. Niece. Here, Stephens, Smith, Thomas,—

SOPHIA (*to* YOUNG WAVERLEY). O Heavens!—You will not suffer me to be ill-treated?

YOUNG WAVERLEY. Never while I breathe! 10

SOPHIA. Guard me, then, from being molested, or pursued!

*Exit.*

OLD WAVERLEY. I'll after her myself, and tell her never to speak to me again while she lives!

*Exit.*

SIR RODERICK. What now? Is the Girl gone? Why if I let her off
so, in ten minutes she'll send me another! Stephens!—
Smith!—Thomas!—after her directly—
YOUNG WAVERLEY (*stopping them*). 'Tis at the risk of your lives you stir a step!
SIR RODERICK. Well, this is a finisher! This is all that was wanted
for a finisher! So I must not as much as send my own servants about now, to turn man, woman, or child out of my own house?
YOUNG WAVERLEY. Believe me, Sir, I wait upon you at this moment, in the humblest manner, to disclaim my foolish
scheme, and beg your forgiveness.
SIR RODERICK. O ho, do you so? what, I suppose you don't know how to squeeze any more Love verses out of your brains?
YOUNG WAVERLEY. I rejoice, Sir, to hear, from Stephens, that her
ladyship has never received that folly.
SIR RODERICK. How? won't you offer yourself to her, then?
YOUNG WAVERLEY. Undoubtedly not, Sir.
SIR RODERICK. And won't you write her any more Love verses?
YOUNG WAVERLEY. No, Sir, indeed!
SIR RODERICK. Prove your words, Jack, and I'll put your name
back again into my Will directly!—Lookee,—it sticks in my throat to speak of any of that cursed Sex,—but there's a Girl came here before that imposter, who says she's my real niece: now—do you hear?—to prove your words, you shall have
her and my money together.
YOUNG WAVERLEY. I am very much indebted to you, Sir, but I must frankly own—the young lady I saw here just now—
SIR RODERICK. Why what have you to do with her? Are you another of her uncles?
YOUNG WAVERLEY. No, Sir, unfortunately, I am nothing to
her—though I wish to be everything!

SIR RODERICK. Well, this surpasses the whole! So, after all I have vowed against it, you are not only resolved to marry, but you must chuse for yourself, must you? Though but a few years ago, you could not walk without a back-string?[1]  50

YOUNG WAVERLEY. Indeed, Sir,—

SIR RODERICK. And pray, what's her fortune? Ha?—O ho! you can give no answer! why then, I suppose she has not a groat in the World? But you are to become master of a family all one? Ha? And you are to have two or three dozen squalling  55 brats? Are you? And to keep half a score drunken servants? And to call about you? And to live at your ease?—And, all the time, your Butcher, I suppose, may find you in meat, and your Baker may treat you with Bread?

YOUNG WAVERLEY. I assure you, Sir,—  60

SIR RODERICK. And who the devil do you think is to treat them? what, I suppose, while you are running up bills, and feasting and rioting, they may go and rot in a Jail?—may they?

YOUNG WAVERLEY. Upon my word, Sir,—

SIR RODERICK. And pray who gave you a title to live at their  65 expence? Ha?—what right have you to starve half a score honest tradesmen, merely to pamper your own luxury? Do you think they don't want to eat and drink as well as you?— what do you suppose they are made of?—Ha?—

YOUNG WAVERLEY. If you'll believe me, Sir,—  70

SIR RODERICK. But I won't believe you, Sir! You are a young driveler, and she is a young impostor; and I'll after her myself, and see her turned out of the Parish! And I would I could do the same by every peticoat in it!

*Exit.*

YOUNG WAVERLEY. What a peppery old fellow! He is all  75 spice!—save that he has heat without flavour! 'Twill be hard, however, if a young woman Lover, cannot get the better of an old woman hater!

*Exit.*

---

1  *a back-string*: a cord attached to young children to keep them from wandering off.

## Scene xi

*The Dressing Room of* LADY SMATTER.

LADY SMATTER. PRIM.

LADY SMATTER.

Love! the most generous passion of the mind,
The softest refuge Innocence can find —[1]
Those were the first verses I ever learnt by heart, Prim. I can't
recollect whether they are Pope's or Swift's. But it's very
5        strange where my niece, and that troublesome woman, can be
gone. Are you sure you ordered Brown to follow, and let
them know I desired they would return immediately?
PRIM. O, yes, my Lady; and he found them presently; but —
LADY SMATTER. What, Prim?
10 PRIM. He could no how persuade Miss Wilmot to come back,
nor old Nurse neither.
LADY SMATTER. Amazing! Where did he meet with them?
PRIM. In that opening in the Wood, my lady, just by.
LADY SMATTER. I'll go thither instantly myself. Some scheme
15      may be afloat, which no one else can fathom. Chiefs must
exert themselves, to merit being cited; for, — as Milton some-
where says — or Spencer, —
What I would do, is not the case;
But what would Brutus in my place?[2]

*Exeunt.*

---

1    *Love! the most generous passion ... find*: from Rochester's "A Letter from Artemiza in the
     Towne to Chloe in the Countrey" (1674), ll. 40-41.
2    *What I would do ... place*: misquoting Swift's "To Stella, Visiting Me in my Sickness"
     (1720?): "How shall I act? is not the Case, / But how would *Brutus* in my Place?"
     (ll. 39-40). Pat Rogers notes that "the Brutus invoked is generally identified ... as
     Lucius Junius Brutus (d. 508 B.C.), the first consul of Rome, who condemned his own
     sons to death for conspiracy: but the figure was merged to some extent with Marcus
     Brutus, the friend of Julius Caesar" (*Jonathan Swift: The Complete Poems* [New Haven:
     Yale University Press, 1983], 693).

Scene xii

*The Wood.*

*Enter* JOYCE *and the* NURSE.

JOYCE. Well, Nurse, scold how you will, and cry how you will, too, I won't go an inch further, till you tell me what you've dragged me away for.

NURSE. O, Miss! Miss!—o, my dear, I should say,—if I had not got you out as I did, you might have been taken up for a 5 cheat! for Sir Roderick's real right earnest niece was just come to his house! I saw a young lady, and I made out from the servants, that she was the daughter of the new comer to the village that I had been told, at Lady Smatter's, was your mama that should be! 10

JOYCE. Well, and what then? How can I help it? Do you think I am to take all your faults upon me? No, Nursy, no! I had rather make you a present of some of mine! Which of them will you have, Nurse? I'll give you your choice.

NURSE. O Miss you'd banter one, if one was going to be set in 15 the stocks! But good by, my dear! I must make my escape.

JOYCE. O la, Nurse, I won't be left to live with Papa, when he knows he i'n't Papa! read, read, reading!—I'd sooner be off with you, or … I'll tell you what, Nurse mammy! … I'd sooner … I'll whisper you!—I'd sooner … now don't you 20 understand me?

NURSE. No, indeed, my dear.

JOYCE. La, you're as stupid! … Why I'd sooner … give me your Ear, … I'd sooner … marry Bob!

NURSE. Fie, Miss, fie! if I a'n't ashamed to hear you! 25

JOYCE. Why he's as good as I am! so I won't be cooped up any longer. I want my liberty, Nurse!

NURSE. O, my dear,—

JOYCE. Don't contradict me, I say, for I'll marry Bob!—I shall like that a great deal better than always studying Books; and sitting 30 with my hands before me; and making courtsies; and never eating half as much as I like,—except in the Pantry!—And

I'll make Bob do every thing I bid him; and you shall be my house-keeper!

35 NURSE. Ah, Miss! —

JOYCE. Don't fret, Nurse-mammy! the less money the less ceremony; and who cares for work, if it's followed by play? so, Nurse, let's be merry — and who will be wise!

NURSE. Laws, my dear, you'd make one dance upon ploughed
40 ground! — O Gemini![1] here comes a Gentleman — and it's your Papa, that was, as sure as a Gun! Let's get out of sight, and pass on when he's gone by.

JOYCE. O, ay, quick, quick, Nurse! — or he'll be sending me back again to old Lady Bookworm's!

*Exeunt.*

## Scene xiii

*Enter* WILMOT, *in a large wrapping Coat.*

WILMOT. That the sum of life can be so short, while its minutes seem so endless! But Misery is a torpid calculator. Yet why should I thus lament delay? What will the coming hours do for me, to make them more blest than the past? Will the sight
5 of her dismay, the execution of her punishment, bring to me the peace, the joy I have tasted from her fancied virtues? Let me look once more at her habitation. — Ha! — the door opens! — Who is it issues forth? — Heavens! — Can it be? — Yes, yes! that grace of Form, that dignity of air — O doating
10 Ideot! O dastard fondness! — Shall I delight again in her attractions? — She moves this way — my forces fail me! — Aid, aid my purpose, O retributive Justice!

*he retires.*

---

1   *O Gemini*: a mild oath, referring to the twin stars Castor and Pollux, whose mythological relation resembles that of Joyce and Sophia.

## Scene xiv

*Enter* ELEONORA.

ELEONORA. She comes not! My poor Sophia! What can thus detain thee? I tremble at every step; yet can rest inactive no longer.—Should accident make her known—or Me!—I must not proceed,—I dare not!—He will demand his daughter—he will upbraid my carrying her off—All the  5 courage that rises when I think upon what I have suffered, dies away when I meditate upon what I may have inflicted. And He—so gentle when at peace with himself, so kind, so benign, when not warped by passion—once enraged, inflamed, how terrible!—O from his Eye in wrath protect me,  10 Heaven!—Who's there?—ah! (*screams*)

WILMOT. She sees me!—nay, nay, (*striking his heart*) throb not thus violently! A few short moment's calm, and thy task will be over!

ELEONORA. 'Tis He!—how shall I support myself?—  15

WILMOT (*advancing*). You are startled, madam, at my sight; you turn from me—with loathing, no doubt! as from you, else, I must turn with horror! I thank, however, the conscious terror that anticipates my design; it spares me a preface I might— even yet!—be weak enough to make with pain.  20

ELEONORA. Your design?—(*turning half towards him; and then covering her face with her hands*) I cannot meet his brow!

WILMOT. Prepare yourself—and quickly;—you accompany me hence.

ELEONORA. Accompany you?  25

WILMOT. Nay, nay, fear not we shall be too long together.

ELEONORA. Is it your intention, then, to deposit me in some place of secret horror?—some dungeon?—

WILMOT. Forbear all useless enquiry, and yet more useless resistance. I purpose, however, nothing against your life:—not  30 shortened,—but bettered I wish it!

ELEONORA. What horrible scheme is meditating? Are, then, seventeen years of absence, of estrangement, thus to terminate?

WILMOT. I come not, madam, to parley—or what would be the

35    words you would hear? from what language might I cull
expressions that might speak to you of those seventeen
years?—But I come not to parley. What you have to settle
must be brief; we go hence to-morrow morning before daylight.

40 ELEONORA. Before daylight?—And I must not ask whither?

WILMOT. No!

ELEONORA. Nor yet—if I am to be left—alone?—

WILMOT. Alone? What mean you? Whom would you propose
for your associate?

45 ELEONORA. Why that dreadful look?—Is it to preclude explanation?—to forbid even petition?—Well, be it so!—My spirit
is borne down from further conflict; and one last request will
finish—on my side, our intercourse. That granted—what is
there,—save Indignation, which yet a little longer may strug-
50 gle with sorrow,—that can keep my heart from bursting?

WILMOT. If I come not to parley, neither come I, madam, to listen: name, and in two words,—your request; I mean not to
refuse it.

ELEONORA. Then even yet Eleonora will bless you! will look
55 upon you as rather insane than barbarous, and will pray for
you!—you will grant to me—my Child?

WILMOT. Ha!—

ELEONORA. Why that direful start?

WILMOT. Will my brain bear this?—perfidious woman!—canst
60 thou name, to Me, thy Child?

ELEONORA. Heavens!

WILMOT. Art thou, then, transformed from all I thought purest,
fairest, to all from which my soul most recoils? Is even Shame
subdued? And liv'st thou what thou wert only in my recollec-
65 tion?

ELEONORA. I am petrified! If even maternal tenderness be a
crime—

WILMOT. Talk'st Thou of maternal tenderness? canst thou name
it? Thou, to whom even this Child is dear but because law-
70 lessly thine? Thou, to whom Nature speaks not more in the
Mother's character, than Honour in the Wife's?—Thou,
Eleonora, talk'st thou of maternal tenderness?

ELEONORA. Whither wouldst thou drive me? To what may I lay claim, if not to maternal tenderness? Even the wrong—the sole wrong of which thou canst justly accuse me, sprung it 75 not from that source? Have I not been bereft of all else?— Ah! menace me with that deprivation, too, and I can submit to my fate no longer! Stormy as thine will be my passions;— as bitter—though not as causeless—my resentment! Wilmot!—deny me not my Child! 80

WILMOT. Incredible! Is then, every chaste duty, every legal tie, dissolved in cherished infamy? Thou dauntless criminal! thou pointest out to me, at least, thy mode of punishment; the Child of thy licentious fondness shall be parted from thee forever. 85

ELEONORA. Hear me, then, Wilmot, and tremble in thy turn! Hear—

Scene xv

*Enter* SOPHIA.

SOPHIA. My Mother!

ELEONORA. My Child!—O pitying Powers!—my Child! my Child! *(falls on* SOPHIA's *bosom)* Here grow! here cling! here fasten!

SOPHIA. Ever, ever, my dearest Mother!—What has thus terri- 5 fied, thus changed you?

WILMOT. Am I turned to stone?—Do I witness this—and suffer it? Would'st thou, Eleonora, force me to extremity?—Part instantly!—or I answer not for my forbearance!

SOPHIA. Ah!—who is that?— 10

ELEONORA. My poor Child!—I cannot speak!—Thou wilt not forsake me?

SOPHIA. Indeed I could not do it,—and live!

ELEONORA. I confide in thy promise, thy tenderness!—Turn, then, my Child—look there!—Thou knowst thy duty! 15

SOPHIA. Ah Heaven!—Is it—O! is it—my Father?

WILMOT *(trembling)*. My feet will scarcely sustain me! Can even Vice be so touching, where the Affections are thus glow-

ing?—Ah! such might have been (*looking at* SOPHIA) my
own poor Child!—No! thou nameless Girl! I am not thy
Father! Not thus would thy Mother have loved, have blessed,
have modelled thee, had such been My share, My happiness,
in thy formation and acquirements! alas!—I am not thy
Father!—

25 ELEONORA. Not her Father?

SOPHIA. Ah, sir! and how have I offended you? And why are you
so unkind as to disown me?—Let me go, my dear Mother,—
support yourself a moment—he looks softer—let me kneel
to him—and perhaps he may bless me!

30 WILMOT. Am I fascinated? Does my understanding fail me? Is
this a Scene for a Man injured as I am?—Advance not,
young woman!—Kneel not to me!—alas! alas! I have no
claim to thy reverence, or affection!

SOPHIA *quits her mother's arms and drops on one knee, without advancing.* ELEONORA *hides her face with her handkerchief, weeping.*

Scene xvi

*Enter* JOYCE, *from the wood, struggling with the* NURSE.

JOYCE. I won't be held, Nurse, I won't! Why I a'n't afraid to speak
to him now he i'n't Papa! And I can't abide to see his own
true flesh and blood upon her knees there for nothing. I'll tell
it all, I will so! I hate a fib.

5 NURSE. O Miss—my dear!—you'll get me sent to Botany Bay![1]

WILMOT. What's this? Sophia here?

JOYCE (*springing forward to him*). Papa, Papa! do you know you a'n't
Papa?

WILMOT. How?

10 JOYCE. Nurse put me upon you for your own, when my mama,
that ought to be,—went off with your real born Child.

SOPHIA *rises*: ELEONORA *uncovers her face: and the* NURSE *conceals herself behind some trees.*

---

1 *Botany Bay*: the site of Australia's first penal colony, founded in 1788.

WILMOT. What do I hear? What execrable stratagem—or what unheard of bliss! Speak, speak again!

JOYCE. Why, Papa, I don't tell it very well; but Nurse says that you a'n't my Papa; and that my Mama, there, that should be, i'n't 15 my Mama; and that that young lady there is your right earnest Daughter; and as for poor I—now who's daughter do you think I am? Why nobody's but old Nurse's, and a shoe-maker's.—And what do you think is my real Christian name? Why Joyce! 20

WILMOT. Where—where is the Nurse?—Let her but give this confirmation—

NURSE. O, I'll run! I'll run! he'll kill me!

*Makes off, followed by* WILMOT.

JOYCE. No, that he sha'n't! She has taken my part hundreds and hundreds of times; and if I don't take hers now—I wish I 25 may be shut up with Aunt Smatter and her Books all the rest of my days!

*Exit.*

ELEONORA. Sophia, my Sophia! what a wonderful discovery seems to be opening new life to me!

SOPHIA. Ah, my dear Mother! did I not say all would end well, 30 and you would still be happy? Come, then; rest on that bank, and let us wait for joyful tydings.

*Exeunt.*

Scene xvii

*Enter* OLD WAVERLEY.

OLD WAVERLEY. I can't overtake her!—yet, I protest, here's Jack overtaking me!

## Scene xviii

*Enter* YOUNG WAVERLEY.

So, Jack!—where are you going?
YOUNG WAVERLEY. O Sir, don't stop me, for goodness!
OLD WAVERLEY. Nay, tell me, at least, whether you are my Son? or whether you are only that old fashioned young Gentleman
5 so remarkably like him?

## Scene xix

*Enter* LADY SMATTER.

LADY SMATTER. Whither can this little Savage have strolled?— Ha! Mr. Waverley! How uncommonly fortunate!
YOUNG WAVERLEY (*aside*). How cursedly unlucky!
LADY SMATTER. I am wandering here, Mr. Waverley, in search of
5 a young person—
YOUNG WAVERLEY (*aside*). So am I!
OLD WAVERLEY (*aside*). Odd enough! that's exactly what I'm doing myself!
LADY SMATTER. Heavens! My Brother!

## Scene xx

*Enter* WILMOT, *perturbed.*

WILMOT. Ah!—Gone?—Which way?—Whither?—

## Scene xxi

*Enter* SOPHIA, *drawing in* ELEONORA.

SOPHIA. He calls!—O meet him, my dearest Mother!—
YOUNG WAVERLEY. Ah!—'tis She!—
OLD WAVERLEY. Yes, yes! there's the little baggage!
LADY SMATTER. How! my Sister-in-law?

WILMOT. Eleonora! I venture not to approach you!—I dare 5
not!—I have been to you a monster!
SOPHIA (*trying to draw her on*). My dearest Mother!
WILMOT. O well may be your step reluctant, your face averted!
Humbled in my own Eyes, in yours I must be debased. I
mean not to torture you for a pardon against which your 10
every feeling must revolt; I come but to do you the little justice yet in my power, of making known to the World your
wrongs—and my Madness!
SOPHIA. Ah! forgive, forgive him!—
ELEONORA (*solemnly*). Are you, then, indeed, satisfied of my inno- 15
cence?
WILMOT. Its full conviction had flashed upon me before my voyage hither; and, impressed with remorse, I came over to pub-
lish it: but a new and dreadful deception again wrought my
senses into phrenzy:—the Nurse, the miscreant Nurse, has 20
now develloped her fraud,—and—had I been less credulous,
less fiery—what a Wife,—what a daughter—might I at this
moment claim!
ELEONORA. And does no lurking doubt—no latent suspicion—
WILMOT. None!—none! 25
ELEONORA. O, Wilmot!—forgive then yourself!—My resentment is gone for ever!
WILMOT (*springing into her arms*). Wife of my Heart! my esteem!
my gratitude! my contrition! Can my whole life's devotion
pay this generous pardon? 30
ELEONORA. My dearest Wilmot! had I not always done justice to
your Heart, how ill should I deserve it!—But let us fly from
sorrows which, explained, are past! A happier theme—(*turning to* SOPHIA) our daughter—
SOPHIA. Ah, my Father! will you now own me? (*kneeling to him*) 35
Will you bless me, my dear Father?
WILMOT. And have I such a daughter? And canst thou wish my
blessing? Rise, rise, my lovely Girl! (*raising and embracing her*)
with joy, with pride I own thee!—May every hour of my
future life offer some kind compensation for the cruelty of 40
the past!
LADY SMATTER. I wish you both much joy!

OLD WAVERLEY. Bless me!—So this young woman, and her mother, are both women of character at last! 'Tis really odd what could put it in their heads to come and take away mine! 'Tis but odd!

## Scene xxii

*Enter* JOYCE.

JOYCE. Pray, is my Papa, that was, here?
WILMOT (*kindly*). My poor Girl! yes!
JOYCE. Because my Nurse-mammy says you want me.
WILMOT. True, I am impatient to assure you of my inalterable interest in your welfare—though the parental tie by which I thought it bound, has changed its object (*turning to* SOPHIA).
JOYCE. (*aside*) Well, I don't care! I hope, at least, he'll make her read all the Books!
OLD WAVERLEY. Bless me! if here a'n't both the two nieces, that popt upon Sir Roderick and I, standing face to face!

## Scene xxiii

*Enter* SIR RODERICK.

SIR RODERICK. Hey day, what's this? Is the Wood got peopled? Have the Gypseys turned their gangs loose upon us?
LADY SMATTER (*aside, and gliding behind* SIR RODERICK). Sir Roderick!—How fortunate! Now will I seize my Golden opportunity, and attack him—as Parnel says—by surprise!
WILMOT. Permit me, Sir Roderick,—
SIR RODERICK. How! Wilmot!
ELEONORA. Let me hope, Brother,—
SIR RODERICK. What the deuce! Eleonora!—
ELEONORA. Ah, Brother! have we not been long enough at war?
LADY SMATTER (*suddenly shewing herself*). Yes, Sir Roderick, yes! And behold Me the herald of Peace!
SIR RODERICK. How?—Ha?—What?—Lady Smatter!—I am all of a shiver!

LADY SMATTER. Accident, at length, having brought us to each 15
other's view—

SIR RODERICK. I shall fall into a trance!

YOUNG WAVERLEY. Lean upon me, Sir Roderick!—I beg!—

SIR RODERICK. O! You are here, also, Sir? Met in the Wood to
go off together? 20

LADY SMATTER. No, Sir Roderick, no! Waller—

JOYCE. La! it's old Sir Roderick, that was going to give me so
many thousand pounds!

SIR RODERICK. What! you are to be at me again, too, are you?
Have I baricadoed myself up from all the sex so long, to be 25
besieged, at last, by whole troops at a time? As I'm alive—

LADY SMATTER. Me, however, Sir Roderick, you will permit—

SIR RODERICK. Now I'm in a quiver again!—I'm all in a quiver!
The moment she comes near me, she puts me all in a quiver!

LADY SMATTER. Nay, at least, Sir Roderick, give me leave to 30
enquire in what it is the Fair Sex has thus offended you?

SIR RODERICK (aside). There's an impudent question, now, after
the trick she has served me! I shake with rage! If I don't give
her a posset,¹ I shall burst!

LADY SMATTER. Come! what can you find to say against us? 35

SIR RODERICK (abruptly facing her). Do you wish to know?

LADY SMATTER. Immensely!

SIR RODERICK. Why then—if you want my opinion—take it!
There i'n't a woman alive, but what is made up of spite, folly,
or extravagance! You all come into the world for no purpose 40
but to tire a man out of it! to ruin his Temper, to spend his
fortune, and wear out the drum of his Ear!

LADY SMATTER. O fie!

SIR RODERICK. Either you know nothing, and a poor fellow,
when noosed, might as well have the charge of a baby, or you 45
know something, and he must pay for it with the peace of his
life; for if once you take to a Book, or a Pen—his House may
go to rack and ruin; his children may have the rickets; his dinners won't be half dressed, and his servants may dance
rigadoons.² 50

---

1  *posset*: a dish of hot milk curdled with ale or wine; a remedy for colds and other afflic-
tions including, proverbially, impudent talk.

2  *rigadoons*: a lively dance for two persons.

LADY SMATTER. For shame! for shame!

SIR RODERICK. Nay, what's the use of such pedantry, to a woman? Must she study mathematics — to count a Hen's nest? — must she understand Latin, — to stitch her sam-
55 pler? — must she pore over a library, to find a Greek receipt¹ for a Pudding?

LADY SMATTER. Nay — this is no better than a lampoon!²

SIR RODERICK. Why what can any of you do, that's of the least use, or value? Answer me to that! What can any of you do?
60 Can you plow the Earth? No! you'd sooner starve! Can you build a house? No! you'd rather freeze! Can you steer a ship? No! you'd prefer to be drowned! Can you fight the enemy? No! you'd like better to fall a squalling!

LADY SMATTER. Quarter! quarter! —
65 SIR RODERICK. You are a poor, helpless, childish race of beings! So ignorant — that you never know a gust of wind from a clap of Thunder; and so feeble, that you can't pare an apple without cutting your fingers, nor mend a Pen — without chopping off a bit of your Thumb. So now — Good by t'ye! (*going*)
70 LADY SMATTER. Hold, Sir Roderick! You did not always think thus of Women!

SIR RODERICK. So much the worse!

LADY SMATTER. Time was — when you and I, Sir Roderick, were Friends!
75 SIR RODERICK. Madam! (*staring*)

LADY SMATTER. Should I hold out — thus! — ah, Sir Roder-ick! — the olive branch —

SIR RODERICK. If I don't believe I am in the moon!

LADY SMATTER. Would you utterly reject it?
80 SIR RODERICK. By the lord Harry, Lady Smatter, if you want to make a fool of me again —

LADY SMATTER. No, upon my word! See the token of Faith! (*playing her hand before his Eyes*)

---

1  *receipt*: recipe.

2  *no better than a lampoon*: alluding to the ending of *The Witlings*, in which the Lady Smatter of that play is made the subject of lampoons by Censor.

SIR RODERICK (*taking it*). O Lady Smatter! what a devilish Jilt you have been to me!

LADY SMATTER. Forget it, my dear Sir Roderick,—and let us, 85 henceforth, be constant Friends.

SIR RODERICK. My head turns round!—O Lady Smatter!—can I believe you?—my dear Sir Roderick did you say?

JOYCE. O, come and look! come and look! here stands a Woman-Hater! 90

SIR RODERICK (*hastily drawing back*). Why what the devil!—you young plague, you!

WILMOT. Heed her not, Sir Roderick, but accept our congratulations. You are but making friends again with Nature, as I have done with Reason! 95

SIR RODERICK. As I'm alive—I believe I am walking in my sleep!

OLD WAVERLEY. Bless my heart! Sir Roderick taking a lady's hand! Well! one man can no more foresee what another will come to, than a periwig can calculate whether it covers any 100 thing besides a scull!

WILMOT. Now, then, my Eleonora, let me hope the tempest of our days is past. What waywardly I have lost, I will study soberly to regain, convinced, by penitent experience, that not all the ills of pain, pestilence, or War, can be compared with 105 the convulsive tortures of acute and ungoverned passions.

ELEONORA. Suffer not retrospective sadness to usurp the place of grateful Joy. Where Error has been felt, Hope may re-animate: be appeased, be happy, then, my dearest Wilmot.

> WILMOT *and* ELEONORA *join the hands of*
> YOUNG WAVERLEY *and* SOPHIA.

JOYCE. Well! I have lost two Papas; but I have learned one thing as 110 perfect as if I had read all the Books and authors in the Universe!—and that is—what is meant by a Woman-Hater! It is,—to hate a woman—if she won't let you love her: to run away from her—if you can't run to her: to swear she is made up of faults—unless she allows you to be made up of perfec- 115

tions: and to vow she shall never cross your Threshhold,—
unless she'll come to be mistress of your whole house!

SIR RODERICK. I sha'n't feel awake again for a twelvemonth.

LADY SMATTER. Come, let us adjourn to my house; recommend-
120     ing to All around a couplet of my favourite Waller—no,
Cowley,—or, I believe, Shakespeare—
Laugh where you must—be candid where you can![1]

1   *Laugh where you must—be candid where you can*: misquoting, for the last time, Pope's *An Essay on Man*: "Laugh where we must, be candid where we can" (I.15). The single line is not, of course, a "couplet," as Lady Smatter claims.

# Appendix A: Burney's Earliest Theatrical Writing: Epilogue to Gerilda

In a letter of 14 February 1781 to Hester Lynch Thrale, Burney expressed her eagerness to see Thrale's newly written prologue to a play by the Reverend John Delap, *The Royal Supplicants*, scheduled to open that evening at the Drury Lane Theatre.[1] In exchange, she offered to show Thrale "a most silly thing of that sort which I wrote, & which was spoken upon the Dublin Theatre; No Creature in all *England* has ever seen it: the story of the occasion is too long for a Letter, & the Composition is terribly feeble, but the less my reasons for my vanity, the greater my power to shew confidence" (*Early Journals*, IV, 299-300). In her critical biography of Burney of 1988, Margaret Anne Doody quoted from this tantalizing letter, regretting that "the 'silly thing' once spoken in a Dublin theater has not come to light."[2]

Thanks to the research of Betty Rizzo and Lars Troide, however, the missing composition can now be tentatively identified. It is probably not a prologue, as Doody assumed, but an epilogue spoken by Jane Barsanti at the Crow Street Theatre, Dublin, on 13 January 1777, the opening night of John Jackson's tragedy *Gerilda; or the Siege of Harlech*. The epilogue was published in *Walker's Hibernian Magazine*, 7 (January 1777), 65, from which it is here reprinted. The *Hibernian Magazine* entitled it an epilogue "written by a Friend." As Rizzo observes, it is "contrived to display Barsanti's dramatic versatility in a variety of styles—comedy heroine, tragedy queen, madwoman. FB probably modelled it on George Colman's 'Occasional Prelude', which he wrote expressly for Barsanti to showcase her talent for mimicry" (*Early Journals*, IV, 541).

Burney had known Barsanti (c. 1755-95) since the late 1760s, when Barsanti, three years younger than Burney, began taking singing lessons from her father. Barsanti went to Ireland for the first time in the winter season of 1776-77, to perform at the Crow Street Theatre. Regrettably, Burney destroyed all of her journal and most of her cor-

---

1  In actual fact, the play opened on 17 February.
2  Doody, *Frances Burney*, 106. Doody adds that "Lars Troide suggests that Jenny Barsanti, actress and singer, who left London for Dublin and married the manager of Dublin Theatre, may have had something to do with Burney's mysterious Irish Prologue" (403, n. 26).

respondence for 1776 (*Early Journals*, II, 199). This material might have provided information on the circumstances that led Burney to write an epilogue to be spoken by Barsanti on the Dublin stage, before she had begun work on *The Witlings*. A few months later, in May 1777, Burney probably wrote a second dramatic piece, also predating *The Witlings*: a scene added to Act II of Arthur Murphy's *The Way to Keep Him,* performed by the Burney family at Barborne Lodge, Worcestershire (*Early Journals*, II, 242 and n. 79). Unlike the epilogue to *Gerilda*, however, this scene has not survived.

These tragic bards must sure be gloomy creatures,
Who deal in nought but melancholy features;
In trumpets, drums, in sieges, battles, dying,
In sable Cupids — and in doleful sighing.
In things most strange that strike the Gods with wonder,
In witches, spirits, traps, and rattling thunder —
What heart but shrinks, when thro' the yawning stage,
Pale spectres rise attention to engage!
What bosom does not feel a taint of fear,
When rolling bullets shake our wooden sphere!
    Melpomene, when pleasures all forsake her,
Stalks forth a mere dramatic undertaker;
A pretty way indeed to be delighted,
First to be drown'd in tears, and then affrighted.
Would sober reason ever strive to borrow
Bright beams of pleasure — from dark clouds of sorrow?
For my own part — I hope you'll all agree —
I like the smiles of laughing comedy;
In which the verbal muse more sweetly sings,
Than when she bellows thro' the throats of kings —
Not but I think a little serious love
*Sometimes does well* — and may fine feelings move,
Tho' nothing practised in the ways of men,
*Love is I scarce know what, and goes I know not when.*
    Yet what's the reason, gentlefolks! that I
Because I make you laugh — can't make you cry?
Upon my life — I've twenty minds to try.
For a small sample — see this polish'd dagger —
    [Taking out her fan.]
I hope the sight won't make your courage stagger. —
*This is thy sheath—there rest and let me die* —
I won't fall down, as here's no lover nigh. —

Shall I like Desdemona yield to death,
And tamely let a husband stop my breath?
One way there is I shou'd not think amiss,
I'd challenge him to stop it with a kiss.
Or would you madness wish, that may affright,
Dishevel'd hair—wild eyes—to strike your sight,
I'll take a touch at them—but not to night.
This piece, no doubt, imported neat from Wales,
You've fairly weigh'd in criticism's scales.
Why shou'd I plead—the author's in no danger,
Hibernia's sons ne'er yet oppress'd a stranger.
What say ye, critics? Is it no or aye?
Your smiles acquaint me that your hearts comply;
Inform him then, behind he anxious stands,
And only lives by your protecting hands.

# Appendix B: Contemporary Letters and Diary Entries *on* The Witlings

### 1. From journal letter: Frances Burney to Susanna Burney, 27 August 1778

Mrs. Thrale then returned to her charge, and again urged me about a Comedy,—and again I tried to silence her,—and we had a *fine fight* together;—till she called upon Dr. Johnson to *back* her,—"Why, Madam," said he, Laughing, "she *is* Writing one!—What a rout is here, indeed!—She is writing one up stairs all the Time.—Who ever knew when she began Evelina? She is working at some drama, depend upon it."

"True, true Oh King!"[1] thought I.

"Well, that *will* be a sly trick!" cried Mrs Thrale;—"however, you know best, I believe, about That, as well as about every other Thing."

### 2. From journal letter: Frances Burney to Susanna Burney, 3 September 1778

Mrs. Thrale suddenly said "Now, Miss Burney, if *you* would write a Play, I have a Notion it would hit *my* Taste in *all* things;—do,— you *must* write one;—a *play* will be something *worth* your Time, it is the Road both to Honour and Profit,—and *why* should you have it in your power to gain these rewards and not do it?"....

"I declare, continued she, I *mean* and *think* what I say with all my Heart and soul!—You seem to me to have the right and true talents for writing a Comedy,— you would give us all the fun and humour we could wish, and you would give us a scene or 2 of the pathetic kind that would set all the rest off. If you would but *try*, I am *sure* you would succeed, and give us such a Play as would be an Honour to all your Family. And, in the *grave* parts, all your sentiments would be Edifying, and such as would *do good*,—and I am sure *that* would be real pleasure to you."—My dear Susy, I *assure* you I recollect her words as exactly as my memory will allow. "Hannah More, added she, got near 400 pounds for her foolish play,[2] & if *you* did not write a better than

---

1   The quotation, from Daniel 3:24, suggests that Burney had already begun writing *The Witlings*.
2   Hannah More's popular tragedy *Percy*, which ran for nineteen performances at Covent Garden Theatre from December 1777 to March 1778.

*hers, I* say you deserve to be *whipped!* — Your Father, I know, thinks the same, — but we will *allow* that *he* may be partial but what can make *me* think it? — and *Dr. Johnson;* — *he*, of all men, would not say it if he did not think it."

She then rejoiced I had published Evelina as I did, without shewing it to any body; "Because You have proved what are your own real resources, she said, and now, — you have nothing to do but to write a *Play*, and both Fame and Profit will attend you. Mr. Johnson, *I* am sure, will be at your service in any thing in his power; — we'll make him write your Prologue, — we'll make him carry your play to the managers; we'll do *any* thing for you, and so, I am sure, he readily will! As to *Plot, situation,* and *Character,* — *Nobody* shall assist you in *them,* for nobody *can!*"

### 3. From journal letter: Frances Burney to Susanna Burney, post 16-21 September 1778

Mrs. Thrale then told me *such* civil Things! — Mrs. Montagu, it seems, talked of nothing else, during my retreat, and enquired very particularly what *kind* of Book it was?[1] "And I told her, continued Mrs. Thrale, that it was a picture of Life, manners, and Characters; But won't she go on? says she, surely she won't stop here?" "Why, said I, I want her to go on in a *new* path, I want her to write a Comedy." — "But, said Mrs. Montagu, one thing must be considered; Fielding, who was so admirable in Novel writing, *never* succeeded when he wrote for the stage."

"Very well said, cried Dr. Johnson; that was an Answer which showed she considered her subject."

So you see, Susy, they make nothing of coupling Fielding and me together! — very affronting! —

Mrs. Thrale continued — "Well, but, apropos, said Mrs. Montagu, if Miss Burney *does* write a play, I beg I may know of it, or, if she thinks proper, *see* it; — and all my Influence is at her service; — we shall *all* be glad to assist in spreading the Fame of Miss Burney."

O dear Susy! — you can't think how I tremble for what all this will *end* in! — I verily think I had best stop where I am, and *never* again attempt writing — for after so much Honour, so much success, — how shall I bear a downfall?

---

1   Burney's *Evelina*; Elizabeth Montagu had not yet read the novel, but she knew of Burney's authorship.

## 4. From journal letter: Frances Burney to Susanna Burney, 11 January 1779

Some time after, Sir Joshua, returning to his *standing* place, entered into *confab.* with Miss Linley¹ and your slave upon various matters;—during which, Mr. Sheridan, joining us, said "Sir Joshua I have been telling Miss Burney that she must not suffer her Pen to lie idle;—*ought* she?"

*Sir Joshua.* No, indeed, ought she not.

*Mr. Sheridan.* —Do *you*, then, Sir Joshua, persuade her. —But perhaps you *have* begun some thing? —may we *ask*? —Will you answer a Question candidly?

*F.B.*—I don't know,—but *as* candidly as *Mrs. Candour*² I think I certainly shall.

*Mr. Sheridan.* What, then, are you about now?

*F.B.*—Why—twirling my Fan, I think!

*Mr. Sheridan.* No, no,—but what are you about *at Home*? —however, it is not a fair Question, so I won't press it.

Yet he *looked* very inquisitive; but I was glad to get off without any *downright* answer.

*Sir Joshua. Any* thing in the *Dialogue* way, I think, she *must* succeed in,—and I am sure *invention* will not be wanting. —

*Mr. Sheridan.* No, indeed;—I think, and say, she should write a *Comedy*.

Lord, Susy, I could not believe my own Ears! *This* from Mr. *Sheridan!*

*Sir Joshua.* I am sure *I* think so; and I hope she *will.*

I could only answer by *incredulous* exclamations. "Consider," continued Sir Joshua, "you have already had all the applause and fame you *can* have given you in the *Clozet*,—but the Acclamation of a *Theatre* will be *new* to you."

And then he put down his Trumpet,³ and began a violent clapping of his Hands.

I actually shook from Head to foot! I felt myself already in Drury Lane, amidst the *Hub bub* of a first Night.

"O no!" cried I, "there *may* be a *Noise*,—but it will be just the *reverse.* —" And I returned his salute with a Hissing.

---

1   Sir Joshua Reynolds, the painter, and Mary Linley, a singer and sister-in-law of Richard Brinsley Sheridan.

2   A character in Sheridan's comedy *The School for Scandal* who claims to be candid without actually being so.

3   A hearing-trumpet; Sir Joshua was deaf.

Mr. Sheridan joined Sir Joshua very warmly.

"O Sir!" cried I, "*you* should not run on so,—you don't know what mischief you may do!"

*Mr. Sheridan.* I wish I *may*,—I shall be very glad to be accessory.

*Sir Joshua.* She has, certainly, something of a knack at Characters;—*where* she got it, I don't know,—and *how* she got it, I can't imagine,—but she certainly *has* it. And to throw it away is—

*Mr. Sheridan.* O she *won't*,—she will write a Comedy,—she has promised me she will!

*F.B.* O!—if you both run on in this manner, I shall—I was going to say *get under the Chair*, but Mr. Sheridan, interrupting me with a Laugh, said "Set about one?—very well, that's right!"

"Ay," cried Sir Joshua, "that's *very* right.—And *you*, (to Mr. Sheridan,) would *take* any thing of *Hers*,—would you not?—*Unsight unseen?*"

What a *point blank* Question! Who but Sir Joshua would have ventured it!

"*Yes*;" answered Mr. Sheridan with quickness,—"and make her a Bow and my best Thanks into the Bargain!"

Now, my dear Susy, tell me, did you ever hear the *fellow* to such a speech as this!—it was all I could do to sit it.

"Mr. Sheridan," I exclaimed, "are you not mocking me?"

"No, upon my Honour! this is what I have *meditated* to say to you the first Time I should have the pleasure of seeing you."

To be sure, as Mrs. Thrale says, if folks *are* to be spoilt,—there is nothing in the World so *pleasant* as spoiling! But I *never* was so much Astonished, and *seldom* have been so much delighted as by this attack of Mr. Sheridan. Afterwards he took my Father aside, and formally repeated his opinion that I should write for the stage, and his desire to see my Play,—with encomiums the most flattering of Evelina.

Consider Mr. Sheridan, as an *Author* and a *manager*, and really this conduct appears to me at once generous and uncommon. As an *Author*, and one so high, and *now* in his first Eclat, to be so lavish of his praise—is it not rare? As a *manager*,[1] who must, of course, be *loaded* with Pieces and recommendations, to *urge* me to write, and to promise to *thank* me for my Writing, instead of making a favour and a difficulty of even *looking* at it,—is it not truly good-natured and liberal-minded?

And now, my dear Susy,—if I *should* attempt the stage,—I think I may be fairly acquitted of presumption, and however I may fail,—

---

1   Of Drury Lane Theatre.

that I was strongly pressed to *try* by Mrs. Thrale,—and by Mr. Sheridan,—the most successful and powerful of all Dramatic living Authors,—will abundantly excuse my temerity.

In short,—this Evening seems to have been *decisive*, my many and encreasing scruples *all* give way to encouragement so warm from so experienced a Judge, who is himself *interested* in not making such a request *par pure complaisance.*[1]

## 5. From Hester Lynch Thrale's diary, 10 February 1779

Our Miss Burney is big with a Comedy for next Season; I have not yet seen the *Ebauche*,[2] but I wish it well: Can I help wishing well to every thing that bears the name of *Burney?* The Doctor is a Man quite after my own Heart, if he has any Fault it is too much Obsequiousness, though *I* should not object to a Quality *my* Friends are so little troubled with.—his following close upon the heels of Johnson or Baretti[3] makes me feel him softer though; like turning the Toothpick after you have rubbed your Gums with the *Brush* and immediately applying the *Spunge* to them. His Daughter is a graceful looking Girl, but 'tis the Grace of an Actress not a Woman of Fashion—how should it?[4] her Conversation would be more pleasing if She thought less of herself; but her early Reputation embarrasses her Talk, and clouds her Mind with scruples about Elegancies which either come uncalled for or will not come at all: I love her more for her Father's sake than for her own, though her Merit as a Writer cannot be controverted. The Play will be a good one too I doubt not—She is a Girl of prodigious Parts—

## 6. From journal letter: Frances Burney to Susanna Burney, post 16 February 1779

"If I,—said Mr. Murphy, looking very archly, had written a certain Book,[5]—a Book I won't name,—but a Book I have lately read,—I would *next* write a Comedy."

"Good God, cried Mrs. Thrale, colouring with pleasure, do *you* think so too?"

---

1 "Only in order to please."
2 "Outline."
3 Giuseppe Baretti, an Italian writer living in England and a friend of Dr. Johnson and the Burneys.
4 "The Burneys are I believe a very low Race of Mortals" (Thrale's note).
5 *Evelina.*

"Yes indeed; I thought so *while* I was reading it,—it struck me repeatedly."

"Don't look at *me*, Miss Burney, cried Mrs. Thrale, for this is no doing of *mine*. Well, I do wonder what Miss Burney will do 20 years hence, when she can blush no more.—for now, she can never bear the Name of her Book."

*Mr. Murphy.* Nay, I name no Book,—at least no *author*,—how *can* I, for I don't *know* the author,—there is no name given to it; I only say, *whoever* writ that Book, ought to write a Comedy. *Dr. Johnson* might write it for ought I know!"

*F.B.* O yes!—

*Mr. Murphy.* Nay, I have often told *him* he does not know his own strength, or he would write a Comedy,—and so I think.

*Dr. Johnson. Laughing!* Suppose Burney and I begin together?—

*Mr. Murphy.* Ah, I wish to God you would!—I wish you would Beaumont and Fletcher us!

*F.B.* My Father asked me this morning how my *Head* stood,—if he should have asked me this *Evening*, I don't know *what* answer I must have made!

*Mr. Murphy.* I have no wish to turn any body's Head,—I speak what I really think;—*Comedy* is the *forte* of that Book,—I Laughed over it most violently;—I lent it to two young ladies, very sensible Girls, of my acquaintance, and they could not go to Bed while it was in reading, *that* seems to me as good a testimony as a Book can have. And if the Author—I won't say *who*.—(all the Time looking *away* from *me*) will write a *Comedy*, I will most readily, and with great pleasure, give any advice or assistance in my power:

"Well, now you are a *sweet* man! cried Mrs. Thrale, who looked ready to *kiss* him,—did not I tell you, Miss Burney, that Mr. Murphy was the man!—

*Mr. Murphy.* All I can do, I shall be very *happy* to do,—and, at least, I will undertake to say I can tell what the sovereigns of the upper Gallery will bear,—for they are the most formidable part of an Audience: I have had so much experience in this sort of Work, that I believe I can always tell what will be *Hissed* at least. And if Miss Burney will write, and will shew me—

*Dr. Johnson.* Come, come, have done with this, now,—Why should you over power her?—Let's have no more of it. I don't mean to *dissent* from what you say,—I think well of it,—and approve of it,—but you have said *enough* of it.

Mr. Murphy, who equally loves and reverences Dr. Johnson, instantly changed the subject.

Am I not, my Susy, as Mrs. Thrale says, an *amazing person*—Think but of encouragement like this from so experienced a Judge as Mr. Murphy! how *amazing*, that this idea of a *Comedy* should strike so many! And how very kind is this offer of service!—Were I disposed to decline it, Mrs. Thrale would not suffer me,—Mr. Murphy is among her first favourites, and she has long quite set her Heart upon making him one of *mine*: but she has most solemnly assured me she had never *hinted* to him the idea of a Comedy.

### 7. From Hester Lynch Thrale's diary, 1 May 1779

Fanny Burney has read me her new Comedy; nobody else has seen it except her Father, who will not suffer his Partiality to overbiass his Judgment I am sure, and he likes it vastly.—but one has no Guess what will do on a Stage, at least I have none; Murphy must read an Act tomorrow, I wonder what he'll say to't. I like it very well for my own part, though none of the scribbling Ladies have a Right to admire its general Tendency —[1]

### 8. From journal letter: Frances Burney to Susanna Burney, 30 May 1779

Mr. Murphy, coming up to me, said "I have had no opportunity, Miss Burney, to tell you how much I have been entertained this morning,—but I have a great deal to say to You about it,—I am extremely pleased with it indeed."

"O yes, no doubt!" cried I, sideling off for fear of being heard.

"The Dialogue, said he, is charming, and the—"

"What's that? cried Mrs. Thrale,—Mr. Murphy always flirting with Miss Burney?—And *here*, too, where every body is watched!"

... Mr. Murphy, checked by Mrs. Thrale's exclamation, stopt the conversation, and said he must run away, but would return in half an Hour. "Don't expect, however, Miss Burney, he said, that I shall bring with me what you are thinking of,—no, I can't part with it yet!—"

"What! at it again! cried Mrs. Thrale,—this flirting is incessant,—but it's all to Mr. Murphy's credit."

... Mrs. Thrale told me, afterwards, that she made these speeches, to divert the attention of the Company from our *subject*, for that she

---

1  "Murphy liked it very well, but her confidential friend Mr. Crisp advised her against bringing it on, for fear of displeasing the female Wits — a formidable Body, and called by those who ridicule them, the *Blue Stocking Club*" (Thrale's note).

found they were all upon the watch the moment Mr. Murphy addressed me, and that the Bishop and his Lady[1] almost threw down their Cards from eagerness to discover what he meant.

### 9. From letter: Frances Burney to Samuel Crisp, 30 July 1779

This seems a strange unseasonable period for *my* undertaking,[2] among the rest,—but yet, my dear Daddy, when you have read my conversation with Mr. Sheridan,[3] I believe you will agree that I must have been wholly insensible, nay, almost *ungrateful*, to resist encouragement such as he gave me,—nay, *more* than encouragement, *entreaties*,—all of which, he warmly repeated to my Father.

Now as to the Play itself,—I own I had wished to have been the Bearer of it when I visit Chesington,—but you seem so urgent, and my Father himself is so desirous to Carry it you, that I have given that plan up....

You will find it of an enormous length, though half as short again as the *original*, but you must advise me as to what parts to curtail.

Oh my dear Daddy, *if* your next Letter were to contain your *real* opinion of it, how should I dread to open it!—Be, however, as honest as your good nature and delicacy will *allow* you to be, and assure yourself I shall be *very* certain that all criticisms will proceed from your earnest wishes to obviate those of others,—and that you would have much more *pleasure* in being my *panegyrist*.

... And now let me tell you what *I wish* in regard to this affair.

I should like that your First reading should have nothing to do with *me*,—that you should go quick through it, or let my Father read it to you, forgetting all the Time, as much as you can, that *Fannikin* is the Writer, or even that it is a play in manuscript, and *capable* of alterations:—And then, when you have done, I should like to have 3 Lines, telling me, as nearly as you trust my candour, its general effect. —

After that,—take it to your own Desk, and lash it at your leisure.

Adieu, My dear Daddy—I shall hope to hear from you *very* soon,—and pray believe me.

Yours ever and ever
Frances Burney.

---

1  John Hinchliffe, Bishop of Peterborough, and his wife, Elizabeth.
2  Crisp believed that Britain was in danger of a French-Spanish invasion.
3  See letter 4, above.

Let it fail *never so much*, the *manager* will have nothing to reproach me with: is not that some comfort?—He would really listen to no denial.

### 10. From letter: Susanna Burney to Frances Burney, 3 August 1779

*The Witlings*—[1] "Good" said Mr. Crisp—"Good—I like the Name—the Dramatis Personae too pleased him, and the name of *Codger* occasion'd a general Grin ... the Milliners Scene and indeed all the first act diverted us *extremely* all round—"It's *funny*—it's *funny* indeed"—said Mr. Crisp who you know does not love to throw away praise—the Second Act I think much improved, and its being more compressed than when I first heard it gives to the whole more *Zest*—it did not flag at all in the reading.—The 3d. is charming—and they all went off with great Spirit ... the fourth act was upon the whole that which seemed least to exhilarate or interest the audience, tho' Charlotte laugh'd till she was almost black in the face at Codger's part, as I had done before her—The fifth was more generally felt—but to own the truth it did not meet all the advantages one could wish—My Father's voice, sight, and lungs were tired ... and being entirely unacquainted with what was coming not withstanding all his good intentions, he did not always give the Expression you meant to be given—Yet he exerted himself ... to give it force and Spirit—and except this Act, I believe only yourself would have read the play better.

For my own part the Serious part seem'd even to improve upon me by this 2^{nd} hearing, and made me for to cry in 2 or 3 places—I wish there was more of this Sort—so does my Father—so, I believe, does Mr. Crisp—however their sentiments you are to hear fully from themselves, which will make me the less eager to write to them—Codger and Jack too seem Characters which divert every body, and would yet more I should imagine in a public Representation.

---

1   On 2 August, Charles Burney had read the play aloud to a gathering at Samuel Crisp's home in Chessington. The audience included Crisp and two of Frances's sisters, Susanna and Charlotte.

## 11. From letter: Frances Burney to Dr. Charles Burney, c. 13 August 1779

The fatal knell then, is knolled! and down among the Dead Men sink the poor Witlings,—for-ever and for-ever and for-ever! —[1] I give a *sigh* whether I will or not to their memory, for, however worthless, they were *mes Enfans*,[2] and *one must do one's Nature*, as Mr. Crisp will tell you of the Dog.

*You*, my dearest Sir, who enjoyed, I really think, even more than myself the astonishing success of my first attempt, would, I believe, even more than myself, be hurt at the failure of my second;—and I am sure I speak from the bottom of a very honest Heart when I most solemnly declare that upon *your* Account any disgrace would mortify and afflict me *more* than upon my own,—for what ever appears with your *knowledge*, will be naturally supposed to have met with your *approbation*, and perhaps with your *assistance*;—and therefore, though all *particular* censure would fall where it *ought*, upon *me*,—yet any *general* censure of the *whole*, and the *Plan*, would cruelly, but certainly, involve *you* in its severity.

Of this I have been sensible from the moment my *Authorshipness* was discovered,—and therefore, from that moment, I determined to have no *opinion* of my own in regard to what I should thenceforth part with out of my own Hands. I would, long since, have Burnt the 4th Act, upon your disapprobation of it, but that I waited, and was by Mrs. Thrale so much *encouraged* to wait, for your finishing the Piece.

You *have* finished it, now,—in *every* sense of the Word,—*partial* faults may be corrected, but what I most wished was to know the general effect of the Whole,—and as *that* has so terribly failed, all petty criticisms would be needless. I shall wipe it all from my memory, and endeavour never to recollect that I ever writ it.

You bid me open my Heart to you,—and so, my dearest Sir, I will,—for it is the greatest happiness of my life that I *dare* be sincere to you,—I expected many Objections to be raised, a thousand errors to be pointed out, and a million of alterations to be proposed;—but—the *suppression of the piece* were words I did *not* expect,—indeed, after the warm approbation of Mrs. Thrale, and the repeated commendation and flattery of Mr. Murphy, how could I? —

---

1  Alluding to *Macbeth*, V.ix.16 ("And so his knell is knoll'd"); John Dyer's poem "Toast: Here's a Health to the King" ("Down among the Dead men"); and Pope's *Rape of the Lock*, III. 154 ("for-ever and for-ever").

2  "My children."

I do not, therefore, pretend to *wish* you should think the decision for which I was so little prepared has given me no disturbance;—for I must be a far more egregious Witling than any of those I tried to draw to imagine you could ever credit that I writ without some remote hope of success *now*, though I literally did when I composed Evelina. But my mortification is not at throwing away the Characters, or the contrivance;—it is all at throwing away the *Time,*—which I with difficulty stole, and which I have Buried in the mere trouble of *writing*.

What my Daddy Crisp says, "that it would be the best *policy*, but for pecuniary advantages, for me to write no more"—is exactly what I have always thought since Evelina was published;—but I will not *now* talk of putting it in practice,—for the best way I can take of shewing that have a true and just sense of the *spirit* of your condemnation, is not to sink, sulky and dejected, under it, but to exert myself to the utmost of my power in endeavours to produce something less reprehensible. And this shall be the way I will pursue, as soon as my mind is more at ease about Hetty and Mrs. Thrale,—and as soon as I have *read* myself into a forgetfulness of my old Dramatis persona,—lest I should produce something else as *Witless* as the last.

Adieu, my dearest, kindest, truest, best *Friend,*—I will never proceed so *far* again without your counsel, and then I shall not only save *myself* so much useless trouble, but *you*, who so reluctantly blame, the kind pain which I am sure must attend your disapprobation. The World will not always go well, as Mrs. Sap.[1] might say, and I am sure I have long thought I have had more than my share of success already.

### 12. From letter: Frances Burney to Samuel Crisp, 13 August 1779

Well!—God's above all!—and there are *plays* that *are* to be saved, and *plays* that are *not* to be saved!—so good Night Mr. Dabler!—good Night Lady Smatter,—Mrs. Sapient, Mrs. Voluble,—Mrs. Wheedle—Censor,—Cecilia—Beaufort,—and you, *you great Oaf*, Bobby! good Night! good Night!—[2]

And good *morning*, Miss Fanny Burney!—I hope, now, You have opened your Eyes for some Time, and will not close them in so drowsy a fit again—at least till the full of the moon.—

---

1 Mrs. Sapient, one of the witlings.
2 Alluding to *Othello*, II.iii.106-7 ("there be souls that must be saved, and there be souls must not be saved"); *Hamlet*, IV.v.72 ("good night, good night"); and Mrs. Voluble's words to Bob in *The Witlings* (p. 106).

I won't tell you I have been absolutely *ravi* with delight at the fall of the Curtain,—but I intend to take the affair in the *tant mieux*[1] manner, and to console myself for your Censure by this greatest proof I have ever received of the sincerity, candour, and, let me add, *esteem* of my dear Daddy.—And, as I happen to love *myself* rather more than my *play*, this consolation is not a very trifling one.

And to all you say of my *rep.*[2] and so forth, I perceive the kindness of your endeavours to put me in humour with myself, and prevent my taking *huff*,—which, if I did, I should deserve to receive, upon any future trial, *hollow* praise from *you*,—and the *rest* from the Public.

As to the M.S. I am in no hurry for it.—Besides, it ought not to come till I have prepared an *ovation*, and the *Honours* of *conquest* for it.

The only bad thing in this affair,—is that I cannot take the comfort of my poor friend Dabler, by calling you a *crabbed fellow*,—because you write with almost more kindness than ever;—neither can I, (though I try hard) persuade myself that you have not *a grain of Taste in your whole composition*.[3]

This, however, seriously, I do believe that, when my two Daddys put their Heads together to concert for me that Hissing, groaning, catcalling Epistle they sent me,[4] they felt as sorry for poor little Miss Bayes[5] as she could possibly do for herself.

### 13. From Hester Lynch Thrale's diary, 18 August 1779

Fanny Burney has pleased me today—She resolves to give up a Play likely to succeed; for fear it may bear hard upon some Respectable Characters.—

### 14. From letter: Dr. Charles Burney to Frances Burney, 29 August 1779

I am glad the objections all fall on the Stocking-Club-Party—as my chief and almost only quarrel was with its Members. As it is, not only the Whole Piece, but the *plot* had best be kept secret, from every body—As to finishing another upon a *new Story*, in a *hurry*, for next

---

1 "Enraptured … so much the better."
2 Reputation.
3 *The Witlings*, 123.
4 This joint letter from Dr. Charles Burney and Samuel Crisp is not extant.
5 I.e. Burney herself, the female dramatist; Bayes is the author of the mock play in Buckingham's comedy *The Rehearsal* (1672).

winter, I think it *may* be done, and would be not only feasible but desirable at any other Time than the present—But public affairs are in such terrible Confusion, and there is so little likelihood of People having more money or more spirits soon, that I own myself not eager for you to come out with any kind of Play, *next Winter.* Many Scenes and Characters might otherwise be preserved, and perhaps save you time—though I am not sure of it—for the adjusting, fine-drawing, and patching neatly is tedious work—

... But all this is no reason why you should not write—tho' it is one against doing anything of such Consequence to your Fame &c— in a *hurry*—don't fear that the Author of Evelina will be soon forgotten!—Come out When you will—something Good, and pleasing, will be expected—You have resources sufficient for Writing a great deal—only, for the stage, I would have you very Careful, and very Perfect—that is, as far so as your own Efforts, and the best advice you can get, can make you. In the Novel Way, there is no danger—and in that, *no Times* can affect ye.

### 15. From letter: Frances Burney to Samuel Crisp, 22 January 1780

As my Play was settled in its silent suppression, I entreated my Father to call on Mr. Sheridan in order to prevent his expecting any thing from me, as he had a good right to do from my having sent him a positive message that I should, in compliance with his exhortations at Mrs. Cholmondeley's,[1] try my fortune in the *Theatrical line*, and send him a Piece for this Winter. My Father did call, but found him not at home,—neither did he happen to see him till about Christmas. He then acquainted him that what I had written had entirely dissatisfied me, and that I desired to decline for the present all attempts of that sort.

Mr. Sheridan was pleased to express great concern,—nay more, to protest he would not *accept* my refusal,—he beg'd my Father to tell me that he could take no denial to *seeing* what I had done—that I could be no fair Judge for myself;—that he doubted not but it would please;—but was *glad* I was not satisfied, as he had much rather see pieces before their Authors were contented with them than afterwards, on account of sundry small changes always necessary to be made by the managers, for Theatrical purposes, and to which they

---

1    Mary Cholmondeley, society hostess. For Sheridan's "exhortations" at her house, see letter 4, above.

were loath to submit when their writings were finished to their own approbations. In short, he said so much that my father, ever easy to be worked upon, began to waver, and told me he wished I would shew the play to Sheridan at once.

This very much disconcerted me,—I had taken a sort of disgust to it, and was myself most earnestly desirous to let it Die a quiet Death. I therefore *cooled* the affair as much as I conveniently could, and by evading from Time to Time the Conversation, it was again sinking into its old state,—when again Mr. Sheridan saw my Father, and asked his leave to call upon me himself.

This could not be refused.

Well,—I was now violently fidgeted,—and began to think of *alterations*, and, setting my Head to Work, I have actually new written the 4th Act from beginning to End except one scene: —Mr. Sheridan, however, has not yet called,—and I have so little Heart in the affair, that I have now again quite dropt it.

Such is the present situation of *my Politics*. Now I wish you much to write me your private opinion what I had best do in case of an emergency,—your Letters are always sacred, so pray write with your ususal sincerity and openness. —I know you too well to fear your being offended if things should be so managed that your Counsel cannot be followed: it will, at any rate, not be thrown away, since it will be a fresh proof of your interest in my affairs.

My Notions I will also tell you; they are: —in case I *must* produce this piece to the manager—

To entirely omit all mention of the *Club*;—

To curtail the parts of Smatter and Dabler as much as possible;—

To restore to Censor his £5000—and not trouble him even to offer it;—

To give a *new* Friend to Cecilia, by whom her affairs shall be retrieved, and through whose means the Catastrophe shall be brought to be happy;—

And to change the Nature of Beaufort's connections with Lady Smatter, in order to obviate the unlucky resemblance the *adopted Nephew* bears to our *Female Pride of Literature*.[1]

This is all I have at present thought of,—and yet, if I am so allowed, even these thoughts shall all turn to Nothing,—for I have so much more Fear than hope, and Anxiety than pleasure in thinking at

---

1    Alluding to Elizabeth Montagu, who had adopted her nephew Matthew Robinson in 1779. In the surviving manuscript of the play, however, Beaufort remains Lady Smatter's adopted nephew, and the other projected revisions are not carried out.

all of the Theatre, that I believe my wisest way will be to *shirk*—
which if, by *evasive and sneaking means* I can, I shall.

### 16. From letter: Samuel Crisp to Frances Burney, 23 February 1780

My great scruple all along has been the Consideration of the great
Stake you are playing for—how much You have to lose; and how
unequal your delicate and tender Frame of mind would be, to sustain
the Shock of a failure of Success, should that be the Case—You can
easily imagine how much it goes against me to say any thing that
looks like discouragement to a Spirit, already too diffident, and apprehensive....

The Play has *Wit* enough, and enough—but the Story and the
incidents dont appear to me interesting enough to seize and keep
hold of the Attention and eager expectations of the generality of
Audiences—This, to me, is its Capital defect—

The omissions You propose are right, I think; but how the business
of the Piece is to go on, with such omissions and Alterations as You
mention, it is impossible for me to know—what You mean to leave
out—the *Club*, and the *larger Share of Smatter and Dabler*, seems to
have been the main Subject of the play—Cecilia's loss, and unexpected restoration of her fortune, is not a new Incident by any means—
however any thing is preferable to Censor's interfering in the business,
by his unaccountable generosity....

What to advise, I profess, I know not—only thus much—I should
have a much greater deference for the Opinion of Sheridan than of
Murphy;—I take him in himself to be much deeper; and he is besides
deeply interested in the fate of whatever he brings forward on his
own Stage—upon the whole, as he is so pressing to see what You
have done, I should almost incline to consent—but we will require
him to observe the strictest Secresy, that it shou'd not be known
among strangers that he has seen it, and indeed not one of your Family told for if shown to him and it should not afterwards be acted, it
would infallibly meet a universal Damnation—it will be said, it was
offer'd the Managers and they refused it.[1]

---

1  This passage was heavily obliterated by Burney; several of the readings are conjec-
   tural.

# Appendix C: Burney and Molière

In a note to her father, Frances Burney denied the charge made by Samuel Crisp that her play, *The Witlings*, was an inferior imitation of Molière's *Les Femmes Savantes*, affirming that "she had literally never read the *Femmes Scavantes* [sic] when she composed *The Witlings*" (*Early Journals* III, 345). Burney's denial of Molière's influence is borne out by the fact that there are virtually no similarities in the wording of any passages in the two plays, and the greater variety of character and incident in her play makes its alleged inferiority an arguable point. Nevertheless, there is enough similarity in the structural elements of the two plays—both of them feature an attractive young woman whose chance to marry is jeopardized by a false report of the loss of her fortune; an older woman who cares more about her reputation as a *philosophe* than she does about her daughter or niece; a witless, dabbling poetaster whose verses are exposed as a fraud by a censorious critic; and a letter that, in restoring the younger woman's fortune, resolves the comedy in her favor—to indicate that *The Witlings* and *Les Femmes Savantes* are in some way related. How then, if Burney's statement is true, could she have written a play that so closely resembles its French forebear?

The answer may lie in the several English translations and adaptations of *Les Femmes Savantes* that were performed and published in eighteenth-century England. In 1693, twenty-one years after *Les Femmes Savantes* was first performed in Paris, a minor dramatist, Thomas Wright, published a free adaptation under the title *The Female Virtuoso's. A Comedy: as it is acted at the Queen's Theatre, by Their Majesties Servants*. Wright's play substituted "Witless, a Cambridge Scholar" for Molière's scribbler Trissotin, and Mariana, who is beloved by Clerimont, for Molière's Henriette and Clitandre, but the key elements of the story are the same as in *Les Femmes Savantes*. In 1721, Colley Cibber produced a new adaptation of *Les Femmes Savantes* titled *The Refusal; or, The Ladies Philosophy* at the Theatre Royal in Drury Lane, which ran for six nights; the scribbling poet in this version is named Witling, while Charlotte and Frankly are the lovers. In a twist, Witling wins the right of first refusal to one of Sir Gilbert Wrangle's daughters in a South Sea stock deal, and is defeated at the end by Charlotte and her father, who collude to outwit Witling and the philosophical Mrs. Wrangle. The publisher Edmund Curll, seeing Cibber's success, hurried into print a second edition of Wright's play, now under the title *No Fools like Wits: or, The Female*

*Vertuosoes. A Comedy as it was acted at the Theatre in Lincolns-Inn-Fields. Or, The Refusal. Or, The Ladies Philosophy, as it is Acted at the Theatre Royal in Drury Lane*, the redundant title emphasizing his belief that Cibber's play was plagiarized from Wright's. Both plays were frequently reprinted through the eighteenth century: Wright's reached its sixth edition in 1764, while Cibber's reached its ninth in 1777, two years before Burney wrote *The Witlings*. There was also an English translation of Molière's works, including *Les Femmes Savantes* (in English, *The Learned Ladies*), published in London in 1714 by John Ozell. Burney could have been familiar with any or all of these English plays while still truthfully writing to her father that she had "literally never read" Molière.

Readers seeking to gauge the degree to which Burney imitated Molière and Wright may do so by comparing the meeting of the "Beaux Esprits" club in Act IV of *The Witlings* with the following passages. The first is from John Ozell's translation of *Les Femmes Savantes*, published as *The Learned Ladies* (1714); the second is from *No Fools like Wits: or, The Female Vertuosoes* (1721), by Thomas Wright.

## 1. From *The Learned Ladies* (1714), Act III, sc. 1

*Trissotin.* A Plate of eight Verses won't be sufficient to satisfie the Hunger you seem to shew, and I believe 'twould do no harm if I join'd to this Epigram or Madrigal the Ragoo of a Sonnet, which a certain Princess thought tolerable. 'Tis true, 'tis season'd throughout with an Attick Salt; I believe you'll like it well enough.

*Armanda.* There's no doubt on't.

*Philaminta.* Let's hearken.

*Belisa (As often as he begins to read, she interrupts him.)* I feel my Heart leap for Joy; I must need confess I love Poetry to Distraction. Especially when the Verses are gallantly turn'd.

*Philaminta.* If we continue talking, he can never read.

*Trissotin.* A Son——

*Belisa.* Silence, Niece.

*Trissotin.* A SONNET.

To the Princess URANIA, upon her Fever.

> *Your Prudence sure is gone to sleep,*
> *To treat so sumptuously,*
> *And so magnificently keep*
> *Your greatest Enemy.*

*Belisa.* How prettily it begins!

*Armanda.* How gallantly 'tis turn'd!

*Philaminta.* Sure none but he possesses the Talent of easie Writing.

*Armanda.* We must yield the Day to *Prudence gone to sleep.*

*Belisa.* How charming is *keeping her Enemy.*

*Philaminta.* I love *sumptuously* and *magnificently*; Those two Adverbs do mighty well.

*Belisa.* Let's hearken to the rest.

*Trissotin.* *Your Prudence sure is gone to sleep,*
   *To treat so sumptuously,*
  *And so magnificently keep*
   *Your greatest Enemy!*

*Armanda.* *Prudence gone to sleep!*

*Belisa.* *Keep her Enemy!*

*Philaminta.* *Sumptuously* and *magnificently!*

*Trissotin.* *Whate'er is said, I'd have you send,*
   *From your rich Room, th'Ingrate,*
  *Who dares attempt to put an end*
   *To a fair Lady's Fate.*

*Belisa.* Ah! for Heav'ns sake let me breathe.

*Armanda.* Pray give us time to admire.

*Philaminta.* One feels, at the hearing of these Verses, something run as it were at the very bottom of the Soul that makes one faint almost—

*Armanda.* From *your rich Room.* How beautiful is *rich Room!* and how wittily is the Metaphor brought in!

*Philaminta.* *Whate'er is said.* *Whate'er is said* is admirable! In my Opinion it cannot be enough admired.

*Armanda.* I'm taken too with *Whate'er is said.*

*Belisa.* I'm of your Opinion, *Whate'er is said* is admirable.

*Armanda.* I wish I had made it.

*Belisa.* 'Tis worth a whole Piece.

*Philaminta.* But do you comprehend the Subtility of it as I do?

*Armanda* and *Belisa.* I can't tell.

*Philaminta.* *Whate'er is said,* that is, whoever takes the Fever's part don't mind 'em, despite all their Bustle. *Whate'er is said, I'd have you send &c. Whate'er is said.* Whate'er is said signifies a great deal more than it seems to do. I don't know whether every one takes it as I do; but I understand in it a Million of Words.

*Belisa.* 'Tis true it says more things than it seems to do.

*Philaminta.* But, Sir, when you made this charming *Whate'er is said,* did you your self comprehend all its Energy? Did you imagine its vast Extent, or think you were writing so much Wit?

*Trissotin.* Ha, Ha.

> ...*Without respect to your high Brood,*
> *Dares he pretend to touch your Blood.*

*Philaminta, Armanda, and Belisa.* Ah!

*Trissotin. And Night and Day torment you so?*

> *If to the Bath you chance to go,*
> *Without a scruple take and drown*
> *With your own Hands the Knavish Clown.*

*Philaminta.* I can hold no longer.

*Belisa.* I faint.

*Armanda.* I die with Pleasure.

*Philaminta.* It gives one a thousand gentle Shiverings....

*Belisa.* What Niece, were you not at all touch'd all this while? You make but a strange Figure there.

*Henrietta.* E'en such a Figure as God made me, Aunt; ev'ry one is not a Wit.


## 2. From *No Fools like Wits: or, The Female Vertuosoes* (1721), by Thomas Wright, Act II

*Catchat.* Make room, make room for the *Virgil* of our Age.

*Lovewit.* What! my old Lover, Sir *Maggot Jingle*, I am in an Extasie for Joy.

*Sir Maurice Meanwell.* Pox of their *Jingle*, and his scandalous Title: Must that starving parasitical Knight be always Rhiming and Bawling at my Table. Curse on him! One may know by his Visits, better than by the Clock, when 'tis Dinner-time at my House. —Sir *Timothy*, I think you and I have nothing to do here, Had not we best go in, and take a Pipe in my little Room?

*Sir Timothy Witless.* With all my Heart, Sir *Maurice*.

*Sir Maurice.* The Ladies will take care of Mr. *Witless*. [*Exeunt Sir Maurice and Sir Timothy.*]

*Lady Meanwell.* Mr. *Witless*, let me have the Honour of presenting you to this Darling of the Muses, this younger Brother of *Apollo*, Sir *Maggot Jingle*.

*Witless.* What, Madam, the Famous Sir *Maggot Jingle* that writ that Incomparable Poem of the Fox?

*Lady Meanwell.* The very same, Sir.

*Witless.* Oh Sir! for the sake of the Fox, let me embrace you, as long as there are Men that love to hunt after Wit and Fancy; your Fox will be sure to run to Posterity. [*Embraces Sir Maggot Jingle.*]

*Sir Maggot.* Sir, your most Humble: I do not love to commend my self; but I take that Piece to be a *Non ultra* in the kind.

*Witless.* What a pity 'tis, Sir, the Court does not understand your Merit.

*Sir Maggot.* I am now favouring the ungrateful World, with a rare Collection of my Songs; for without Vanity, let it be spoken, I am the best Lyrick Poet in *England.*

*Catchat.* How Wittily his Muse expresses her self.

*Lady Meanwell.* I'm now in my Element—*Nimble,* bring Chairs,— [Nimble *brings a Chair, and falls with it.*] There lies a Booby now, for want of understanding the *Æquilibrium* of Things.

*Nimble.* And so this, I saw it, as soon as I was down.

*Sir Maggot.*　　*'Tis well for you, Son of an Ass,*
　　　　　　　*Nature did not make you of Glass.*

*Lovewit.* What! an *impromptu* with so much Wit! Wonderful?

*Catchat.* Surely this Man is the Phoenix of Poetry. [*Chairs are brought in, all sit.*]

*Sir Maggot.* Well Ladies, Is the Day fix'd for the opening of your Academy of *Beaux Esprits.*

*Lady Meanwell.* Tuesday is the Day, Sir *Maggot.*

*Sir Maggot.* Woe then to the Royal Society; the Glory of it will suffer a manifest Eclipse.

*Catchat.* Nay, Sir *Maggot,* we will not be so Cruel neither to those Gentlemen as to refuse to join to our Learned Body, the most able Mathematicians amongst 'em; to the end, that by a free Communication of our Discoveries, we may penetrate together into such Dark Secrets of Nature, as have hitherto been deem'd unfathomable by human Capacity.

*Lady Meanwell.* Our Society shall be as the Inquisition, a Tribunal without Appeal, or Mercy? where, with a Sovereign Authority, we shall Judge of all Books that come out: no Authors shall write well but those we approve of; and no body pretend to Wit, but we and our Friends.

*Lovewit.* But you, Sir *Maggot,* has your witty Muse conceiv'd of late: What News pray from *Apollo's* Levee?

*Sir Maggot.* Very little, Madam, that deserves to be nam'd to such Sapphoes of our Age, as I see here.

*Lovewit.* Come Sir *Maggot,* no Compliments: You know we had rather hear fine Things, that our selves commended.

*Sir Maggot.* This is another *impromptu,* Ladies, only made at Leisure. [*Pulling out a Paper.*]

*Catchat.* Oh! I shall fall into a Swoon—
*Sir Maggot.* Hum, Hum, Hum. —

To the Countess of *Squeezingham,*
upon her AGUE.

> *Your Prudence surely, is Asleep,*
> *Whilst you magnificently Treat;*
> *And in your rich Apartment Keep*
> *Your cruel Enemy in State.*

*Lady Meanwell.* Oh the *Jantèe* Beginning!
*Catchat.* What a gallant Turn is there!
*Lovewit.* Nothing can be more *degagée.*
*Sir Maggot.*    *Ah force it out, say what they will,*
> *From your Apartment, rich and rare;*
> *Th' Ungrateful that attempts to kill*
> *And rob you of a life so fair.*

*Lady Meanwell.* Oh give me Leave to breathe.
*Lovewit.* I am all Rapture, I vow.
*Catchat.* Bless me! what a pretty Metaphor that *rich Apartment* is.
*Lady Meanwell.* The Parenthesis in my Mind, is worth a Million—
    *Force it out, say what they will,* it implies a Challenge, a Defiance to
    Criticks.
*Lovewit.* I'd freely give my Portion to be the Author of a Thing, so
    much out of the common Road.
*Sir Maggot.* What follows, Ladies, will not disgrace the Beginning I'm
    sure.

> *What! thus regardless of your Race,*
> *In your high Blood it self to place!*
> *And Night and Day torment you so.*

> *Though it has all this Favour found,*
> *Oh, yet at length some Anger show;*
> *And when next to the* Bath *you go,*
> *With your own Hands let it be Drown'd.*

*Lady Meanwell.* I can hold no longer.
*Catchat.* I die away! Support me! Oh, Support me, some body! Alas!
    Alas!
*Lovewit.* I'm lost in Pleasure!

*Lady Meanwell.* Though it has all *this Favour found*; though you have indulg'd it, humour'd it so long—

*Lovewit.* Oh, *yet at length some Anger show*, some Passion, some Indignation, some Resentment for its Ingratitude.

*Catchat. With your own Hands let it be Drown'd:* — That is, take hold of it, Madam, and plunge it into the Water—Oh! Oh!—

*Lady Meanwell.* Well, Mr. *Witless,* did you ever hear the like? What do ye think now the Author of so excellent a Piece deserves?

*Witless.* What does he deserve, Madam? —He deserves to be Hang'd.

# Appendix D: Contemporary Critical Essays on "Laughing" and Sentimental Comedy

In an essay published in 1773, Oliver Goldsmith called for a return to "laughing" comedy, which he contrasted with the recent fashion for "sentimental" comedy.[1] By "laughing" comedy, Goldsmith meant plays written in the satirical tradition of Terence and Molière, whose comedies ridiculed the vices of "low" characters rather than eliciting sympathy for them, as the latter sort of comedy often did. Burney's choice of materials for *The Witlings* in 1779 may have been in part a response to Goldsmith's call for a revival of the former sort of comedy, excerpted below.

... Yet notwithstanding [the authority of the best critics] and the universal practice of former ages, a new species of dramatic composition has been introduced, under the name of *sentimental* comedy, in which the virtues of private life are exhibited, rather than the vices exposed; and the distresses rather than the faults of mankind make our interest in the piece. These comedies have had of late great success, perhaps from their novelty, and also from their flattering every man in his favorite foible. In these plays almost all the characters are good, and exceedingly generous; they are lavish enough of their *tin* money on the stage: and though they want humour, have abundance of sentiment and feeling. If they happen to have faults or foibles, the spectator is taught not only to pardon but to applaud them, in consideration of the goodness of their hearts; so that folly, instead of being ridiculed, is commended, and the comedy aims at touching our passions without the power of being truly pathetic. In this manner we are likely to lose one great source of entertainment on the stage; for while the comic poet is invading the province of the tragic muse, he leaves her lovely sister quite neglected. Of this, he is no way solicitous, as he measures his fame by his profits....

But there is one argument in favor of sentimental comedy, which will keep it on stage in spite of all that can be said against it. It is, of all others, the most easily written. Those abilities that can hammer out a novel are fully sufficient for the production of a sentimental comedy. It is only sufficient to raise the characters a little; to deck out the hero

---

1 "An Essay on the Theater; or, A Comparison between Laughing and Sentimental Comedy," *Westminster Magazine* (Dec. 1772-Jan. 1773).

with a riband, or give the heroine a title; then to put an insipid dialogue, without character or humour, into their mouths, give them mighty good hearts, very fine clothes, furnish a new set of scenes, make a pathetic scene or two, with a sprinkling of tender melancholy conversation through the whole, and there is no doubt but all the ladies will cry and all the gentlemen applaud.

Humour at present seems to be departing from the stage, and it will soon happen that our comic players will have nothing left for it but a fine coat and a song. It depends upon the audience whether they will actually drive those poor merry creatures from the stage, or sit at a play as gloomy as at the Tabernacle. It is not easy to recover an art when once lost; and it will be but a just punishment, that when, by our being too fastidious, we have banished humour from the stage, we should ourselves be deprived of the art of laughing.

William Cooke expressed similar views in Chapter XVII, "Of Sentimental Comedy," in his book *The Elements of Dramatic Criticism* (1775), from which the following excerpt is taken:

Tho' the laws of the drama know no species of comedy under this title [i.e., sentimental], yet as the prevalence of custom has not only of late admitted it, but given it a first rate place on our theatres, it very properly becomes an object of enquiry in this work.

Were we to reason by analogy, we should never be able to find out the cause of so unclassical a supersession, for whoever will make the comparison between that comedy left us by antiquity, and so ably continued to us by several of our English poets with this, will find the features too dissimilar to claim the most distant reference; in the former, we have a fable founded on the laws of probability and nature; characters speaking the language of their conformation, and the whole stage reflecting the manners of the world; in the latter, names instead of characters, poetical egotisms for manners, bombast for sentiment, and instead of wit and humour (the very essence of comedy), a driveling species of morality, which as a term generally applied to ethics, may properly enough be called *good*, but from being falsely applied to comedy (however it may excite the *piety* of the crowd) must nauseate men of sense and education.

There is a circumstance which we think has been a leading assistant in the establishment of this false taste. Without meaning to turn reformers, and inconsiderately fall in with the vulgar opinion of generally condemning the present age, merely because it is the present age; thus much we think we are warranted to assert; that the present age, however it may be free from great, and leading vices, is peculiarly marked by a *slavish effeminacy of manners*, and *universality of indolent dissipation*, unknown to former ages; hence the people of fashion, unwilling to see such just emblems of themselves on the stage as comedy *should* represent, thought it better to assume a virtue which they had not, by crying up the *theory* of morality as a kind of cover for the *breach* of it. The lower kinds of people having no other models in their eye, than those whom they often mistakenly call their *betters*, without weighing this opinion, followed their example; so that between the two parties nature began to be called vulgar, and every thing partaking of the low, humourous, or vicious (principal ingredients in comedy) began to be under-rated, because the former had an interest in decrying them, and the latter permitted themselves to be duped by the artifice....

Comedy being thus debauched, like an unhappy female, began to be viewed in the light of *common game*, by those poets who dare not look up to her in the days of her chastity; such finding the intercourse easy, and the profits great, immediately hired themselves in her service. The success of one fool drew many; they had nothing to do but exchange the *vis comica* for the pathetic, and substitute tame individual recital for natural dialogue; in short, a novel furnished them with the plot; a servile allusion to all the little chat of the times, for wit, and humour; and the Whole Duty of Man, Pamela, or the Oeconomy of Human Life, for sentiments. Thus an art originally invented to lash the follies and imperfections of mankind, through the vehicle of ridicule; an art which should ever be considered as the greatest test of wit, breeding, and observation; an art, "whose end both at the first, and now was, and is, to hold as 'twere the mirror up to nature, to shew virtue her own features, scorn her own image, and the very age and body of the time his form and pressure,"[1] is changed into what is vulgarly called a moral kind of entertainment, where a citizen, 'tis true, may bring his wife and daughter to, with as much *safety* as to a Methodist chapel, but with equal prospect of improvement.

---

1   *Hamlet* III.ii.

# Appendix E: Literary Allusions in The Witlings and The Woman-Hater

In *The Witlings*, Lady Smatter alludes frequently to her favourite poets, but names only seven: Shakespeare, Dryden, Prior, Parnell, Swift, Pope, and Thomson. In *The Woman-Hater*, she quotes from a much larger number of authors, though with no improvement in accuracy. All the writers to whom Lady Smatter alludes in these plays are listed below.

Addison: Joseph Addison (1672-1719), co-author with Richard Steele of *The Tatler* (1709-11) and *The Spectator* (1711-12; 1714); author of a neo-classical tragedy *Cato* (1713).

Armstrong: John Armstrong (1709-79), Scottish author of *The Art of Preserving Health* (1744) and other poems.

Bacon: Francis Bacon (1561-1626), author of *Essays* (1597; 1612; 1625) and other prose works.

Beaumont: Francis Beaumont (1584-1616), author of *The Knight of the Burning Pestle* (1607?) and (with John Fletcher) many other plays, including *The Woman Hater* (1607).

Butler: Samuel Butler (1613-80), author of *Hudibras* (1663-80) and other satirical poems.

Churchill: Charles Churchill (1731-64), author of *The Rosciad* (1761; 1763) and other topical verse satires.

Congreve: William Congreve (1670-1729), author of four comedies, including *The Way of the World* (1700), a tragedy, and a novel.

Cowley: Abraham Cowley (1618-67), author of *The Mistress* (1647) and other collections of poems.

Dryden: John Dryden (1631-1700), author of *Absalom and Achitophel* (1681-82) and other poems; *The Conquest of Granada* (1672) and some thirty other plays; and *Of Dramatick Poesy* (1668) and other critical essays.

Fletcher: John Fletcher (1579-1625), prolific dramatist, who collaborated on many plays with Francis Beaumont and others.

Gay: John Gay (1685-1732), author of *The Beggar's Opera* (1728) and other comedies, and several collections of verse.

Goldsmith: Oliver Goldsmith (1730?-74), author of *The Deserted Village* (1770) and other poems; two comedies, including *She Stoops to Conquer* (1773); a novel, *The Vicar of Wakefield* (1764 ), and numerous prose works.

Gray: Thomas Gray (1716-71), author of *An Elegy Written in a Country Church-Yard* (1751) and other poems.

Hammond: James Hammond (1710-42), author of *Love Elegies* (1732), and the subject of one of Samuel Johnson's *Lives of the Poets*.

Locke: John Locke (1632-1704), author of *An Essay Concerning Human Understanding* (1690) and other treatises.

Milton: John Milton (1608-74), author of *Paradise Lost* (1667), *Paradise Regained* (1671) and other poems and prose works.

Newton: Sir Isaac Newton (1642-1727), author of *Opticks* (1704) and other works on physics and mathematics.

Otway: Thomas Otway (1652-85), author of tragedies, including *The Orphan* (1680) and *Venice Preserv'd* (1682), and other plays.

Ovid: Publius Ovidius Naso (43 BC-AD 18), Latin poet, author of love elegies *Amores* (16 BC) and other works.

Parnel: Thomas Parnell (1679-1718), author of *Poems on Several Occasions* (1721), published posthumously by Pope.

Pliny: Gaius Plinius Secundus (Pliny the Elder) (AD 23-79), Roman encyclopaedist, naturalist, and statesman.

Pope: Alexander Pope (1688-1744), author of *The Rape of the Lock* (1712; 1714; 1717), *The Dunciad* (1728-43), *An Essay on Man* (1733-34), and other poems.

Prior: Matthew Prior (1664-1721), author of occasional verses and prose works.

Rochester: John Wilmot, second earl of Rochester (1647-80), lyric poet and satirist, notorious for both the wildness of his life and the unrestrained depiction of sexuality in his poetry.

Rowe: Nicholas Rowe (1674-1718), author of tragedies, including *The Fair Penitent* (1703) and *Jane Shore* (1714), and an edition of Shakespeare.

Sapho: Sappho (c. mid-seventh century BC), Greek lyric poet and principal figure in a group of women who honoured the Muses and Aphrodite.

Seneca: Lucius Annaeus Seneca (Seneca the Younger) (4 BC-AD 65), author of several dialogues, moral epistles, and nine tragedies.

Shakespeare: William Shakespeare (1564-1616), author of some thirty-six comedies, tragedies, and history plays, as well as narrative poems and sonnets.

Shenstone: William Shenstone (1714-63), author of *Poems Upon Various Occasions* (1737) and other, mainly pastoral poems.

Spenser: Edmund Spenser (c. 1552-99), author of *The Shepheardes Calender* (1579), *The Faerie Queene* (1590; 1596) and other poems.

Swift: Jonathan Swift (1667-1745), author of *A Tale of a Tub* (1704) and *Gulliver's Travels* (1726), and other prose works and poems.

Thompson: James Thomson (1700-48), author of *The Seasons* (1730; 1744; 1746) and other poems and tragedies.

Waller: Edmund Waller (1606-87), author of several collections of poems.

Wycherley: William Wycherley (1641-1715), author of *The Country Wife* (1675) and three other comedies.

# *Appendix F: Burney's Cast-List for* The Woman-Hater

*The Woman-Hater* was intended for production at Drury Lane Theatre, as Burney's projected cast-list shows. Beside the names of eight of the principal characters in the fair copy, she pencilled in the names of members of the Drury Lane Company, as follows:

| | |
|---|---|
| Sir Roderick | Thomas King (1730-1805) |
| Wilmot | John Philip Kemble (1757-1823) |
| Old Waverley | John Quick (1748-1831) |
| Young Waverley | John Bannister (1760-1836) |
| Lady Smatter | Jane Pope (1744?-1818) |
| Eleonora | Sarah Siddons (1755-1831) |
| Miss Wilmot | Dorothy Jordan (1761-1816) |
| Sophia | Maria Theresa De Camp (1775-1838) |

The parts of Bob Sapling, his sister Henny, the Nurse and the various servants were not assigned.

In selecting her cast, Burney avoided all the actors in the disastrous Drury Lane production of *Edwy and Elgiva* of March 1795, with the natural exception of the two star performers, Sarah Siddons and John Philip Kemble. For the other parts, Burney could draw on her familiarity with Drury Lane actors from their appearances in recent productions. On 3 November 1797, she had seen a performance of Frederick Reynolds's *Cheap Living!*, with John Bannister as Spunge, Dorothy Jordan as Sir Edward Bloomly, Jane Pope as Mrs. Scatter, and Maria De Camp as Elinor Bloomly; she found the play "full of absurdities—but at times irresistibly comic" (*Journals and Letters*, IV, 29).[1] Some months later, on 22 February 1798, she saw Hannah Cowley's *The Belle's Strategem*, with Bannister as Flutter and Pope as Mrs. Racket (*Journals and Letters*, IV, 129). And on 6 June 1801, Burney saw a performance of David Garrick's *The Country Girl*, with Jordan in the leading role (*Journals and Letters*, IV, 494).

In casting Siddons, the greatest tragedienne, and Jordan, the greatest comedienne, of the day—together with another leading actress,

---

1 The cast-lists for these productions are given in *The London Stage 1660-1800, Part V: 1776-1800*, ed. Charles Beecher Hogan (Carbondale, IL: Southern Illinois University Press, 1968) V, 2013, 2019.

De Camp—for the parts of Eleonora, Miss Wilmot, and Sophia, Burney revealed her ambitions for *The Woman-Hater* on stage. Pope was also aptly cast as Lady Smatter; Hazlitt described her as "the very picture of a dunenna, a maiden lady, or antiquated dowager."[1] King, a senior actor in the company, was well known for his performance as Sir Peter Teazle in Sheridan's *The School for Scandal*, and Bannister had played Tony Lumpkin in Goldsmith's *She Stoops to Conquer*. Quick, George III's favourite actor, was the original Tony Lumpkin; Burney had seen him play the part on 17 July 1789 (*Journals and Letters*, IV, 301). Later he achieved fame for his portrayal of "whimsical or irascible old men."[2] His presence in the cast-list helps to date Burney's plans for staging the play. An actor at the Covent Garden Theatre for many years until 1798, he came to Drury Lane for the 1801-02 theatre season, playing there for the first time on 19 November 1801. This suggests that Burney drew up her cast-list between November 1801 and her departure from England to live in France the following April—a move that brought an end to any plans for a production of her comedy.

In one of the draft outlines for a play growing out of *The Witlings* and preceding *The Woman-Hater*, Burney cast a set of characters using most of the same Drury Lane actors. This draft has John Philip Kemble in the part of Dignitatas; Charles Kemble as Dignitatas's son; John Bannister as Jack; Maria Theresa De Camp as Dignitatas's daughter; Dorothy Jordan as Miss Megrim; and Maria Ann Pope as Mrs. Sapient.[3]

---

1   Philip H. Highfill, Jr., Kalman A. Burnim, and Edward A. Langhans, *A Biographical Dictionary of Actors, Actresses, Musicians, Dancers, Managers and Other Stage Personnel in London, 1660-1800* (Carbondale, IL: Southern Illinois University Press, 1973-93) XII, 83.

2   *The London Stage*, V, 1992.

3   "Miscellaneous Pieces of Manuscript, 1772-1828," folder V, Berg Collection, New York Public Library.

# Appendix G: Similarities between The Witlings, The Woman-Hater, and Burney's Novels

Readers of *The Witlings* and *The Woman-Hater* will immediately recognize situations and characters in those plays that also appear in Burney's fiction. Her first novel, *Evelina* (1778), concerns a young woman whose rightful identity and inheritance have been denied her by her father, who repudiated his marriage to Evelina's mother, and by a nurse, who switched the infant Evelina with the nurse's own child, thus causing her to be brought up in Evelina's place. In *The Woman-Hater*, the child Sophia returns from the West Indies with her mother Eleonora to reclaim her inheritance, which she had lost when her father Wilmot repudiated his wife, only to learn that her place has been usurped by a "Miss Wilmot" who is in fact the daughter of her old nurse. In Burney's second novel, *Cecilia* (1782), the orphaned heiress Cecilia Beverley loses her inheritance through the financial betrayals of her guardians, leading her prospective mother-in-law, Mrs. Delvile, to condemn the marriage. In *The Witlings*, written a few years earlier, the heiress Cecilia Stanley loses her inheritance through the bankruptcy of her guardian, Stipend, whereupon her prospective mother-in-law, Lady Smatter, endeavours to prevent her marriage to Beaufort. Burney evidently adapted the same story lines for both drama and fiction, constructing her plots around the trials of a young woman who has been injured by the betrayals, deceptions, and prejudices of her supposed guardians.

The similarities of the heroines' situations, however, are not the only ways in which the novels resonate with the plays; there are also recurring characters. Cecilia Beverley is courted by Mr. Belfield, a supercilious young man whose habit of mis-quoting bits of poetry reminds a reader of the poetaster Dabler in *The Witlings* and of his ancestor Trissotin from Molière's *Les Femmes Savantes*. Burney draws Belfield's character in the following paragraph:

But the principal figure in the circle was Mr. Belfield, a tall, thin young man, whose face was all animation, and whose eyes sparkled with intelligence. He had been intended by his father for trade, but his spirit, soaring above the occupation for which he was designed, from repining led him to resist, and from resisting, to rebel. He eloped from his friends, and contrived to enter the army. But, fond of the polite arts, and eager for the acquirement of knowledge, he found not this way of life much better adapted to his inclination than that from which he had escaped; he soon grew weary of it, was reconciled to his father, and entered at the Temple. But here, too volatile for serious study, and too gay for laborious application, he made little progress: and the same quickness of parts and vigour of imagination which united with prudence, or accompanied by judgment, might have raised him to the head of his profession, being unhappily associated with fickleness and caprice, served only to impede his improvement, and obstruct his preferment. And now, with little business, and that little neglected, a small fortune, and that fortune daily becoming less, the admiration of the world, but that admiration ending simply in civility, he lived an unsettled and unprofitable life, generally caressed, and universally sought, yet careless of his interest and thoughtless of the future; devoting his time to company, his income to dissipation, and his heart to the Muses. (*Cecilia*, 11-12)

Burney's final novel, *The Wanderer; or, Female Difficulties* (1814), also resonates with *The Witlings* and *The Woman-Hater*. The "Cecilia character" in that novel is Juliet Granville, a refugee from the troubles in France, who has had to disguise her identity and appear as Miss Ellis, a harp teacher. Since her students seldom pay, she is reduced to penury; to relieve her distress, her friend, Mr. Giles Arbe, calls on some wealthy patrons to assist her. One of them is Lady Kendover, who denies her in much the way that Lady Smatter turns her back on both Cecilia Stanley and Eleanora's daughter, Sophia:

[Giles Arbe's] next visit was to Lady Kendover, by whom he was received, he said, with such politeness, and by whom Ellis was mentioned with so much consideration, that he thought he should quite oblige her ladyship, by giving her an opportunity to serve a young person of whom she spoke with so much civility. "Upon which," continued he, "I told her about your debts, and how much you would thank her to be as quick as possible in helping you to pay them. But then she put on quite a new face. She was surprised, she said, that you should begin your new career by running into debt; and much more at my supposing that she should sanctify such imprudence, by her name and encouragement. Still, however, she talked about her concern, and her admiration, in such elegant sentences, that, thinking she was coming round, 'Madam,' said I, 'as your ladyship honours this young lady with so generous a regard, I hold it but my duty to tell you how you may shew it the most to her benefit. Send for all her creditors, and let them know your ladyship's good opinion of her; and then, I don't doubt, they'll wait her own convenience for being paid.' Well! all at once her face turned of a deep brick red, as if I had offered her an affront in only naming such a thing! So then I grew very angry indeed; for, as she is neither young nor pretty, there is no one thing to excuse her. If she had been young, one might have hoped she would mend; and if she were pretty, one might suppose she was only thinking of her looking-glass. But her ladyship is plain enough, as well as old; so I felt no scruple to reprimand her. But I gained no ground; for just as I was beginning to cry down the uselessness of that complimentary language, if it meant nothing; she said that she was very sorry to have the honour to leave me, but that she must go and dress for dinner. But then, just as I was coming away, and upon the point of being in a passion, I was stopt by little Lady Barbara; that sweet fine child; who asked me a hundred kind questions about you, without paying any regard to the winking or blinking of her aunt Kendover. She is a mighty agreeable little soul. I have taken a great kindness to her. She let out all their secrets to me; and I should like nothing better than to tell them all to you; only Lady Kendover charged me to hold my tongue. The ladies are very fond of giving that recommendation to us men! I don't know (smiling) whether they are as fond of giving the example!" (*The Wanderer*, 301-2)

# Select Bibliography

This bibliography lists works that discuss Burney as a dramatist or that are directly relevant to the study of her plays.

## Primary Works

Burney, Frances. *A Busy Day*. Ed. Tara Ghoshal Wallace. New Brunswick, NJ: Rutgers University Press, 1984.

———. *A Busy Day*. Adapted by Alan Coveney. London: Oberon Books, 2000.

———. *The Complete Plays of Frances Burney*. Ed. Peter Sabor; associate editor (*Tragedies*) Stewart J. Cooke; contributing editor (*Comedies*) Geoffrey M. Sill. 2 vols. London: Pickering & Chatto, 1995.

———. *The Early Journals and Letters of Fanny Burney*. Ed. Lars E. Troide *et al.* 6 vols. Oxford: Clarendon Press, 1988-.

———. *Edwy and Elgiva*. Ed. Miriam J. Benkovitz. Hamden, CT: Shoe String Press, 1957.

———. *Journals and Letters*. Ed. Peter Sabor and Lars E. Troide. London: Penguin, 2001.

———. *The Journals and Letters of Fanny Burney (Madame d'Arblay)*. Ed. Joyce Hemlow *et al.* 12 vols. Oxford: Clarendon Press, 1972-84.

———. *The Witlings*. Ed. Clayton J. Delery. East Lansing, MI: Colleagues Press, 1995.

## Secondary Works

Adelstein, Michael E. *Fanny Burney*. New York: Twayne, 1968.

Backscheider, Paula R. *Spectacular Politics: Theatrical Power and Mass Culture in Early Modern England*. Baltimore: Johns Hopkins University Press, 1993.

Bevis, Richard W. *English Drama: Restoration and Eighteenth Century, 1660-1789*. London: Longman, 1988.

———. *The Laughing Tradition: Stage Comedy in Garrick's Day*. Athens: University of Georgia Press, 1980.

Booth, Michael R., *et al.*, *The Revels History of Drama in England*. Vol. VI, *1750-1880*. London: Methuen, 1975.

Chevalier, Noel. "Redeeming the Nabob: Frances Burney, Warren Hastings and the Cultural Construction of India in *A Busy Day*." *The Burney Journal* 2 (1999): 24-39.

Chisholm, Kate. *Fanny Burney: Her Life, 1752-1840*. London: Chatto & Windus, 1998.

Cox, Jeffrey N., ed. *Seven Gothic Dramas 1789-1825*. Athens: Ohio University Press, 1992.

Darby, Barbara. "Feminism, Tragedy, and Frances Burney's *Edwy and Elgiva*." *Journal of Dramatic Theory and Criticism* 10 (1997): 3-23.

———. "Financial and Social 'Discrimination' in Frances Burney's Comedies." *The Burney Journal* 2 (1999): 4-22.

———. "Frances Burney's Dramatic Mothers." *English Studies in Canada* 23 (1997): 37-58.

———. *Frances Burney, Dramatist: Gender, Performance, and the Late Eighteenth-Century Stage*. Lexington: University Press of Kentucky, 1997.

Donkin, Ellen. *Getting into the Act: Women Playwrights in London 1776-1829*. London: Routledge, 1995.

Donohue, Joseph. *Dramatic Character in the English Romantic Age*. Princeton: Princeton University Press, 1970.

———. *Theatre in the Age of Kean*. Oxford: Blackwell, 1975.

Doody, Margaret Anne. "Fanny Burney." *Dictionary of Literary Biography* 39, *British Novelists, 1660-1800*. Ed. Martin C. Battestin. Detroit: Gale Research, 1985. 90-101.

———. *Frances Burney: The Life in the Works*. New Brunswick, NJ: Rutgers University Press, 1988.

Ellis, Frank. *Sentimental Comedy: Theory and Practice*. Cambridge: Cambridge University Press, 1991.

Gagen, Jean Elisabeth. *The New Woman: Her Emergence in English Drama, 1600-1730*. New York: Twayne, 1954.

Harman, Claire. *Fanny Burney: A Biography*. London: HarperCollins, 2000.

Hemlow, Joyce. "Fanny Burney: Playwright." *University of Toronto Quarterly* 19 (1950): 170-89.

———. *The History of Fanny Burney*. Oxford: Clarendon Press, 1958.

Loftis, John. *Sheridan and the Drama of Georgian England*. Cambridge, MA: Harvard University Press, 1977.

Newey, Katherine. "Women and History on the Romantic Stage: More, Yearsley, Burney, and Mitford." *Women in British Romantic Theatre: Drama, Performance, and Society, 1790-1840* Ed. Catherine Burroughs. Cambridge: Cambridge University Press, 2000. 79-101.

Nicoll, Allardyce. *A History of English Drama 1660-1900*. Vol. III, *Late Eighteenth Century Drama*, 2nd ed. Cambridge: Cambridge University Press, 1952.

Price, Cecil. *Theatre in the Age of Garrick*. Oxford: Blackwell, 1973.

Rogers, Katharine M. *Frances Burney: The World of Female Difficulties*. London: Harvester Wheatsheaf, 1990.

——, ed. *The Meridian Anthology of Restoration and Eighteenth-Century Plays by Women*. New York: Meridian, 1994.

Sabor, Peter. "'Altered, Improved, Copied, Abridged': Alexandre d'Arblay's Revisions to Burney's *Edwy and Elgiva*." *Lumen* 14 (1995): 127-37.

——. "The Rediscovery of Frances Burney's Plays." *Lumen* 13 (1994): 145-56.

Schofield, Mary Anne, and Cecilia Macheski, eds., *Curtain Calls: British and American Women and the Theater, 1660-1820*. Athens: Ohio University Press, 1991.

Sherman, Sandra. "'Does Your Ladyship Mean an Extempore?': Wit, Leisure, and the Mode of Production in Frances Burney's *The Witlings*." *Centennial Review* 40 (1996): 401-28.

Simons, Judy. *Fanny Burney*. London: Macmillan, 1987.

Thaddeus, Janice Farrar. *Frances Burney: A Literary Life*. London: Macmillan, 2000.

Watkins, Daniel P. *A Materialist Critique of English Romantic Drama*. Gainesville: University Press of Florida, 1993.